Chinese Literature and Culture in the World

Series Editor
Ban Wang
Stanford University
Stanford, CA, USA

As China is becoming an important player on the world stage, Chinese literature is poised to change and reshape the overlapping, shared cultural landscapes in the world. This series publishes books that reconsider Chinese literature, culture, criticism, and aesthetics in national and international contexts. While seeking studies that place China in geopolitical tensions and historical barriers among nations, we encourage projects that engage in empathetic and learning dialogue with other national traditions. Imbued with a desire for mutual relevance and sympathy, this dialogue aspires to a modest prospect of world culture. We seek theoretically informed studies of Chinese literature, classical and modern - works capable of rendering China's classical heritage and modern accomplishments into a significant part of world culture. We promote works that cut across the modern and tradition divide and challenge the inequality and unevenness of the modern world by critiquing modernity. We look for projects that bring classical aesthetic notions to new interpretations of modern critical theory and its practice. We welcome works that register and analyze the vibrant contemporary scenes in the online forum, public sphere, and media. We encourage comparative studies that account for mutual parallels, contacts, influences, and inspirations.

Shouhua Qi

Culture, History, and the Reception of Tennessee Williams in China

palgrave
macmillan

Shouhua Qi
Western Connecticut State University
Danbury, CT, USA

ISSN 2945-7254   ISSN 2945-7262   (electronic)
Chinese Literature and Culture in the World
ISBN 978-3-031-16933-5   ISBN 978-3-031-16934-2   (eBook)
https://doi.org/10.1007/978-3-031-16934-2

© The Editor(s) (if applicable) and The Author(s), under exclusive licence to Springer Nature Switzerland AG 2022
This work is subject to copyright. All rights are solely and exclusively licensed by the Publisher, whether the whole or part of the material is concerned, specifically the rights of translation, reprinting, reuse of illustrations, recitation, broadcasting, reproduction on microfilms or in any other physical way, and transmission or information storage and retrieval, electronic adaptation, computer software, or by similar or dissimilar methodology now known or hereafter developed.
The use of general descriptive names, registered names, trademarks, service marks, etc. in this publication does not imply, even in the absence of a specific statement, that such names are exempt from the relevant protective laws and regulations and therefore free for general use.
The publisher, the authors, and the editors are safe to assume that the advice and information in this book are believed to be true and accurate at the date of publication. Neither the publisher nor the authors or the editors give a warranty, expressed or implied, with respect to the material contained herein or for any errors or omissions that may have been made. The publisher remains neutral with regard to jurisdictional claims in published maps and institutional affiliations.

Cover illustration: Shanghai Cityscape and Tennessee Williams By permission of Qianman Wan at MICA

This Palgrave Macmillan imprint is published by the registered company Springer Nature Switzerland AG.
The registered company address is: Gewerbestrasse 11, 6330 Cham, Switzerland

Acknowledgments

In 1985, after freshly graduating from an MA in English program and as a rookie teacher at a college in China, I gave my students a compressed version of Scene VI of Tennessee Williams's *The Glass Menagerie* (which I had read a few years before during one of the earliest Fulbright programs in China housed at Peking University), titled "The Gentleman Caller," for them to perform on stage. It was a stage reading rather than theatrical production or performance by any stretch of the term. Now, almost four decades later, as I present this book to likeminded Williams enthusiasts the world over, it seems that my early burgeoning interest in the American playwright has finally come to some fruition.

My heartfelt gratitude to all the scholars and theatre artists in China, the United States, and elsewhere in the world whose endeavors have enriched my understanding and deepened my appreciation of Tennessee Williams and made this book possible. More particularly, I want to thank Angelique Richardson, Annette Saddik, Claire Conceison, Alexander Pettit, Donald Gagnon, Wei Zhang, and Zhixiang Zhuang for their continued friendship and support; the two anonymous reviewers for their encouraging and constructive feedback; Ban Wang for including this book in the "Chinese Culture and Literature in the World" series; and editors at Palgrave Macmillan, especially Allie Troyanos, for believing in the project, and the production team for taking the project to the finish line.

I also want to thank the interlibrary loan staff at Western Connecticut State University for their support despite the challenges of the COVID-19 pandemic. This book project was supported in part by Connecticut State University's research grants.

Praise for *Culture, History, and the Reception of Tennessee Williams in China*

"Tennessee Williams stands alongside Eugene O'Neill and Arthur Miller as the most influential American playwrights in China—Shouhua Qi tells us why in this thoroughly researched and engaging study that places Williams' work in an entirely new context of China's social and political shifts of the past half-century in terms of national ideology, ideas about sexuality, and reception of foreign literature."
    —Claire Conceison, *Quanta Professor of Chinese Culture and Professor of Theater Arts, MIT, author of* Significant Other: Staging the American in China

"Shouhua Qi's valuable contribution to the field of Williams scholarship explores the reception of Williams' plays in China through a rare bilingual/bicultural lens that adds to our understanding of the complexities involved in adapting art across cultural divides."
    —Annette J. Saddik, *Distinguished Professor of Theatre and Literature, City University of New York*

"Shouhua Qi's persuasive and readable study discovers important intersections of reception, adaptation, and craft. A playwright who has seemed at times definitionally and perhaps oppressively American thus assumes a newfound breadth of meaning and appeal."
    —Alexander Pettit, *Professor of English, University of North Texas, Editor* Eugene O'Neill Review

CONTENTS

CHAPTER 1

Introduction

Towards the end of Tennessee Williams' *A Streetcar Named Desire*, when the Doctor and the Matron come to take Blanche DuBois to the mental institution, she struggles for a while, surrenders, and (as she is being led through the portieres by the Doctor, holding tight to his arm) says this famous line:[1]

> Whoever you are—I have always depended on the kindness of strangers.

To a large extent this line encapsulates the reception of Tennessee Williams (1911–1983) in China.[2] He remained a "stranger" to the Chinese for decades after his string of successes in the US (*The Glass Menagerie*, 1944; *A Streetcar Named Desire*, 1947; and *Cat on a Hot Tin Roof*, 1955) and elsewhere in the world, just as the Chinese remained not much more than strangers to him. Compared to Eugene O'Neill (1888–1953) and Arthur Miller (1915–2005), Tennessee Williams is a late comer to the Chinese drama/theatre scene, an acquired taste, and a much belated bloomer on the Chinese stage, so to speak. Unlike O'Neill and Miller,[3] Williams never visited China. Other than the title of his first play ever to receive a production (*Cairo, Shanghai, Bombay!* 1935)[4] and a few passing references, possibly as "exotic other," in plays such as *A Streetcar Named Desire* and *The Night of the Iguana* (1959), China does not figure much in meaningful ways in the dramatic world created by Williams. His international travels

S. Qi, *Culture, History, and the Reception of Tennessee Williams in China*, Chinese Literature and Culture in the World, https://doi.org/10.1007/978-3-031-16934-2_1

1

did take him to Japan and Thailand for a few times; otherwise, the world would find the American playwright a frequent traveler on the other side of the Atlantic: Williams and Europe were "tempestuous lovers" after all[5] and he could not stay away from what his heart and mind desired for too long.

CHINA AS "EXOTIC OTHER" GLIMPSED FROM AFAR

Among the oft-cited albeit few China/Chinese culture references in Williams dramatic oeuvre are those that appear in *A Streetcar Named Desire* and *The Night of the Iguana*.[6] On the notorious "Poker Night" (Scene Three) in *A Streetcar Named Desire* (*Streetcar*, hereafter), as the poker players—Stanley, Steve, Mitch, and Pablo ("men at the peak of their physical manhood, as coarse and direct and powerful as the primary colors") are absorbed in another night of poker fun in the kitchen, we hear this request from Pablo, possibly a diversion tactic, which is shut down by Stanley right away:[7]

PABLO: Why don't somebody go to <u>the Chinaman's</u> and bring back a load of chop suey?
STANLEY: When I'm losing you want to eat! Ante up! Openers? Openers! Get y'r ass off the table, Mitch. Nothing belongs on a poker table but cards, chips and whiskey. (*underline added*)

Shortly after, during their first direct encounter in the dimly lit bedroom separated from the poker scene by no more than the portieres, Blanche asks Mitch to do something for her:[8]

MITCH: Sure. What?
BLANCHE: I bought this adorable little <u>colored</u> <u>paper lantern</u> at a <u>Chinese shop</u> on Bourbon. Put it over the light bulb! Will you, please?
MITCH: Be glad to.
BLANCHE: I can't stand a naked light bulb, any more than I can a rude remark or a vulgar action.
MITCH
[*adjusting
the lantern*]: I guess we strike you as being a pretty rough bunch.
BLANCHE: I'm very adaptable—to circumstances. (*underline added*)

Apparently, this little colored paper lantern bought at a Chinese shop would assume much more psychological meaning than mere stage props as the drama unfolds on the stage. As Blanche explains to Stella in the aftermath of the poker night scene, telling her sister what has happened back home and how Belle Reve has slipped "through [her] fingers,"[9]

BLANCHE: I never was hard or self-sufficient enough. When people are soft—soft people have got to shimmer and glow—they've got to put on soft colors, the colors of butterfly wings, and put a—paper lantern over the light ... It isn't enough to be soft. You've got to be soft and attractive. And I—I'm fading now! I don't know how much longer I can turn the trick. [*The afternoon has faded to dusk. Stella goes into the bedroom and turns on the light under the paper lantern. She holds a bottled soft drink in her hand.*] (*underline added*)

Mitch, who was "glad" to help put the little colored lantern over the bulb, would be the one to tear it down to have some "realism" (and in that very act, also tearing down the gentlemanly façade he himself has put on, showing his own true colors, perhaps only a few shades different from Stanley's), once he feels he has been cheated by Blanche and perhaps by life, despite Blanche's desperate pleadings ("I don't want realism. I want magic! ... Yes, yes, magic!").[10] This would prove a prelude to what would happen during the final confrontation between Blanche and Stanley, her executioner:[11]

STANLEY: I've been on to you from the start! Not once did you pull any wool over this boy's eyes! You come in here and sprinkle the place with powder and spray perfume and cover the light bulb with a paper lantern, and lo and behold the place has turned into Egypt and you are the Queen of the Nile! Sitting on your throne and swilling down my liquor! I say—Ha!—Ha! Do you hear me? Ha—ha—ha! (*underline added*).

He goes on to tear whatever shred of pretense of dignity Blanche desperately holds on to by raping her ("We've had this date with each other from the beginning.").[12] During the last scene of the play, when Blanche, dazed and confused as she is being led away by the Matron, Stanley has to rub it in to hasten her departure from the world in which he is king and can lord it over again:[13]

STANLEY: You left nothing here but spilt talcum and old empty per-
             fume bottles—unless it's the paper lantern you want to
             take with you. You want the lantern? [*He crosses to dressing*
             table and seizes the paper lantern, tearing it off the light
             bulb, and extends it toward her. She cries out as if the lantern
             was herself]. (*underline added*)

If the lantern bought from a Chinese store functions as an alter ego or stand-in for Blanche's vulnerable and fragilized ego, personhood, and world, Williams would have her directly confront Stella as if her sister is the one who lives in a pretense of her making, urging her to leave Stanley, get out, and make a new life.[14] When Stella tells her she is not in anything, she wants to get out and in fact she is quite content where she is ("Oh, well, it's his pleasure, like mine is movies and bridge. People have got to tolerate each other's habits, I guess."), Blanche is perplexed:[15]

BLANCHE: I don't understand you. [*Stella turns toward her*] I don't
             understand your indifference. Is this a Chinese philosophy
             you've—cultivated?
STELLA: Is what—what?
BLANCHE: This—shuffling about and mumbling—"One tube
             smashed—beer bottles—mess in the kitchen!"—as if noth-
             ing out of the ordinary has happened! (*underline added*)

Williams' understanding, or lack thereof, of Chinese philosophy aside, such explicit evocations, along with the recurrent colored lantern motif, certainly add to the thematic depth, character portrayal, and emotive tapestry and potency for the play although it might lead to false impressions of the Chinese culture because they were not based on any substantive knowledge and/or understanding.

Similarly, in *The Night of Iguana* (1961; *Iguana*, hereafter), written more than ten years after *Streetcar*, China is evoked quite a few times to serve not much more than an "exotic other." Early in the play, when Shannon tells Hank, the bus driver, to go and get the women tourists (from Texas) to stay at a "rather rustic and very Bohemian hotel" sitting on a jungle-covered hilltop, one of the selling points he pitches is this:[16]

> So go on back down there and get them out of that bus before they suffocate in it. Haul them out by force if necessary and herd them up here. Hear me? Don't give me any argument about it. Mrs. Faulk, honey? Give him a menu, give him one of your sample menus to show the ladies. She's got a Chinaman cook here, you won't believe the menu. The cook's from Shanghai, handled the kitchen at an exclusive club there. I got him here for her, and he's a bug, a fanatic about-whew!-continental cuisine ... can even make beef Strogonoff and thermidor dishes. (*underline added*)

Not long after that, when Hannah, while sketching Shannon, asks him how long he has been inactive in the Church, Shannon responds with a counterquestion—a diversion:[17]

SHANNON: What's that got to do with the price of rice in China?
HANNAH (*gently*): Nothing.
SHANNON: What's it got to do with the price of coffee beans in Brazil?
HANNAH: I retract the question. With apologies. (*underline added*)

In another dialogue between the two, Hannah asks Shannon what he would do if he gets sacked:[18]

SHANNON: Got the sack? Go back to the Church or take the long swim to China. *(underline added)*

Much in the same vein as the folksy myth of digging a hole through earth to China,[19] Shannon will threaten to swim out to China a few more times in the play:[20]

HANNAH: Where are you going? What are you going to do?
SHANNON: I'm going swimming. I'm going to swim out to China!

HANNAH: No, no, not tonight, Shannon! Tomorrow ... tomorrow,
             Shannon! (*underline added*)

For Hannah, however, Shannon's threat to swim out to China sounds not
much more than a copout:[21]

HANNAH: Not quite yet, Mr. Shannon. Not till I'm reasonably sure
             that you won't <u>swim out to China</u>, because, you see, I
             think you think of the ... "<u>the long swim to China</u>" as
             another painless atonement. I mean I don't think you
             think you'd be intercepted by sharks and barracudas
             before you got far past the barrier reef. And I'm afraid you
             would be. It's as simple as that, if that is simple.
SHANNON: What's simple?
HANNAH: Nothing, except for simpletons, Mr. Shannon.
SHANNON: Do you believe in people being tied up?
HANNAH: Only when they might <u>take the long swim to China.</u>
SHANNON: All right, Miss Thin-Standing-Up-Female-Buddha, just
             light a Benson & Hedges cigarette for me and put it in my
             mouth and take it out when you hear me choking on it-if
             that doesn't seem to you like another bit of voluptuous
             self-crucifixion. (*underline added*)

Five pages worth of dramatic development later, we see Hannah once
again trying to stop Shannon from choosing the easy way out:[22]

HANNAH: I think I'll think of something because I have to. I can't
             let Nonno be moved to the Casa de Huéspedes, Mr.
             Shannon. Not any more than I could let you take <u>the long
             swim out to China.</u> You know that. Not if I can prevent it,
             and when I have to be resourceful, I can be very resource-
             ful. (*underline added*)

She will hammer on the same message again another four pages of dramatic development later:[23]

SHANNON: Yes, well, if the conversation is over—I think I'll go down
             for a swim now.
HANNAH: <u>To China?</u>

SHANNON: No, <u>not to China</u>, just to the little island out here with the sleepy bar on it … called the Cantina Serena. (*underline added*)

The Chinaman cook, silent (silenced?) throughout the play, does get to speak once, albeit indirectly, through Maxine, saying something much in line with what Blanche says to Stella alluded to earlier, in heavily accented broken English (as was typically portrayed in Hollywood films much of the twentieth century):[24]

MAXINE: The Chinaman in the kitchen says, "No sweat." … "No sweat." He says that's all his philosophy. All the Chinese philosophy in three words, "Mei yoo guanchi" which is Chinese for "No sweat."

Maxine will evoke this exotic other one more time before the curtain falls:[25]

HANNAH: He [Shannon] will quiet down again. I'm preparing a sedative tea for him, Mrs. Faulk.
MAXINE: Yeah, I see. Put it out. Nobody cooks here but the <u>Chinaman in the kitchen</u>.

Finally, in one of the most important speeches in the entire play, Hannah has this to say about an experience she had in Shanghai, from where the Chinaman cook was imported, trying to reawaken or enlighten Shannon who seems to have lost his way:[26]

In Shanghai, Shannon, there is a place that's called the House for the Dying—the old and penniless dying, whose younger, penniless living children and grandchildren take them there for them to get through with their dying on pallets, on straw mats. The first time I went there it shocked me, I ran away from it. But I came back later and I saw that their children and grandchildren and the custodians of the place had put little comforts beside their death-pallets, little flowers and opium candies and religious emblems. That made me able to stay to draw their dying faces. Sometimes only their eyes were still alive, but, Mr. Shannon, those eyes of the penniless dying with those last little comforts beside them, I tell you, Mr. Shannon, those eyes looked up with their last dim life left in them as clear as the stars in the Southern Cross, Mr. Shannon.

It is not clear from what source(s), for example, reports from Western missionaries in China,[27] Tennessee Williams drew inspiration for this speech by Hannah as illustration of her transcendent philosophy about life and death. Williams could have had Hannah evoke either of the other two "exotic" places from the title of his first play, *Cairo, Shanghai, Bombay*, or Jerusalem, Rome, Bangkok, for that matter, to achieve the same emotive and thematic effect. One would be hard put to draw the same conclusion, as some Chinese scholars apparently have done, that Williams evoked China in his plays as the final spiritual home he so longed for.[28]

It is not known whether Williams ever entertained the idea of traveling to China and seeing with his own eyes the land, people, and culture he evoked now and then in some of his plays. As alluded to earlier, Eugene O'Neill visited China in the 1920s, although it was not as fruitful a trip as he had hoped. Arthur Miller travelled to China twice in the late 1970s and early 1980s and got to direct *Death of a Salesman* in Beijing. But for much of the decades before China began to "reform and opening up" toward the end of the 1970s, Western intellectuals, writers, and artists rarely had opportunities (getting invitations and visas) to visit China.[29] Given the misgivings the Chinese had about Williams (the perceived "decadence" in his plays, if nothing else) even in the early 1990s when they began to pay more serious attention to this American playwright, via both scholarly discussions and translations, one cannot imagine an invitation sent to him in his lifetime.

THE CALL OF THAILAND AND JAPAN

Williams did travel to Asia, though—to Thailand and Japan, more specifically. In 1970, after cruising the Pacific aboard the S.S. President Cleveland and stopping off at a few ports (e.g., Honolulu and Yokohama, Japan), he flew in from Hong Kong to Bangkok, the City of Angeles. Williams did not cancel his plans for a trip to Bangkok even after he had discovered a swelling in the breast and suspected he had developed breast cancer because, as Williams indicated in his *Memoirs*, "I had my heart set on continued voyaging;" "my determination to proceed to the Orient was reinforced by the assurance of a friend that he knew the king's surgeon personally" (which turned out to be untrue).[30] Williams had a fabulous time visiting the "fabled city of Bangkok," including having opportunities to sample "underground Bangkok" (meaning, the "gay bars").[31]

While stopping off at Yokohama on route to Bangkok, where he stayed for a couple of days, Williams got to see Yukio Mishima (1925–1970), the famed Japanese writer and Shintoist, for the last time—Mishima drove out to the port one evening to have dinner with his long-time American friend[32] and then committed *hara-kiri* barely a month after the meeting. Williams' interest in Japanese literature goes back to his college years, well before he met Mishima and began the storied friendship in 1957.[33] While still a university student, young Williams wrote a play titled *The Lady from the Village of Falling Flowers* (subtitled "A Japanese Fantasy in One Act"). Drawing inspiration from the eleventh-century Japanese classic *The Tale of Genji* (via Arthur Wiley's capable English translation), *Falling Flowers* is about an Emperor who enlists his Prime Minister to help him find a wife who has to be a gifted poet. This rediscovered early play has seen many a world premier; although, as pointed out by Onoda Power, director of a recent puppet production (staged for live audiences in 2019 and then redesigned for viewing online in 2020), any Westerner writing the play today could be accused of "cultural appropriation."[34] Power's puppet adaptation of the play mixes Japanese *kamishibai*-style ("paper play")[35] street theatre with storytelling performers.

In the April 15, 1960, issue of *Japan Report*, a semi-monthly information bulletin published jointly by the Embassy of Japan in the US and Consulates General of Japan in New York, Chicago, San Francisco, and Los Angeles, which includes news items of President Eisenhower's forthcoming visit to Japan in June that year, it was reported that Tennessee Williams had penned an enthusiastic pitch for the premier of Kabuki in New York in June as "a benefit performance for the Friends of the City Centre."[36]

Tennessee Williams Hails Kabuki

The noted American playwright Tennessee Williams greets the coming of the Grand Kabuki Company in the following message: "The great traditional theatre of Japan, the Noh plays and the Kabuki theatre which grew out of them, deserve to be ranked in importance and influence with such historical flowering of drama, verbal and plastic, as the ancient Greek and the Elizabethan theatres and the theatre of Chekhov and Stanislavsky. We are receiving a great honor in their coming to America, and I hope that all our theatre artists and craftsmen will be as thrilled, influenced, instructed and inspired as I was when I saw them last Fall in Japan."

In the same year that Williams wrote this enthusiastic pitch for Japanese traditional theatrical arts, ten years before the last meeting between Williams and Mishima in Yokohama, there was a Japanese premiere of Williams' play *The Day on Which a Man Dies*, inspired by the death of Jackson Pollock (1912–1956), an expressionist American painter Williams had met in the late 1950s. In this play (written between 1957 and 1959, drastically rewritten in the early 1970s, "in memory of my friend, Yukio Mishima, with great respect for his art"[37]), as in Japanese *Gutai* performance art,[38] paintings are created and destroyed in the course of the performance. This play was premiered in Chicago in 2007 and saw another production in Provincetown in 2009.[39]

Indeed, the influence of traditional Japanese theatre arts on Williams is particularly acute in his later works, for example, *The Day on Which a Man Dies* (1957–1959), *The Milk Train Doesn't Stop Here Anymore* (1962), and *In the Bar of a Tokyo Hotel* (1969).[40] In writing *The Milk Train Doesn't Stop Here Anymore*, Michael Paller posits, Williams was writing a *noh* play: "*Milk Train* was an outré work in which Williams replaced Western Theatre conventions with those of Japanese Noh."[41] This bold dramaturgical experimentation by Williams caused confusion on the part of critics and led to some extremely negative reviews. *In the Bar of a Tokyo Hotel*, an intense one-act play which has seen several productions in the US,[42] was also written "based thematically and structurally in Noh theatre."[43] In this play, Mark, an American painter on the verge of a nervous breakdown, has holed up in his Tokyo hotel room, trying desperately to salvage his career by spraying paint on canvases to invent a new style; his wife, Miriam, fearful of losing the lifestyle she is used to, shamelessly flirts with the bartender in the hotel lounge; near the end of the play Mark comes downstairs, his body covered with blood (from shaving cuts and spattered paint) and dies, after mumbling out his last speech of protest ("Nobody ever gave me a magnum or a quart or a baby's bottle of confidence, and I didn't have a long, white beard and a stepladder to the vault of the Sistine chapel to paint the creation of creation); and Miriam screams "I have no plans. I have nowhere to go" as the stage darkens.[44]

Williams' fascination with Thailand and Japan, especially the latter's culture and theatrical tradition, was such that one could easily change the title of his first play from *Cairo, Shanghai, Bombay* to something like *Cairo, Bangkok, Tokyo*! Nonetheless, in his heart of hearts, both as a person and as a theatre artist, Williams remained a Westerner, an outsider looking in as far as traditional Japanese performing art was concerned (although he saw enough to get inspired and, unlike Mark in *In the Bar of a Tokyo Hotel*, succeeded in creating a new style).[45] His emotive and spiritual home, if he could choose, was Europe. At a press conference at the Hotel Orient during his 1970 Bangkok visit, when he was asked this question, "Is it true, Mr. Williams, that you have come to Bangkok to die?" his answer was: "The only place I'd go to die, if I had any choice, is Rome, not because it's the home of the Vatican but because it's always been my favorite city in the world."[46]

POLITICS, SEXUAL MORES, AND THE RECEPTION OF TENNESSEE WILLIAMS IN CHINA

Although he achieved huge success on Broadway around the same time as Arthur Miller in the 1940s, Williams did not catch any comparable attention from the Chinese. Ying Ruocheng, who had read Miller's *Death of a Salesman* in college when it was first published and dreamed of one day mounting it on the Chinese stage, did put out a translation of Williams' 1953 play *Something Unspoken* in the third issue of *World Literature* (*shijie wenxue* 世界文学) in 1963. This compact one-act play portrays a Southern grand dame, Cornelia, who craves for, or rather, demands absolute, unanimous vote of confidence—despite an acute inner sense of insecurity—and will not accept any office except the highest until Grace, her companion/secretary, gathers up the courage to tell her the inconvenient truth, especially concerning the nature of their relationship (something that has remained unspoken until then).[47]

It is not clear why out of so many of Williams' plays Ying Ruocheng chose *Something Unspoken* to translate at a time when China had just suffered a horrendous "Three-Year Famine" (1958–1961), largely resulted from the feverish leftist policies of Mao Zedong who, despite the disaster, continued to strike back against and indeed crack down on anyone who dared to speak the truth and criticize. Intended or not, opaque or explicit, the potentially subversive theme of the short play that speaks to the sociopolitical reality of China at the time is unmistakable. After all, what Ying did with that translation, wittingly or not, was much in the same vein as the long tradition of Chinese intelligentsia: "using the past (ancient times) to satirize the present" (*jie gu feng jin* 借古讽今), or its variation, "using the foreign to satirize the domestic" (*jie wai feng nei* 借外讽内). It is not known whether this audacious translation was included in the charges against Ying during the Cultural Revolution (1966–1977) when he served jail time and was forced to do manual labor on a farm to reform.[48]

According to Chinese scholars, one of the reasons why Williams did not catch as much attention as O'Neill and Miller was that elements of "decadence," "warped psychology," and homosexuality (however opaquely portrayed) were hard for the Chinese to relate to and appreciate.[49] Zhou Peitong, a Central Academy of Drama professor who was critical of *The Merchant of Venice* staged by the China National Youth Theatre (1980–1982) for diluting its racial theme,[50] felt that Williams' plays suffer from their exclusive focus on the dark, gloomy side of life, too "indulgent in sick, twisted 'beauty' to have any energy left to see and represent what is bright, positive, and truly beautiful in life."[51] Huang Zuolin, a prominent figure in modern Chinese theatre who was instrumental in introducing and adapting Bertolt Brecht for the Chinese stage,[52] could not bring himself to like Williams, either. In 1987, when asked how he felt about a production of *Cat on a Hot Tin Roof* mounted by students of the Shanghai Theatre Academy, Huang said, "I don't like Tennessee Williams' plays. Plays by Americans are too far away from China."[53]

Although Chinese scholars and theatre artists, in their rejection and/or misgivings of Williams, were primarily informed by the dominant leftist-socialist ideology and sexual mores, they happened to be in tune, albeit unwittingly, with the negative reception Williams was subjected to in the West in much of his post-1950s career. The negative reception of Williams in the West, especially in the US, has been well studied by scholars since the 1990s.[54] Also having been well studied are William's affinities with Hart Crane (who writes with explicit or implicit homosexual themes) due to "quasi-identification" and with Oscar Wilde "based on a feeling of existential affinity" because "both became world famous in their lifetime but were later ostracized, largely because of their homosexuality."[55] Even the Swedish Academy, when reviewing and deliberating the nominations of Williams for the Nobel Prize for Literature in the 1950s, could not avoid letting their bias against homosexuality influence their decisions. He was nominated as "one of the most solid and most noticed dramatic authors of our time" who was "experimenting and driven by a conscious artistic will" and who, "concerning human content, warmth and the seriousness of intention," did not "stand behind any of the above named [Strindberg, Ibsen, Pirandello, Brecht, Ionesco] and probably surpasses most of them." However, Williams the person, an author who "not only frequently dealt with the subject of homosexuality, but also, moreover, was rumored to be sexually deviant," made the Academy uncomfortable and unready to award the prize in the homophobic climate. Officially, homosexuality in Sweden was classified as a mental disease between 1944 and 1979, yet, as in many other Western countries, "the general paranoia of the immediate post-war period conflated homophobia and the fear of communism, marking homosexuals as constituting a possible threat to national security and the corruption of the nation's youth."[56]

In the popular imagination of the West, Williams was seen as one of the world's greatest living playwrights, but that reputation was closely associated with the salacious aspects of plot and character in the best-known of his plays (which for several years secured Williams' reputation "as American's most scandalous playwright:"[57]

[Williams] is the nightmare merchant of Broadway, writer of *Orpheus Descending* (murder by blowtorch), *A Streetcar Named Desire* (rape, nymphomania, homosexuality), *Summer and Smoke* (frigidity), *Cat on a Hot Tin Roof* (impotence, alcoholism, homosexuality), *Sweet Bird of Youth* (drug addiction, castration, syphilis), *Suddenly Last Summer* (homosexuality, cannibalism), and *The Night of Iguana* (masturbation, underwear fetishism, coprophagy).

Much of the negativity directed at Williams came from confusion and misunderstanding of his late plays. As Annette Saddik and other scholars have argued, Williams' late "outrageous" plays written from the 1960s to the early 1980s were his "response to a critical establishment that swung from hailing him as 'American's Greatest Playwright' during the 1940s and '50s, to viciously dismissing both him and his work after *The Night of the Iguana* in 1961."[58] Growing interest in Williams since the 1990s has led to "a series of festivals, conferences, and journals dedicated to his work" and new scholarship to reassess "the Williams canon through a variety of new theoretical lenses," including the politics of sexuality in Williams oeuvre." Saddik, for example, in her *Tennessee Williams and The Theatre of Excess* (2015), looks at Williams' late plays "through the theoretical lenses of Mikhail Bakhtin, Antonin Artaud, and Julia Kristeva as well as through the sensibilities of the carnivalesque and the grotesque, German Expressionism, and psychoanalytic, feminist, and queer theory, in order to contextualize these plays in terms of a subversive politics of excess and laughter that celebrates the irrational."[59] One irony concerning the literary reputation of Tennessee Williams is that in the 1990s, some gay critics felt that Tennessee Williams was not "gay *enough*" for them because "he was incapable of producing a 'positive image' of a gay person." Paller, however, contends that "none of Williams' gay characters is simply the product of its author's alleged self-loathing, but an amalgam of personal, social, and historical forces" and that "his work was the place where he struggled with and overcame" whatever self-loathing he may have had.[60]

Much of the early Chinese rejection and/or misgivings of Tennessee Williams, especially by Chinese theatre artists, was informed by the dominant ideology and discourse in arts and literature. As is well-known to scholars of modern Chinese culture (including arts and literature) and history, for decades, the country's cultural policies and ideologies were based on Mao Zedong's "Yan'an Talk" in 1942, in which Mao, while recognizing the necessity and benefit of drawing from both foreign and classic literatures, called on the artists and writers to go to the common people for both inspiration and material:[61]

> Art and literature of all levels have their root in human beings' reflection upon the masses' lives. Books and existing artistic products are only the streams from this source; they were born as our ancestors and foreigners created upon the foundations of the people's literature and art. We should critically learn from these traditional and foreign elements while we reshape the raw materials we take from people's present arts and literature ... Such learning determines the difference between naiveté and refinement, and distinction between crudeness and elegance.

Further, Mao asked artists and writers to focus on the "brightness" of the revolutionary causes (instead of dwelling on the darker sides). He went on to issue the decree that all art and literature must serve the workers, peasants, and soldiers and be subservient to politics—the objectives of the Communist revolution and the Party.[62]

These cultural policies and ideologies were also influenced by the dominant ideology of Soviet Russian literature, the so-called socialist realism, which has a four-part "dictum": "party-mindedness," which decrees that every artistic act is a political act and the Communist Party is the ultimate source of all knowledge; "idea-mindedness," which decrees that "idea" (or content) of all artwork should embody and promote whatever the Party's top priority was at the moment, socioeconomic or moral; "class-mindedness," which decrees that all artwork should serve the cause of the proletariat; "people- or folk-mindedness," which decrees that all artwork should draw from the masses in both matter (traditions and values) and manner (e.g., language) in order to be accessible and appealing to them.[63] One can only imagine how Tennessee Williams would fare under the scrutiny of such dogmatic policies and ideologies.

Ironically, although the Chinese leftist cultural and literary ideology was heavily influenced by the socialist realism ideology of the Soviet Union, Williams fared quite well on the Soviet stage.[64] Soviet press mentioned Williams for the first time at the end of the 1940s, alluding to the staging of a new play "with the wild name *A Streetcar Named Desire* written by a certain Williams," which shows the moral degradation and spiritual decay in capitalistic society that had "run into absurdity." In the 1950s, the theaters of Moscow began to open their doors to Western companies: La Comedie Francaise with Moliere and Corneille, the TNP Theatre from Paris with Musset, Hugo, and Balzac, the Berliner Ensemble with Brecht's *Mother* Courage (which was soon followed by the staging of Brecht's *The Threepenny Opera* and *The Caucasian Chalk Circle* at the Mayakovsky Theatre, directed by Okhlopkov). In 1960, the magazine *Inostrannaya Literatura* (Foreign Literature) published a translation of Williams *Orpheus Descending*, which was staged in the Mossoviet Theatre in 1961. In 1967, when the Proletarian Cultural Revolution in China (which, among other things, was meant to abolish all things feudalistic and bourgeois), had reached its feverish height, an anthology of ten of Williams's plays (*The Glass Menagerie and Nine Other Plays*, all translated into Russian) was published. In 1968, eight years after the Mossoviet Theatre's *Orpheus Descending*, the Ermolova Theatre staged *The Glass Menagerie*, which was followed two years later, in 1971, by the staging of *A Streetcar Named Desire* at the Mayakovsky Theatre. During the 1970s and the first half of the 1980s, Tennessee Williams "became a favorite Western playwright, and also one of the most frequently staged authors in the Soviet theatre."[65]

Another important reason for Chinese early rejection and/or misgivings of Williams has to do with Chinese sexual mores, consciously or unconsciously—given that Chinese scholars might not have known a lot about Tennessee Williams and were not aware of the negative reception he was experiencing in the West due to his homosexuality (not just an orientation, but a lifestyle he pursued, sometimes recklessly). Homosexuality has existed in China since ancient times and, according to some scholars, Chinese attitude toward homosexuality, as was the case of ancient Athens and Rome, was accepting, as evidenced by classical poems celebrating male friendship and stories of homosexual love involving imperial figures. One such story concerns the relationship between Emperor Wen of Chen (Chen Wen Di 陈文帝, 522–566) and his favorite male lover, Han Zigao (韩子高). According to *Book of Chen* (Chen Shu 陈书), the official history of the Chen dynasty, one of the Southern Dynasties of China, Chen famously said to Han: "People say I am destined to be an Emperor. If it comes true, you will become my queen." Chen did become an Emperor in 559, but he was unable to keep his promise to Han and so he instead made Han a general. Han spent all his time with Emperor Wen of Chen until he later died in 566.[66]

Another story concerns the homosexual love between Emperor Ai of Han (Han Ai Di 汉哀帝, 27 BCE–1 BCE) and Dong Xian (董贤, 23 BCE?–1 BCE). The story goes that one afternoon after falling asleep for a nap on the same bed, Emperor Ai cut off his sleeve rather than disturb the sleeping Dong Xian when he had to get out of bed, hence the expression "the passion of the cut sleeve" (*duan xiu zhi pi* 断袖之癖) used to refer to homosexual love. Thanks in part to this relationship, Dong advanced rapidly and soon became the supreme commander of the armed forces. When Emperor Ai of Han died suddenly (at the young age of 26), Dong, cornered by court intrigues against him, committed suicide.[67]

According to some scholars, negativity toward homosexuality in China was a much more recent development as the country began to try to "modernize" (read Westernize, adopting Western values and ways of thinking and doing things) itself since the nineteenth century in the face of challenges and aggressions from the West[68] whereas other scholars believe that such negativity is deeply rooted in the teachings of Confucius (551 BC–479 BC) that admonish against not having posterity, or rather, having no male heir (through heterosexual unions) as one of the greatest sins against filial piety.[69] For most of the twentieth century, homosexual sex was banned in China until it was legalized in 1997. As recently as 1993, *Farewell My Concubine* (*Ba wang bie ji* 霸王别姬), a historical film directed by Chen Kaige, starring Leslie Cheung, Gong Li, and Zhang Fengyi, was banned for domestic viewing due to its portrayal of homosexuality and the Cultural Revolution (1966–1976). The ban was reluctantly lifted (with the release of a heavily censored version) after the film won the Palme d'Or at the 1993 Cannes Film Festival.[70] The ban (for domestic release) on the 1996 film, *East Palace, West Palace* (*Dong gong xi gong* 东宫西宫), directed by Zhang Yuan, starring Hu Jun and Si Han, and inspired by real events in Beijing (the title of the film referring to the two parks near the Forbidden City where homosexuals congregated during the night), was never lifted.[71]

It is in part through the pioneering work of scholar activists such as Li Yinhe (李银河)[72] that the push for changes, both in societal attitudes and governmental policies, gathered momentum. Li, who received her PhD in sociology from the University of Pittsburgh (1998), in partnership with her husband Wang Xiaobo, conducted a first-time-ever extensive study of homosexuality in China, which was published in their 1992 book *Their World: A Study of Male Homosexuality in China* (*Tamen de shijie: Zhongguo nan tongxinglian qunluo toushi* 他们的世界: 中国男同性恋群落透视).[73] Li and Wang argued for the importance of conducting this first-time-ever extensive study of this "subculture" in China based on a basic philosophy that all humans, despite their differences in education, lifestyle, marital status, and so on, are equal; no one should automatically occupy the center and no one, including the homosexuals, should be marginalized.[74] In the context of China in the early 1990s, this amounted to a manifesto of equal rights for the homosexuals, not unlike Maria Wollstonecraft's *A Vindication of Rights for Women* (1792). Li has since continued to conduct extensive studies of homosexuality, sexuality, and gender equality in China and, along with many other LGBTQ rights activists, advocating for same-sex marriage legislation and other social and policy changes.

Neglected or rejected during much of the 1960s and the 1970s, Williams' fortune in China began to change in the 1980s as China opened its door to the outside world and embarked on reforms, as attitudes and policies and laws toward homosexuality began to evolve, albeit slowly. Since then, interest in this American playwright has gained momentum, as evidenced not only by the many published translations of his plays but also by the hundreds of articles published in journals as well as graduate theses and dissertations approaching Williams' plays from a myriad of critical perspectives. The volume alone is testimonial of how far China has come in the last few decades toward embracing this "wounded genius" from America. Williams' plays, such as *The Glass Menagerie, A Streetcar Named Desire*, and *Cat on a Hot Tin Roof*, have also seen quite a few notable productions on the Chinese stage.

This book studies how the reception of Tennessee Williams in China, from rejection and/or misgivings to cautious curiosity and finally to full-throated acceptance, has developed over time through literary translation, critical interpretation, and theatrical adaptation in the context of profound changes in China's socioeconomic and cultural life and mores during the decades since the end of the Cultural Revolution (1966–1976) and the beginning of "reform and opening up." During those decades, China has developed from an economy teetering on the edge of collapse to that of the second largest in the world today. Compared to the days of "Eight Model Plays" (e.g., *Red Detachment of Women*—a ballet presented to Richard Nixon by Madame Mao during his historical visit to China in 1972),[75] today's sociocultural life in China is exponentially richer and offers exponentially more choices and possibilities, from stage (professional and armature) to screen (big and small), from print to all kinds of new social media platforms despite censorship, "The Great Firewall" (legal and technological barriers set up by the government to block access to selected foreign websites and to slow down cross-border internet traffic)[76] and other treacherous limits and constraints. A significant sign that Chinese society has also become "kinder" was the decriminalization of homosexual sex in 1997 and its removal from the list of mental disorders in 2001 by the Chinese Society of Psychiatry; it had concluded that homosexuality is not a perversion (c.f., The American Psychiatric Association did so in 1973; the World Health Organization in 1993). This was a big step forward toward a kinder, more accepting society, especially compared to the recent past when homosexual activities were not only banned but also prosecuted sometimes, although even today homosexuals could still face prejudice and harassment of various kinds.[77]

This study is also situated in the larger context of the reception of Western ideas and arts and literature since the post-Opium War (1839–1841) decades as China searched for ways to strengthen itself in the brave new world and to reclaim its glory, real and imagined, on the world stage. Indeed, cultural and people renewal for national survival has been the motivating force behind much of the Chinese translation, interpretation, and adaptation endeavors since the turn of the twentieth century. It is what has inspired many Chinese intellectuals and artists living by the "literature/art as a vehicle of the way (*wen yi zai dao* 文以載道) mantra upheld by the Chinese intelligentsia for centuries although the *dao* (道 the way) has never been a "constant" but a "variable" and translation, interpretation, adaptation and such artistic, literary, and intellectual practices have, inevitably, always been molded by the complex dynamics of texts (literary and socio-historical), contexts (Chinese and Western), and intertexts (translations, adaptations, performances), of dominance (language, culture, ideology) and resistance, and of tension and convergence.

This study draws from critical perspectives from translation studies, comparative drama and comparative literature, adaptation studies and other pertinent fields of inquiry that have many points of both convergence and diversion between and amongst them, which will lend this study an assortment of lenses, so to speak, to both see the big picture—broad contours and topographies—and sharpen the view of subtle nuances. It is the first comprehensive and interdisciplinary study of the reception of Tennessee Williams in China that examines the literary translation, critical interpretation, and theatrical adaptation of Williams' dramatic works in the context of profound socioeconomic and cultural changes in China since the end of the Cultural Revolution and indeed since the turn of the twentieth century. As such, this book fills a notable gap in scholarship in the reception of Tennessee Williams, one of the greatest American playwrights ("The American Shakespeare"[78]) whose works enjoy vibrant afterlives all over the world, in cultures other than American and European. It joins book-length studies of the reception of Williams in the West and Chinese reception of Shakespeare, Ibsen, O'Neill, Brecht, and other important Western playwrights whose dramatic works have been more eagerly embraced and appropriated, through translation, interpretation, and adaptation, for the national renewal project and have had catalytic effect on modern Chinese cultural life.

This book has five chapters. Chapter 1 introduces the subject and scope of the study, its historical and cultural context, and the critical perspectives drawing from translation studies, comparative drama and comparative literature, and adaptation studies that inform the study. Chapter 2 focuses on Chinese translations of Tennessee Williams: *what* gets translated, *why*, and *how*, for example, how do Chinese translators deal with explicit sexuality and gender themes/politics in Williams works, including his *Memoirs* (1972; "A raw display of private life"). Chapter 3 presents a critical overview/assessment of recent Chinese scholarship on Williams dramatic oeuvre, especially a dozen or so monographs based on the authors' doctoral dissertations. Chapter 4 is a study of Chinese staging of Williams plays, especially *A Streetcar Named Desire*, in the last few decades—from trying to understand the complexity of Blanche (1988) to presenting an overtly more sympathetic portrayal of Blanche through the creation of a frame narrator and insertion of fantastic scenes (2002), and finally to highlighting the humanness of the modern tragedy (2016, reproduced thereafter), embracing Blanche and such psychological and sociocultural and economic migrants and outcasts as amongst "us." Chapter 5 concludes the study with a forward look not only of the reception of Tennessee Williams in China in the years ahead, but also, more importantly, of Western arts and literature in general, including drama/theatre, as cultural and ideological control continues to be tightened, as has been the case since much of the second decade of the twenty-first century.

NOTES

1. Tennessee Williams, *Tennessee Williams Plays 1937–1955* (New York: The Library of America, 2000), 563. Hereafter, Williams, *1937–1955*.
2. This introductory overview of the reception of Tennessee Williams in China draws from Wei Zhang and Shouhua Qi, "The Kindness of Strangers: Tennessee Williams's *A Streetcar Named Desire* on the Chinese Stage," *Comparative Drama* 54.1 (2021): 97–115, https://scholarworks.wmich.edu/compdr/vol54/iss1/5.
3. Eugene O'Neill visited China in 1927 to search for the "Right Way" and to recharge his battery, so to speak, with wisdom of Chinese philosophy. See Eric Grode, "A Touch of Eugene O'Neill," *The Sun*, April 25, 2007, http://www.nysun.com/arts/touch-of-eugene-oneill/53172/. Arthur Miller visited China in 1978 as a tourist and then again in 1983 to direct *Death of a Salesman* in Beijing. See Arthur Miller, *Salesman in Beijing* (New York: Viking, 1984).
4. It was not staged again until 2013 as one of the three short plays of *The Chorus Girl Plays* during the Provincetown Tennessee Williams Theatre Festival. In this burlesque play, two young women, Millie and her friend Aileen, pick up two sailors and bring them home to the Bronx. See "Provincetown Tennessee Williams Theater Festival-2013 Shows," https://www.twptown.org/archives.
5. John S. Bak, ed., *Tennessee Williams and Europe: Intercultural Encounters, Transatlantic Exchanges* (Amsterdam and New York: Rodopi, 2014), 1.
6. At least one Chinese scholar interpreted these China/Chinese culture references in Williams plays as indications of the American playwright regarding China as the last spiritual and emotional refuge (see Chap. 4, pp. 119–122), which seems a misreading and hasty overgeneration based more on wishful thinking than on any textual or biographical evidence.
7. Williams, *1937–1955*, 492–493.
8. Ibid., 499.
9. Ibid., 515.
10. Ibid., 545.
11. Ibid., 552.
12. Ibid., 554–555.

13. Ibid., 562.
14. Ibid., 505–507.
15. Ibid., 506.
16. Tennessee Williams, *Tennessee Williams Plays 1957–1980* (New York: The Library of America, 2000), 333. Hereafter, Williams, *1957–1980*.
17. Ibid., 366–367.
18. Ibid., 385.
19. The first notable use of the "digging a hole to China" idea occurred in the middle of the nineteenth century. In 1854, Henry David Thoreau wrote in *Walden*, "As for your high towers and monuments, there was a crazy fellow in town who undertook to dig through to China, and he got so far that, as he said, he heard the Chinese pots and kettles rattle; but I think that I shall not go out of my way to admire the hole which he made." There seems not much curiosity or adventurous spirit on the part of the famed transcendentalist about the world so far out of his reach. For more on the possible origins and cultural significance of this saying, see Andy Wright, "The Hole Truth about Why We 'Dig to China,'" October 19, 2015, https://www.atlasobscura.com/articles/the-hole-truth-about-why-we-dig-to-china.
20. Williams, *1957–1980*, 399.
21. Ibid., 405.
22. Ibid., 410.
23. Ibid., 414.
24. Ibid., 391.
25. Ibid., 406.
26. Ibid., 411–412.
27. Here is a quote from the "Foreword" of a 1948 book entitled *They Went to China*:

    China missionaries of the Disciples of Christ have known privation and danger, distrust and suspicion, indifference and opposition; they have experienced revolutions from within and invasion from without; but they have also known the high joys of suffering alleviated, of ignorance dispelled, of souls illuminated and lives regenerated by the love of God, of fellowship with Chinese Christian friends in soul-testing and in heartwarming experiences, of seeing come into being, and of being a part of a vital, growing church in China.

    See The United Christian Missionary Society, *They Went To China: Biographies of Missionaries of the Disciples of Christ* (Indianapolis, Indiana: The United Christian Missionary Society, 1948), https://digitalcommons.acu.edu/crs_books/477.

28. See Chap. 3, pp. 119–122.

29. In autumn 1955, per invitation from the Chinese as part of their people's diplomacy strategy (to eventually establish official relations with the guests' countries), Jean-Paul Sartre, along with Simone de Beauvoir, made a two-month visit to China, a highly programmed tour to showcase the new People's Republic. The distinguished French guests had tea with Mao Zedong (1893–1976) although no substantive conversation happened. They also had the honor to join Mao on the Tiananmen podium during the National Day celebration and went on to tour Shenyang, Shanghai, Hangzhou, and Guangzhou. Sartre was probably an exceptional case, being a Communist sympathizer, although he did not join the French Communist Party; moreover, he was actively involved in the French resistance against the Nazis during World War II. See Shouhua Qi, *Adapting Western Classics for the Chinese Stage* (London and New York: Routledge, 2018), 162.

30. Tennessee Williams, *Memoirs* (New York: New Directions Publishing, 2006), 235.

31. Eddie Woods, *Tennessee Williams in Bangkok* (Dixon, CA: Inkblot Books, 2013), 1–6.

32. Williams, *Memoirs*, 236.

33. John Lahr, *Tennessee Williams: Mad Pilgrimage of the Flesh* (New York: Norton, 2014), 351.

34. See John Stoltenberg, "Tennessee Williams's *Lady from the Village of Falling Flowers* Returns," December 19, 2020, *DC Metro*, https://dcmetrotheaterarts.com/2020/12/19/natsu-onoda-power-crafts-a-tennessee-williams-puppet-show/; and Christopher Henley, "Review: *The Lady from the Village of Falling Flowers*," December 11, 2019, *DC Theatre Scene*, https://dctheatrescene.com/2019/12/11/review-the-lady-from-the-village-of-falling-flowers/.

35. See "Kamishibai," https://en.wikipedia.org/wiki/Kamishibai.

36. See The Embassy of Japan, *Japan Report* (日本) 6.8, April 15, 1960, 5, https://books.google.com/books?id=7VeHgPX7m1MC&printsec=frontcover&source=gbs_ge_summary_r&cad=0#v=onepage&q&f=false.

37. See "*The Day on Which a Man Dies: An Occidental Noh-Play*," https://www.themorgan.org/literary-historical/184607.

38. See "Gutai group," https://en.wikipedia.org/wiki/Gutai_group.

39. See David Kaplan, "*The Day on Which a Man Dies*: Chicago 2007, Chicago, East Hampton, Provincetown 2009," http://davidkaplandirector.com/the-day-on-which-a-man-dies/; and Tom Williams, "The Day On Which A Man Dies: Unique Lost Tennessee Williams One Act is Riveting," Chicago Critic, https://chicagocritic.com/the-day-on-which-a-man-dies/.

40. See Sarah Elizabeth Johnson, *The Influence of Japanese Traditional Performing Arts Tennessee Williams Late Plays*, MFA (Master of Fine Arts) thesis, University of Iowa, 2014), https://doi.org/10.17077/etd.92wlztti.

41. Michael Paller, *Gentlemen Callers: Tennessee Williams, Homosexuality, and Mid-Twentieth-Century Drama* (New York: Palgrave Macmillan, 2005), 163.

42. See Clive Barnes, "Theater: *In the Bar of a Tokyo Hotel*," *New York Times*, May 12, 1969, https://archive.nytimes.com/www.nytimes.com/books/00/12/31/specials/williams-tokyo.html; Mark Blankenship, "*In the Bar of a Tokyo Hotel*," *Variety*, February 6, 2007, https://variety.com/2007/legit/reviews/in-the-bar-of-a-tokyo-hotel-1200510564/; and Alexa Criscitiello, "Photo Flash: *In The Bar of A Tokyo Hotel* Opens Tomorrow at 292 Theatre," *Broadway World*, March 14, 2017, https://www.broadwayworld.com/article/Photo-Flash-IN-THE-BAR-OF-A-TOKYO-HOTEL-Opens-Tomorrow-at-202-Theatre-20170314.

43. Paller, 169.

44. Tennessee Williams, *In the Bar of a Tokyo Hotel* (New York: Dramatist Plays Service, 1969), 40.

45. It is interesting to note that in his *Memoirs*, Japan gets mentioned only once (236) and Mishima twice (236, 248).

46. Williams, *Memoirs*, 236–237.

47. "In that velvet dressing-gown you look like the Emperor Tiberius!—In his imperial toga!—Your hair and your eyes are both the color of iron! Iron grey. Invincible looking! People nearby are all somewhat—frightened of you. They feel your force and they admire you for it. They come to you here for opinions on this or that." Williams, *1937–1955*, 869.

48. See Ying Ruocheng and Claire Conceison, *Voices Carry: Behind Bars and Backstage during China's Revolution and Reform* (New York: Roman and Littlefield, 2009).

49. Wu Wenquan 吾文泉, "*Kua wenhua shixue yanjiu yu wutai biaoshu: Tiannaxi weiliansi zai zhongguo*" (跨文化诗学研究与舞台表述:田纳西·威廉斯在中国 Transcultural poetics studies and theatrical expressions: Tennessee Williams in China," *Xiju* (Drama) 4 (2004): 68.

50. Qi, *Adapting Western Classics*, 92.

51. Zhou Peitong 周培桐. "*Duju yige de meiguo juzuojia: Jieshao Tiannaxi weiliansi*" (独具一格的美国剧作家—介绍田纳西·威廉斯 An idiosyncratic American playwright: an introduction of Tennessee Williams), *Xiju bao* (Theatre Gazette) 8 (1987): 33–34.

52. Wei Zhang, *Chinese Adaptations of Brecht: Appropriation and Intertextuality* (New York: Palgrave Macmillan, 2019), 15–18.

53. See Wu Wenquan. In 2016, almost 30 years later, the graduating class of acting students at the recently founded Shanghai Institute of Visual Arts mounted a production of *Cat on a Hot Tin Roof*. It had a full week run from November 27 to December 3, to packed audiences. See "*Biye daxi Re tiepi wuding shang de mao*" (Graduation performance *Cat on a Hot Tin Roof*, December 1, 2016, http://www.siva.edu.cn/site/site1/newsText.aspx?si=16&id=3787.

In 2012, *Cat on a Hot Tin Roof* was one of the three Williams plays performed by the Amsterdam Company Urban Aphrodite during the Shanghai Pride celebration to highlight their homosexual themes (the other two plays being *The Chalky White Substance* and *Something Unspoken*). See "Shanghai PRIDE 2012 Theater," http://www.shpride.com/pride2012theater/?lang=en.

54. See Annette Saddik, *The Politics of Reputation: The Critical Reception of Tennessee Williams' Later Plays* (Plainsboro, NJ: Associated University Presses, 1999) and David Kaplan, ed., *Tenn at One Hundred: The Reputation of Tennessee Williams* (East Brunswick, NJ: Hansen Publishing Group, 2011).

55. Gilbert Debusscher, "Creative Rewriting: European and American Influences on the dramas of Tennessee Williams," in *The Cambridge Companion to Tennessee Williams*, edited by Matthew C. Roudané (Cambridge, UK: Cambridge University Press, 1997), 172, 183.

56. Dirk Gindt, "Tennessee Williams and the Swedish Academy: Why He Never Won the Nobel Prize," in Kaplan, *Tenn*, 157–160.

57. Qtd. in Thomas Keith, "Pulp Williams: Tennessee in the Popular Imagination," in Kaplan, *Tenn*, 170.

58. Annette Saddik: "The Grotesque and Too Funny for Laughter," in Kaplan, *Tenn*, 263.

59. Annette J. Saddik, *Tennessee Williams and The Theatre of Excess: The Strange, The Crazed, The Queer* (Cambridge, UK: Cambridge University Press, 2015), 5.

60. Paller, 2.

61. Qtd. in Hung-yok Ip, *Intellectuals in Revolutionary China, 1921–1949* (London and New York: Routledge, 2005), 145.

62. Shouhua Qi, *Western Literature in China and the Translation of a Nation* (New York: Palgrave Macmillan, 2012), 91–92.

63. Caryl Emerson, *The Cambridge Introduction to Russian Literature* (Cambridge, UK: Cambridge University Press, 2008), 200.

64. This brief overview of the reception of Tennessee Williams in the Soviet Union draws from Irene Shaland, *Tennessee Williams on the Soviet Stage* (Lanham, NY and London: University Press of America, 1987).

65. Shaland, 2–5.
66. Damien Chaussende, "Chen Shu 陈书," in *Early Medieval Chinese Texts: A Bibliographical Guide*, edited by Cynthia Louise Chennault, et al. (Berkeley, CA: Institute of East Asian Studies University of California, 2018), 44–47.
67. See Bret Hinsch, *Passions of the Cut Sleeve: The Male Homosexual Tradition in China* (Oakland, CA: University of California Press, 1990).
68. See Hinsch; and Wenqing Kang, *Obsession: Male Same-Sex Relations in China, 1900–1950* (Hong Kong: Hong Kong University Press, 2009).
69. In Confucian teachings, filial piety is regarded as "the foundation of all virtues, and the seed of all education," and, according to Mencius (372–289 BC or 385–303 or 302 BC), of the three sins against filial piety (disobeying one's parents; not taking care of one's parents when they are old; and having no male heir), having no male heir is "the greatest of all." See The American Ethical Union, *The Standard*. Vol III (New York: the American Ethical Union, 1916–1917), 194–195. See also Fu Youde and Wang Qiangwei, "A Comparison of Filial Piety in Ancient Judaism and Early Confucianism," translated by Noah Lipkowitz, *Journal of Chinese Humanities* 1 (2015), https://brill.com/view/journals/joch/1/2/article-p280_6.xml?language=en.
70. See Nicholas D. Kristof, "China Bans One of Its Own Films; Cannes Festival Gave It Top Prize," *The New York Times*, August 4, 1993, https://www.nytimes.com/search?query=Nicholas+D.++Kristof%2C+%22China+Bans+One+of+Its+Own+Films%3B+Cannes+Festival+Gave+It+Top+Prize%22; and Patrick E. Tyler, "China's Censors Issue a Warning," *The New York Times*, September 4, 1993, https://www.nytimes.com/search?query=Patrick+E.+Tyler%2C+%22China%27s+Censors+Issue+a+Warning%22.
71. See "*Dong gong xi gong*" (东宫西宫), (https://baike.baidu.com/item/%E4%B8%9C%E5%AE%AB%E8%A5%BF%E5%AE%AB/2540476;   and Lawrence Van Gelder, "*East Palace, West Palace*: Powerful Drama and Courageous Politics," *The New York Times*, July 24, 1998, https://archive.nytimes.com/www.nytimes.com/library/film/072498palace-film-review.html.
72. See "Li Yinhe," https://en.wikipedia.org/wiki/Li_Yinhe; and "Li Yinhe" (李银河), https://baike.baidu.com/item/%E6%9D%8E%E9%93%B6%E6%B2%B3/648256.
73. Li Yinhe and Wang Xiaobo 李银河 王小波, *Their World: A Study of Male Homosexuality in China* (*Tamen de shijie: Zhongguo nan tongxinglian qunluo toushi* 他们的世界—中国男同性恋群落透视) (Hong Kong: Cosmos Press, 1992; Xi'an: Shanxi People's Press 陕西人民出版社, 1993).
74. Li and Wang, 5–6.

75. "Yangbanxi" (model drama), https://www.britannica.com/art/yangbanxi.
76. "Great Firewall," https://en.wikipedia.org/wiki/Great_Firewall.
77. See Tom Mountford, *China: The Legal Position and Status of Lesbian, Gay, Bisexual and Transgender People in The People's Republic of China*, 2009, https://outrightinternational.org/content/china-legal-position-and-status-lesbian-gay-bisexual-and-transgender-people-people%E2%80%99s; and John Gittings, "China Drops Homosexuality from List of Psychiatric Disorders," *The Guardian*, March 7, 2001, https://www.theguardian.com/world/2001/mar/07/china.johngittings1.
78. See Matthew Biberman, "Tennessee Williams: The American Shakespeare." *Huffington Post*, March 26, 2011, https://www.huffpost.com/entry/tennessee-williams-the-am_b_838552.

CHAPTER 2

Speaking the Unspoken and the Unspeakable: Translating Tennessee Williams

Early in the opening scene of Tennessee Williams' one-act play *Something Unspoken* (1953), we are told that between the two women characters, Miss Cornelia Scott and Miss Grace Lancaster, there is "a mysterious tension, an atmosphere of something unspoken."[1] As the play progresses on that particular day, we find out that an annual election of the local chapter of the Confederate Daughters is being held and Cornelia has a personal stake in its outcome although she feigns indifference. The tension between the two grows until Grace has this to say to Cornelia:[2]

> You say there's something unspoken. Maybe there is. I don't know. But I do know some things are better left unspoken.

Grace does eventually gather enough courage to speak the unspoken about their relationship, complicated by their politics (different social status) and personality despite the intimacy of having lived under the same roof for the last fifteen years (as signified by the fifteen roses Cornelia has given Grace to mark the anniversary).

In many ways, how to speak the unspoken or the unspeakable through translation has been the challenge facing Chinese translators of "Western" ideas, from Xuanzang (玄奘 602–664) who travelled to India to seek true scriptures of Buddhism[3] to those who took on tremendous translation

© The Author(s), under exclusive license to Springer Nature Switzerland AG 2022
S. Qi, *Culture, History, and the Reception of Tennessee Williams in China*, Chinese Literature and Culture in the World,
https://doi.org/10.1007/978-3-031-16934-2_2

projects in modern times, for example, Yan Fu (严复 1854–1921), who translated Thomas Huxley's *Evolution and Ethics* as (*Tianyan lun* 天演论, On Evolution), Adam Smith's *The Wealth of Nations* (*Yuan fu* 原富, On Wealth), Lin Shu (林纾 1852–1924), who (co)translated Harriet Beecher Stowe's *Uncle Tom's Cabin* (*Heinu yutian lu* 黑奴吁天录, Black Slave Cry to Heaven), Charles Dickens' *David Copperfield* (*Kuairou yusheng lu* 块肉 余生录, Life of a Piece of Flesh), and many other fictional works. Translation, carrying ideas from source language(s) and culture(s) to target language(s) and culture(s), especially in the context of China, is so much more than the "technical" question of being faithful or freewheeling, literal or free, and for the stage or for the reader (performability versus readability, in the case of dramatic works) although they are all important questions. It is fraught with politics, morality, and social and cultural norms. This is even truer in the case of Tennessee Williams, given how his literary reputation was maligned for quite some time in the US due to his open homosexuality and how he was not eagerly accepted in China for much of the same reasons—his perceived obsession with the dark and ugly side of life.[4] Indeed, Williams was introduced and translated into Chinese much later than his American compatriots such as Eugene O'Neill and Arthur Miller and many other Western authors, largely due to the sociopolitical and cultural agendas translation has taken on, self-consciously, in modern times.

TRANSLATION AS AGENT OF CHANGE FOR CULTURAL RENEWAL

Translation has always been an important part of Chinese march toward modernity.[5] In so many ways, translation has played a key role in the shaping of modern China, its culture, its memories, its psyche, and every facet of its sociopolitical life. China's experience with foreign texts can be traced back to the epic-scale Buddhism scripture translation projects that lasted from the first century (AD) to about the thirteenth century. The Chinese during those centuries and all the way to the early nineteenth century saw themselves as "central in the world," their culture was relatively "homogeneous;" therefore, they were in a position to acculturate the foreign through the "domesticating" method of translation, for example, using the native Daoist concepts as well as classical Chinese (the sanctioned style of language for formal and public communication by the literati, the scholar-official class, the court, and the monastery) to assimilate Buddhism into the Chinese culture.[6] It was with the same elite readership in mind that Yan Fu, Lin Shu, and Liang Qichao (梁启超 1873–1929) in the late 1890s jumpstarted a translation campaign to strengthen and hence save China in a world in which the old view of China being the "Middle Kingdom" had been shattered by the West.

The more "radical" members of the New Culture and New Literature Movement in the early decades of the twentieth century leaned toward the "foreignizing" style not only for the translated text but also for creative writing in the vernacular. For them, the hope for creating a refreshing *baihua* (白话 vernacular) for literature lay in the creation of a new, Europeanized literary language that would transcend the language that had been long in use. They argued that a main task of the New Literature Movement was to change the old mindset about literature and the style of writing that had been in use for thousands of years and stifled free expressions of thoughts and feelings. The push for Europeanizing the literary language and for the "foreignization" method of translation was driven by the overarching sociopolitical and cultural agenda of the New Culture and New Literature Movement. Inter-culturally speaking, the Chinese language, though having its great traditions and splendid achievements in literature and other writings, was the dominated language, to borrow from Pascale Casanova, whereas the European languages, riding on the hegemonic powers of their host countries, were the dominating language and culture.[7] The irony, it seems, is that many iconoclasts in the dominated language and culture were eager to adopt, or at least adapt, the dominating language and culture in order to renew their own, to renew their nation, and ultimately, to resist the hegemonic powers of the dominating language and culture. Intra-culturally, the position of dominance and resistance shifted as the New Culture and New Literature Movement gained momentum. The traditional, classical (or quasi-classical) style that had dominated for centuries gradually yielded ground to the new, Europeanized *baihua*. Although the debate has never been settled completely, *baihua* has enjoyed unchallenged dominance ever since.

Any discussion of translation with regard to drama/theatre, in the case of this chapter, would inevitably entail the question of literary translation for reading versus translation for stage performance (playability or performability.) In the early 1980s, Bassnett put forth the idea that a dramatic text is a fully rounded unit only when it is performed because it is only in the performance that its full potential is realized (1991b, 120–121). She later further developed this idea into the concept of playability or perform-ability: on the one hand, performability implies a distinction between the idea of the written text and the physical aspect of the performance, and, on the other hand, it presupposes that the theatre text contains within its structure some features that make it performable.[8] Some scholars believe that the theoretical polarization of performability and readability is reductive because in practice, there are no precise divisions between a performance-oriented translation and a reader-oriented translation, but rather there exists a blurring of borderlines.[9]

In the context of China, the debate or discussion of performability versus readability in the translation of dramatic texts is a much more recent phenomenon. For many reasons, dramatic texts, from classical Greek tragedies through Shakespeare to more modern classics, have almost always been translated as "literary" texts for readability. Only in a few cases, such as Ying Ruocheng's translation of Arthur Miller's *Death of Salesman* for staging in 1983, that considerable attention was given to performability.[10] In the case of Tennessee Williams, questions of translation have more to do with politics, cultural norms, and sexual mores than performability versus readability or anything else. Below is an incomplete list of works by Tennessee Williams that have seen published Chinese (re)translations:

1963 *Something Unspoken*
1981 *The Glass Menagerie*
1982 *Cat on a Hot Tin Roof*
1985 *The Glass Menagerie*
1987 *A Streetcar Named Desire*
1991 *A Streetcar Named Desire*
1991 *The Glass Menagerie*
1992 *The Glass Menagerie*
1992 *Cat on a Hot Tin Roof*
1992 *A Streetcar Named Desire*
1992 *The Night of Iguana*
2015 *A Streetcar Named Desire*
2018 *Memoirs*

From the incomplete list above, it is clear that while *A Streetcar Named Desire* and *The Glass Menagerie* have each seen multiple translations, no later plays of Williams have had any such luck (c.f., "dark" and absurdist plays by Beckett, Camus, Ionesco, Albee, and others that have been trans-lated since "reform and opening up" in the late 1970s without encountering undue resistance). Somehow Williams remains known to the Chinese as the author of *The Glass Menagerie*, *A Streetcar Named Desire*, and *Cat on a Hot Tin Roof*, mostly through both translations and theatrical adaptations although other plays of his, for example, *Suddenly Last Summer*, *Smoke and Youth*, *The Night of Iguana*, and even some of his later plays, have begun to receive their share of scholarly attention recently.[11]

Speaking the Unspoken and the Unspeakable Through Translation: Politics

The first known Chinese translation of Williams' dramatic works was his one-act play *Something Unspoken* (1953), rendered by Ying Ruocheng and published in *World Literature* (*Shijie wenxue*世界文学) (1963).[12] It is not known how Ying Ruocheng obtained a copy of this one-act play in the early 1960s of China, when scholars and artists had very limited access to contemporary Western plays such as those written by Williams. It is also interesting, and potentially quite revealing, to consider why, out of so many dramatic works of Williams, including award-winning and highly successful plays such as *The Glass Menagerie* and *A Streetcar Named Desire*, Ying Ruocheng chose this rather "obscure" one-act play to translate by way of introducing this American playwright to China. Given the larger sociocultural and political contexts of the early 1960s in China and the peritextual context of this published translation,[13] one cannot help but see this translation as fraught with sociopolitical relevance and significance although one cannot speculate now whether readers of this particular issue of *World Literature* in 1963 would see and hear such resonances in their socio-political life at the time. Was Ying applying the classical stratagem of "using the foreign to satirize the domestic" (*jie wai feng nei* 借外讽内) or the stratagem of "doing one thing under cover/facade of another" (*ming xiu zhan dao, an du chen cang* 明修栈道, 暗度陈仓)? If so, he did not let on by anything, explicit or implicit, anywhere in his writings, not even in his memoir, cowritten with Claire Conceison, when he knew his life's journey was coming to an end.[14] Nonetheless, a close reading of Ying's rendition of the play would reveal palpable, hard-to-miss relevance and resonance with the sociopolitical life of the 1960s China, which amounts to speaking, intentionally or not, the unspoken or the unspeakable through the camouflage of translated text; camouflage being a necessary stratagem for survival, given the all but certain dire consequences of doing so openly, as was the case of General Peng Dehuai (彭德怀 1898–1974).[15]

This is part of the stage description for the opening scene of the play, as written by Tennessee William, followed by Ying's Chinese rendition (the same arrangement hereafter):[16]

> Miss Cornelia Scott, 60, a wealthy southern spinster seated at a small mahogany table which is set for two … An imperial touch is given by the purple velvet drapes directly behind her figure at the table. (*underline added*)
> 考尔尼丽亚·司考脱小姐，六十岁，一个有钱的美国南部的老处女…. 正好在她身后垂下来的紫色丝绒帷幕给她增加了一种帝王般的威严。

The Chinese expression 帝王般的威严 (*diwang ban de weiyan*, imperial majesty) is a close denotative equivalent of "imperial touch," but is connotatively a notch or two more intense in conveying the regality of the person being described. Shortly after, the playwright describes Grace's "insubstantial quality in sharp contrast to Miss Scott's Roman grandeur," which Ying translates as 罗马式的威严 (*luoma shi de weiyan*).[17] Still in the opening scene of the play, Cornelia places her first phone call, pretending to be Grace, her secretary/companion:[18]

> Is this Mrs. Horton Reid's residence? I am calling for Miss Cornelia Scott.
> 是霍尔登·雷德夫人的公馆吗？我是为考尔尼丽亚·司考脱小姐打电话。

"Residence" is translated as 公馆 (*gongguan*), a near equivalent to "mansion" in English (a closer Chinese equivalent for "residence" would be 住所 *zhusuo* or 家 *jia*). Although 公馆 used to be associated with residences of the rich and powerful, for example, in the old Shanghai, it could also, semantically and socio-politically, evoke a more regal association, as in the expression 离宫别馆 (*ligong bieguan*, mansions or palaces outside the capital for the emperor when going on inspecting tours).[19]

The Chinese renditions of "imperial touch" (帝王般的威严), "Roman grandeur" (罗马式的威严), and "residence" (公馆) set the tone, in both linguistic and paralinguistic ways, for the topical theme of the play in its Chinese reincarnation, overdetermined by the sociopolitical ecology of the early 1960s China.

A short while after the opening scene, Grace answers a phone call:[20]

Miss Scott's residence (This announcement is made in a tone of reverence, as though mentioning <u>a seat of holiness</u>. (*underline added*)
司考脱小姐 公馆(她说这话时充满了敬意, 好像是在宣布这里是个什么圣地)。

圣地 (*shengdi*) in Chinese, like "seat of holiness" in English, is typically associated with religious holy places such as Mecca, Jerusalem, Vatican City and loaded with significance; it has also been used quite often in terms such as 革命圣地 (*geming shengdi*, revolutionary holy land/seat) in references of places such as 延安 (Yan'an), which served as the headquarters of the Chinese Communist Party from 1935 (the end of the Long March) to 1947.[21]

Sometimes, Ying chooses to keep "foreign" (French) expressions in the original in his Chinese rendition. In this phone conversation, Cornelia thus speaks to Esmeralda Hawkins:[22]

Of course, I know that you're calling me from the meeting, *ça va sans dire, ma petite*? Ha ha! But from which phone in the house, there's two you know, the one in the downstairs hall and the one in the chatelaine's *boudoir* where the ladies will probably be removing their wraps.
我知道你是从开会的地方打来的, *ça va sans dire, ma petite*? 问题是你用的是哪一架电话; 你知道, 那儿有两架, 楼下门厅里有一架, 夫人的 *boudoir* 里还有一架。

Ying keeps "*ça va sans dire, ma petite*?" ("It goes without saying, my little one") and *boudoir* (a woman's dressing room, bedroom, or private sitting room) untranslated to relay the flavor of the old southern culture as well as Cornelia's pretentiousness, in keeping with the practice of French being the language of aristocracies and royal courts in many European countries from medieval to early modern times.

Reading some of the dialogues between Cornelia and Grace, in their English original or in Ying's capable Chinese renditions, in the sociopolitical ecology of the early 1960s or from the vantage point of today, one cannot help but see and feel the barbed politics in the text and the subtext. As a matter of fact, Ying's Chinese renditions make whatever fiery political expressions in the original even fierier and more poignant. When Grace tries to talk Cornelia into going to the Annual Election being run on that day, Cornelia insists that she does not want to go:[23]

Intrigue, intrigue, and duplicity, revolt me so that I wouldn't be able to breathe in the same atmosphere!
全是<u>阴谋</u>, <u>阴谋</u>, <u>两面三刀</u>, 我对这些厌恶死了, 和她们在一起我就觉得恶心得喘不过气来!

Both 阴谋 (*yinmou*, plotting in the dark) and 两面三刀 (*liangmian sandao*, two faces and three daggers) are good Chinese equivalents to "intrigue" and "duplicity" respectively, but they are much more evocative and therefore more likely to "cut to the quick," so to speak, when experienced by Chinese readers of the translation.

Indeed, Cornelia suspects that there is a conspiracy against her amongst members of the local chapter and this election is a test of something: [24]

> It's a test of something. You see I have known for some time, now, that there is <u>a little group, a clique,</u> in the Daughters, which is hostile to me! ... There is <u>a movement against me.... An organized movement to keep me out of any important office</u> ... I don't "want" to be anything whatsoever. I simply want to break up this movement against me and for that purpose I have rallied my forces." (*underline added*)
> 这次是个考验。我可以告诉你, 我知道, 而且已经知道了不少日子, 在这些"女儿"当中有一个 <u>敌视我的小集团</u>, <u>一个派系...现在有一个反对我的运动....一个有组织的运动</u>, 目的在于防止我取得任何重要的职位....无论什么职位我都不用当。我只不过要 <u>粉碎这个反对我的运动</u>; 为了这个目的, 我已经 <u>把我的队伍动员起来了</u>。

Cornelia defends her own record at the local chapter of the Confederate Daughters:[25]

> I'm not a snob. I'm nothing if not <u>democratic</u>. (*underline added*)
> 我绝不是势利眼。没有比我再<u>讲民主</u>的了。

"讲民主" (*jiang minzhu*, being democratic),[26] 敌视我的小集团 (*dishi wo de xiao jituan*, a clique hostile to me), 一个派系 (*yige paixi*, a clique), 反对我的运动 (*fandui wo de yundong*, a movement against me), 有组织的运动 (*you zuzhi de yundong*, an organized movement), 粉碎这个反对我的运动 (*fensui zhege fandui wo de yundong*, to blast into powder this movement against me, which is much more evocative than the English original, "to break up this movement against me"), 把我的队伍动员起来了 (*ba wo de duiwu dongyuan qilai le*, which carries the same forcefulness as the war metaphor used the English original: "I have rallied my forces")—it is as if

Tennessee Williams had been writing these dialogues, or rather, Ying Ruocheng was translating these dialogues in 1963, with the Anti-Rightest Campaign (1957–1959), Lushan Conference (1959), and Four Cleanups Movement (1963) in mind.[27]

Having not many cards to play to ensure her coming out victorious from the election, Cornelia calls the branch of the Confederate Daughters bluff:[28]

> But if, on the other hand, the—uh—*clique!*—and you know the ones I mean1—is bold enough to propose something else for the office—Do you understand my position? In that eventuality, hard as it is to imagine—<u>I prefer to bow out of the picture entirely</u>!" (*underline added*)
> 如果那个—呃—*派系*!—你知道我指的是谁!—如果她们胆敢提出另外一个人来担任这个职位—你明白我的立场吗?如果事情演变到那一地步, 虽然这难以想象—<u>我宁可洁身引退, 完全退出</u>!

Later in the play, when Esmeralda, an offstage character, calls again to inform Cornelia of what the most likely results of the election would be, Cornelia thus responds:[29]

> Who asked if I would accept the vice regency, dear? Oh, Mrs. Colby, of course!—that treacherous witch!—*Esmeralda*! Listen! I—WILL ACCEPT—NO OFFICE—EXCEPT—THE HIGHEST. Did you understand that? I—WILL ACCEPT NO OFFICE EXCEPT—*ESMERALDA*!
> 谁提出的问我是否愿意接受副理事长的职位的, 亲爱的?噢, 寇儿比太太, 这还用说!—那个<u>两面三刀</u>的老妖婆!—埃斯默热达!听着!我—<u>除了—最高位置以外—什么—也不接受</u>!你听明白了没有?我—<u>除了最高的职位以外什么也</u>—埃斯默热达!

洁身引退, 完全退出 (*jieshen yintui, wanquan tuichu*, retreat/resign with a clean, impeccable reputation) is a good translation of "bow out of the picture," with the bonus of expressing the speaker's pride and sense of her moral superiority. 除了—最高位置以外—什么—也不接受! (*chule zui gao weizhi yiwai shenmo ye bu jieshou*) is an almost literal translation of the original: will accept no office except the highest. Once again, the parallels between what Cornelia says here at this high-stake moment in her life and what happened in China in the tumultuous sociopolitical and economic life of the country from late 1950s to early 1960s—Mao Zedong retreated to the second line of leadership (退居二线 *tuiju erxian*) in 1959 due to the disastrous results of the Great Leap Forward although the real power never left him as the supreme leader of the Communist Party—are hard to miss.[30]

However, there is nothing Cornelia can do when someone else, Mrs. Hornsby, a dark horse, is elected, but to resign to the reality, or rather, to resign from the local chapter of Confederate Daughters and be comforted by the new membership of the "more elite" Daughters of the Barons of Runymede and her eligibility for the Colonial Dames and "the Huguenot Society," declaring that she "couldn't possibly have taken it on if they'd—wanted" her to be the regency."[31]

The political strand of the story told in Williams' one-act play, especially in Ying's capable Chinese rendition, gives utterance to what was unspoken or unspeakable in the sociopolitical life of China then. The more personal strand of the story also speaks about an unspeakable aspect of social life, albeit much less visible or exigent at the time. Indeed, this may not even be the reason why Ying chose the play for translation in the first place. Perhaps Tennessee Williams intended the politics of Confederate Daughters branch election as a backdrop for the drama of the personal, the unspoken romantic feelings between the two elderly women. For Chinese readers, however, the political strand of the story would take the center stage because it was too visible, and the parallels were too eerily close for them not to see. Ying Ruocheng, in his translator's note published in the same 1963 issue of *World Literature*, "condemns" the kind of bourgeois decadence, hypocrisy, and spiritual nihilism represented in the story, especially when the characters do get to speak what is unspoken between them.[32] When it becomes impossible for Grace to dodge and equivocate anymore, what she speaks would assume political significance too, although the lesbian theme is just as clear.

One interesting "mistranslation," whether made unwittingly or by choice, concerns this dialogue about the flowers Cornelia has given to Grace on that particular day to mark their special relationship:[33]

> Cornelia: Dearest, isn't there something you've failed to notice?
> Grace: Where?
> Cornelia: Right under your nose.
> Grace: Oh! You mean <u>my flower</u>?
> Cornelia: Yes! I mean <u>your flower</u>!

> 考   亲爱的, 这儿是不是有点东西你没有注意到呢?
> 格   —在哪儿?

考　　就在你鼻子跟前。
格　　哦!你指的是<u>我这朵花</u>?
考　　对了!我指的是<u>你这朵玫瑰花</u>!

Although我这朵花 (*wo zhe duo hua*) and 你这朵玫瑰花 (*ni zhe duo meiguihua*) are fair translations of "my flower" and "your flower" respectively, even with the insertion of 玫瑰 (*meigui*, rose), based on the context, fuller translations should be 我<u>的</u>这朵花 (*wo de zhe duo hua*) and 你<u>的</u>这朵玫瑰花 (*ni de zhe duo meiguihua*). Missing the possessive marker 的 (*de*) renders the meaning of the dialogue ambiguous in Chinese: it could mean "my flower" and "me the flower" and "your flower" and "you the flower" respectively, which serves to signify the romantic (and possibly sexual) nature of the relationship between the two women even more suggestively than the original.

Then, Cornelia talks feelingly about the fifteen roses for the fifteen years they have spent together:[34]

> Cornelia: Fifteen years my companion! A rose for every year, a year for every rose!
> 我十五年来的<u>伴侣</u>!每朵玫瑰花是一年, 每一年都是一朵玫瑰花!

Once again, 伴侣 (*banlü*) is a fair translation of "companion" denotatively. However, 伴侣 in Chinese is typically used to refer to married couples, as in终身伴侣 (*zhongshen banlü*, lifetime partners). The idea and feeling invoked by 伴侣 as used here in Ying's translation suggests a more intimate and serious relationship, almost like a married couple, between the two women.

When Grace is finally forced to speak the unspoken for the last 15 years, what she says is fraught with a mix of political and personal, employer and employee, and indeed the mistress and the maid. There is no equality or "democracy" to speak of; the barrier between them is unbridgeable:[35]

> You're the strong one of us two and surely you know it.—both of us have turned grey!—but not the same kind of grey. In that velvet dressing-gown you look like the <u>Emperor Tiberius—In his imperial gota!</u>—your hair and your eyes are both the color of iron! Iron grey. <u>Invincible looking! People nearby are all somewhat—frightened of you. They feel your force and they admire you for it. They come to you here for opinions on this or that ...— On, you're a fountain of wisdom!</u> ... I am—very—different!—Also turning grey but my grey is different. Not iron, like yours, <u>not imperial</u>, Cornelia,

but grey, yes, grey, the—color of a … cobweb … (She starts the record again, very softly)—Something white getting soiled, the grey of something forgotten. (*underline added*)

在你我之间你是强者，这你当然清楚。—我们两个都老了，头发灰白了!—但是灰得不一样。你穿着那身丝绒的睡衣就象是<u>罗马皇帝泰比里乌斯</u>!—<u>穿着他的皇帝的长袍</u>!—你的头发和你的眼睛都是铁的颜色!灰铁色。<u>不可战胜的样子</u>!<u>差不多所有的人对你都有点说不出来的—恐惧。大家都感觉得到你的力量，大家也因为这个佩服你。他们到你这里来请教你对各式各样的事情的看法…</u>—哦，你是智慧的泉源!…. 我和你—很—不一样!—我的头发也灰白了，但是我灰得不一样。不象铁，不象你，<u>没有皇帝一样的威严</u>，考尔尼丽亚，我的灰白，是的，我的灰白是—蜘蛛网—的颜色….(她又放那张唱片，声音很小。)—是白东西被弄脏了的颜色，是被遗忘了的东西的灰色。

Expressions such as 皇帝的长袍 (*Huangdi de changpao*, imperial gota), 不可战胜的样子 (*buke zhansheng de yangzi*, invincible looking), 都有点说不出来的—恐惧 (*dou youdian shuobuchulai de kongju*, all somehow frightened of you), 智慧的泉源 (*zhihui de quayuann*, fountain of wisdom), 皇帝一样的威严 (*Huangdi yiyang de weiyan*, imperial grandeur), and so on, would inevitably remind Chinese readers of Mao Zedong venerated as the greatest and wisest leader of China although the cultish titles of 四个伟大" (*si ge wei da*, four greats): "great teacher, great leader, great supreme commander, and great helmsman" would not be lavished on him by Lin Biao, soon to be Mao's handpicked successor, until a few years later in 1966 for Lin's own ambitious agenda.[36]

Given the taboo subject, both sociopolitical and moral, of *Something Unspoken* and the potential yet real danger it could bring to the translator and *World Literature*, the literary magazine that published it, one wonders, once again, why Ying Ruocheng chose this one-act play, out of many other possible (and politically safer) dramatic works by Williams, and for the same reason (of political risk), one understands why there has been no Chinese scholarship on Ying's translation of this play, let alone any theatrical adaptation for the Chinese stage even today.

PUSHING THE BOUNDARIES THROUGH TRANSLATION: SEXUAL MORES

In 1981, 18 years after the publication of Ying Ruocheng's translation of *Something Unspoken*, and barely a few years after the Cultural Revolution (1966–1976) was over, *Contemporary Foreign Literature* (*dangdai waiguo wenxue* 当代外国文学), a quarterly created by the Nanjing University Foreign Literature Research Institute with an inaugural issue in the summer of 1980, published a full-text translation of Tennessee Williams' *The Glass Menagerie*, rendered by Dong Xiu (东秀).[37] The front cover art of this issue features a picture of Williams (taken in a bar in Turkey, 1948), signifying the official debut of the American playwright in China: He has finally arrived—albeit rather belatedly. The back cover art features "Boating on the River Epte" by the French Impressionist painter Oscar-Claude Monet (1840–1926). In this issue are Chinese translations of *A Kiss for the Leper* by François Mauriac (1885–1970); "The Pot of Gold" by John Cheever (1912–1982), a capable translation by Zhang Boran (张柏然), although its Chinese title *Jin fanwan* (金饭碗) is potentially misleading because it is, much more appropriately, the Chinese title for *The Golden Bowl*, a1904 novel by Henry James (1843–1916); and a few short stories by Soviet and Austrian authors. Featured in the middle is Dong Xiu's translation of *The Glass Menagerie*. This issue of *Contemporary Foreign Literature*, from cover to content, is a far cry from the 1963 issue of *World Literature* discussed in the preceding section; it is so much more "Western" and "modernistic," representing how far China has travelled in just a few years in the introduction and reception of contemporary foreign (mostly Western) literature.

Nonetheless, the editors of *Contemporary Foreign Literature* still found it necessary to defend and justify their choices by citing Lu Xun (鲁迅, 1881–1936), bona fide standard-bearer of modern Chinese literature, also a translator of foreign literature, to align with him ideologically, and to be "politically correct," or rather, safe.

There are four excerpts from Lu Xun "strategically" placed at various spots in this issue:[38]

What I like to see is that China has many good translators. Short of this, I'd be in favor of 'hard translation' [literal translation]. The reason is for many Chinese readers they could draw some nourishment from such translated literature which is not all dishonest falsehood; it'd be more beneficial than an empty plate. Personally, I have always been grateful to translations. Take [Bernard] Shaw as an example. The arguments we are having now about Shaw's literary reputation and his subject matters and so on have long been resolved definitively in foreign literary circles.

Therefore, as I've said before, if we really want to understand, we should "read more foreign books," to break through such encirclement. ... There are English books or translations of English books about New Literature. Not too many, but the few we have, they are substantive and reliable. We will have a lot of clarity if we read foreign literary theories and works first and then take a look at our new literature in China. It'd be beneficial to introduce such foreign theories and works to China: Translation is not easier than casual creative writing, but it is more beneficial to the development of new literature and to us all.

To sum it up, we have to take. We can put it to use, in storage, or destroy it. Indeed, when the new owner moves in, the house will become new too. To make it happen, one has to be calm, courageous, perceptive, and unselfish. Without take-ism, one cannot become a new person. Without take-ism our literature cannot become new literature.

One way to enrich our literature is to adapt good practice from foreign literature and make it work for us; another way is to draw from our own Chinese heritage and interject some new vitality to reinvigorate our literature.

These excerpts from Lu Xun, whose reputation did not suffer even during the Cultural Revolution, are included not as space fillers (typically occupying half or one-third of a page); rather, they are included not only because they are topically relevant, but also, and perhaps more importantly, because they provide a paratextual argument and justification, socio-politically as well as literarily, for what the journal sets out to do: to introduce new works by new foreign authors, even the contemporary ones.

Also included in this issue are short essays about contemporary German literature, "*A Kiss for the Leper*," Tennessee Williams, and modernist literature authored by Yuan Kejia (袁可嘉, 1921–2008), a well-known foreign literature scholar based at the Chinese Academy of Social Sciences.[39] *The Glass Menagerie* would see two more notable Chinese translations: a 1985 rendition by Zhao Quanzhang (赵全章), as one of the selections in a volume of *Modernist Foreign Literary Works* published by Shanghai Literature and Art Press;[40] and a 1991 rendition by Lu Jin (鹿金), included in a volume of *Classic Foreign Tragedies* published by Henan People's Press.[41]

In 1982, Chinese translations of two other major plays by Tennessee Williams were published, *A Streetcar Named Desire* and *Cat on a Hot Tin Roof*. This early Chinese translation of *Streetcar* appeared in an issue of *Foreign Film Scripts Series* (*waiguo dianying juben congkan* 外国电影剧本丛刊) published by China Film Press (*Zhongguo dianying chubanshe* 中国电影出版社). It is interesting to note that this translation, rendered by Yi

Kuang (一匡), was based on a Russian translation in a Russian magazine titled *American Film Collection* published by Soviet Art Press in 1960. The first full-blown Chinese translation of *Streetcar*, as written by Tennessee Williams, would be a translation rendered by Liang Bolong (梁伯龙), a Central Academy of Drama professor (Beijing), who played an instrumental role in the first known professional Chinese staging of a Williams play (by Tianjin People's Art Theatre) in 1987.[42] This translation was printed on paper of rather poor quality (non-printing press bounding), for internal use and stage production rather than public reading. The first Chinese translation of *Cat*, rendered by Chen Liangting (陈良廷), was published by China Social Sciences Press (中国社会科学出版社).[43] This translation was included in a volume of *World Literature Series* (*shijie wenxue congkan* 世界文学丛刊), which also featured Chinese translations of *Roots*, a 3-act play by the English playwright Arnold Wesker (1932–2016), *Topaze*, a 4-act play by the French playwright Marcel Pagnol (1895–1974), *In the Matter of J. Robert Oppenheimer* by the German writer Heinar Kipphardt (1922–1982), and *Biedermann und die Brandstifter* (The Arsonists) by the Swedish writer Max Frisch (1911–1991). On the cover of the volume is the Chinese title for *Cat*, 热铁皮屋顶上的猫 (*Re tiepi wudin shang de mao*), as the volume's sales pitch, testimonial of the "hotness" of the play and the increased enthusiasm for its author.

The early 1990s would see quite a few more notable translations of Williams' dramatic works. A bilingual edition (with Chinese rendition and English original put side by side, like a double-entry) of *Streetcar*, rendered by Sun Baimei (孙白梅), was published by the Shanghai Translation Press (*Shanghai yiwen chubanshe* 上海译文出版社) in 1991.[44] A volume in a series titled *Foreign Contemporary Plays* (*Waiguo dangdai juzuo xuan*, 外国当代剧作选) devoted to Chinese translations of four Williams plays, was put out by China Drama Press (*Zhongguo xiju chubanshe* 中国戏剧出版社): *Streetcar*, rendered by Qi Qing (奇青);[45] *The Glass Menagerie*, rendered by Dong Xiu (东秀), a reprint of the 1981 translation; *Cat*, rendered by Chen Liangting (陈良廷), another reprint; and *The Night of Iguana* (*Xiyi de yewan* 蜥蜴的夜晚), rendered by An Man (安曼).[46] Another translation of *A Streetcar*, rendered by Feng Tao (冯涛), based on the English edition with a preface by Arthur Miller, was published by Shanghai Translation Press (上海译文出版社) in 2015.[47] A noteworthy event in the reception of Tennessee Williams in China is the publication of a Chinese translation of his *Memoirs* (*Tiannaxi weiliansi huiyilu* 田纳西·威

廉斯回忆录), rendered by Feng Qianzhu (冯倩珠) and published by Henan University Press (*Henan daxue chubanshe* 河南大学出版社) in 2018.[48]

Taking a close look at these translations, that is, how they each handle the somewhat "racy" (albeit tame by Western standards) dialogues, one can see a gradual loosening up, so to speak, and indeed a trajectory of development, albeit not in a simple, straightforward fashion, from Dong Xiu's 1981 rendition of *The Glass Menagerie* onward, moving from trying to dance around more "explicit" sexual references and repackage and camouflage them in flowery but much less vivid and authentic poetic diction to more "faithful" translations that convey the "raciness" of the original both in content and style (and register) much more effectively.

In *The Glass Menagerie*, Tom Wingfield talks about how his mother, Amanda, tries to sell those journals to make a living:[49]

> Journal that features the serialized sublimations of ladies of letters who think in terms of delicate <u>cup-like breasts, slim, tapering waists, rich creamy thighs, eyes like wood-smoke in autumn, fingers that soothe and caress like strains of music</u>, and bodies as powerful as Etruscan sculpture

This is Dong Xiu's 1981 translation:[50]

> 她们大肆吹捧女主人公<u>身材窈窕、体态婀娜、眼如秋水、手如柔荑、肤如凝脂</u>,身体健壮宛若古罗马利伊特肯雕像。

This translation uses the so-called poetic diction, that is, trite four-character phrases in praising women's beauty: 身材窈窕 (*shencai yaotiao*, beauteous body), 体态婀娜(*titai e nuo*, willowy waist), 眼如秋水 (*yanru qiushui*, eyes like autumnal water), 手如柔荑 (*shouru routi*, hands like budding leaves), 肤如凝脂 (*furu ningzhi*, cream-like skin) are evocative enough for Chinese readers familiar with classics such as *Romance of the West Chamber*,[51] yet "cup-like breasts" and "rich creamy thighs" have disappeared and swept under a thick layer of trite, stock expressions. If such renditions gain anything in "elegance," they lose in the vivid specificity of cup-like breasts, thighs, tactile, titillating sensation of fingers as soothing and caressing as strains of music. They take the author of the source language/culture to the readers, to the literary repertoire of quasi-classical style of a bygone era, which leaves a taste of affectedness and makes Tom, in his Chinese reincarnation, appear unworthy being the nickname

"Shakespeare" bestowed on him by Jim O'Connor, the gentleman caller, although the other boys in the warehouse regarded him "with suspicious hostility"[52]

In contrast, only a few years later, Zhao Quanzhang in 1985 shows much more confidence and comfort in giving a more "faithful" and hence more vivid and effective rendition of the same lines by Tom:[53]

> 这些女作家们想的是柔软的杯状的乳房，苗条纤细的腰部，丰满奶油色的大腿，象秋日林烟似的眼睛，象音乐一样能安抚的手指，象伊特拉斯坎雕像那样强壮的身体。

柔软的杯状的乳房 (*rouruan de beizhuang de rufang*, soft, cup-shaped breasts), 苗条纤细的腰部 (*miaotiao qianxi de yaobu*, slender waist), 丰满奶油色的大腿 (*fengman naiyouse de datui*, full, cream-colored thighs) are much closer in conveying the English original.

Similarly, Lu Jin's 1991 translation gives a direct rendition that could have titillating effect on many a young reader back then:[54]

> 那些女作家想到的无非是娇嫩、浑圆的乳房啦，苗条、纤细的腰身啦，丰满的乳白色大腿啦，象秋天里的木材烟雾那样的蓝眼睛啦，抚摸起来象乐曲似的充满柔情蜜意的手指头啦，象伊特拉里亚雕像那样健美的肉体啦。

娇嫩、浑圆的乳房 (*jiaonen hunyuan de rufang*, tender, round and smooth breasts), 苗条、纤细的腰身 (*miaotiao qianxi de yaoshen*, slender, slim waist), 丰满的乳白色大腿 (*fengman de rubaise datui*, full, milk-white thighs) are as "explicit" and evocative to the Chinese readers as can be.

Sexual references in *A Streetcar Named Desire*, *Cat on a Hot Tin Roof*, and *The Night of Iguana* proved just as challenging to Chinese translators. In *Streetcar*, this is how Stella responds to Stanley after he tells her about Blanche's past concerning Allen, the young husband who died:[55]

> This beautiful and talented young man was a <u>degenerate</u>. Didn't your supply-man give you that information?

This is Liang's rendition in 1987:[56]

> 那个又漂亮又聪明的年轻人是个<u>同性恋者</u>。那个送货员，没有谈到这点吗?

同性恋者 (*tongxin lian zhe*, same-sex love person) is a mis- or over-translation of "degenerate," which reflects the sexual mores in China at the time: homosexuality regarded as being debased, decadent, and deviant behavior. A few years later, in 1991, Sun Baimei gave the same translation in the bilingual edition of the play published by Shanghai Translation Press:[57]

这个才貌出众的年轻人竟然是个<u>同性恋者</u>。你那个供销员有没有告诉你这件事?

However, one year later in 1992, Qi Qing chose a more "precise" or "technical" Chinese term, 性变态者 (*xing biantai zhe*, sexual deviant), for "degenerate":[58]

发现这位又英俊又有才华的年轻人是个<u>性变态者</u>。你们的供销员没给你讲这个情况吗?

Feng's 2015 translation dropped 性(*xing*, sexual)and simply translated "degenerate" as 变态(*biantai*, deviant):[59]

这个美丽超群又天姿卓越的年轻人竟是个<u>变态</u>。

The term "degenerate" is typically defined as "one degraded from the normal moral standard," "an immoral or corrupt person" and "sexual pervert" (especially as used in the context of the play).[60] Translating it as 同性恋者 (same-sex lover person, or homosexual) may have the benefit of making it clear to Chinese readers what Stella meant and Stanley understood it to mean, yet it certainly put "homosexual" in the category of "degraded," "immoral," and "corrupt." This translation was probably overdetermined by the sociocultural and moral context of China in1991 when 同性恋 (homosexual) was possibly a "dirtier" term than 变态 (degenerate). It is not possible to know whether the term 性变态or 性心理变态 (sexual deviant)[61] was already in currency in China then, but apparently it has more of a medical/clinical ring. The 2015 rendition alluded to above drops 性 (*xing*, sex) altogether and keeps only 变态 (*biantai*, deviant), which removes much of the biased moral judgment and sounds less pejorative than the English original "degenerate."

If we think of all translations as mistranslations (just as we can think of all reading as misreading[62]) because there is no such a thing as one hundred percent perfect equivalents between languages and cultures, both denotatively and connotatively, some of the mistranslations, as far as

Williams dramatic works are concerned, were probably caused by misunderstanding of the English original, for example, colloquial or slang expressions used by the playwright for character portrayal. This is the case of Chinese renditions of what Blanche says to Stella in Scene Five of *Streetcar* about her budding romance with Mitch:[63]

> Especially when the girl is over—thirty. They think a girl over thirty ought to—the vulgar term is—<u>"put out."</u> ... And I—I'm not "putting out." Of course he—he doesn't know—I mean I haven't informed him—of my real age!

As a "vulgar" slang expression, "put out," as is used here, possibly means "easy to grant sexual favors or engage in sexual act."[64] Here are a few attempts at translating this expression into "proper" Chinese:[65]

> 尤其是—女人过了三十岁，他们认为，超过三十岁的女人—说句实话—<u>便宜货</u>。可是，我不是<u>便宜货</u>。
> 尤其当女方已经—年过三十。他们认为一个年过三十的女人就该—说得粗俗些—<u>"放荡"</u>.... 而我—我并不"放荡"。
> 尤其是对一个年过三十的女子。他们认为过了三十的女人应该—用俗话说—"滚蛋".... 而我—我偏不"滚蛋"。
> 特别是当那个姑娘年过—三十以后。他们认为一个姑娘只要过了三十就该—用那个粗俗的说法就是—"<u>人尽可夫了</u>".... 而我—我可不是"人尽可夫"的。

Of these four translations, Qi Qing's 滚蛋 (*gundan*, go to hell) is a complete mistranslation due to miscomprehension; Liang's 便宜货 (*pianyihuo*, cheap and easy) and Sun's 放荡 (*fangdang*, loose, promiscuous) come closer to the original while Feng's 人尽可夫 (*ren jin ke fu*, any man can be my husband), though not too far off in in meaning, sounds too polished and "literary" in Chinese.

Cat on Hot Tin Roof proved another site of challenges for Chinese translators in terms of sexuality, especially sex-themed dialogues. As alluded to earlier, the first (and the only known) full-text translation of the play, rendered by Chen Liangting (陈良廷), was published by China Social Sciences Press (中国社会科学出版社) in 1982. Upon first reading, this rendition feels so fluent (bringing Tennessee Williams home to the Chinese readers) that one all but forgets that one is actually reading a translation of a play originally written in another language. One is "easily" drawn into the story, watching and listening in through the fourth wall, so to speak, as Brick and Margaret talk and fight, as Brick and Big Daddy clash, and as they all try to dodge yet are forced to confront the ghosts from the past, speak the unspoken and unspeakable, and come to grips with the truths even though they cut to the quick and hurt badly. However, when comparing this Chinese translation with the English original by Williams, one would soon find so many instances of over- or under-translation apparently due to misreading (intentional or unintentional) and/or sexual more concerns.

This is Williams's description of the room of Margaret and Brick (followed by Chen's 1982 translation):[66]

> Perhaps the style of the room is not what you would expect in the home of the Delta's biggest cotton-planter. It is Victorian with a touch of the Far East. It hasn't changed much since it was occupied by the original owners of the place, Jack Straw and Peter Ochello, a pair of old bachelors who shared this room all their lives together. In other words, the room must evoke some ghosts; <u>it is gently and poetically haunted by a relationship that must have involved a tenderness which was uncommon.</u> (*underline added*)
> 这屋子是带点远东风味的维多利亚款式。公馆旧主杰克·斯特劳和彼得·奥契柯洛是一对老光棍，他们俩一生都厮守在这间屋子里，从他们住下那天起直到现在，屋子都没有什么变样。换句话说，<u>这屋子一定闹鬼；这地方有一种必是不比寻常的暧昧关系富有诗意地隐隐作祟。</u>

This line "it is gently and poetically haunted by a relationship that must have involved a tenderness which was uncommon" would be challenging for any translator. While Chen's rendition tried hard and relayed to some degree the ambiance of the original, it tripped on the word "tenderness." "A relationship that must have involved a tenderness which was uncommon" implies a relationship that was not exactly socially sanctioned at the time. 暧昧 (*aimei*), which denotes a kind of relationship straddling between friendship and sexual attraction, typically between a man and a woman, seems to relay what is being conveyed in English, but it is tinged with negativity and disapproval not present in the original. A more "literal" translation 温情 (*wenqing*) would have worked better and more accurately captured the "tenderness" embodied in the original English description.

As is known to anyone who has read *Cat*, there is something special between Margaret and Big Daddy. Here is how Margaret describes to Brick that bond between her and Big Daddy:[67]

MARGARET: Big Daddy shares my attitude toward those two! As for me, well—I give him a laugh now and then and he tolerates me. In fact!—<u>I sometimes suspect that</u> Big Daddy <u>harbors a little unconscious 'lech' fo' me ...</u>

BRICK: What makes you think that Big Daddy <u>has a lech for you</u>, Maggie?

MARGARET: Way he always drops his eyes down my body when I'm talkin' to him, <u>drops his eyes to my boobs an' licks his old chops</u>! Ha ha!

BRICK: That kind of talk is disgusting. (*underline added*)

玛格丽特　大阿爹对他们两口子跟我是一个看法!我呀，　咳，　我时常和他打哈哈，　他都不吱声。其实啊!我有时心里感觉到，　大阿爹无意中竟然对我<u>动心</u>啦....

布里克 你怎么想到大阿爹对你<u>动心</u>了呢?玛吉?

玛格丽特 每当我跟他说话的时候，他的眼睛老在我身上直打转，<u>眼珠盯着我的奶子, 直咽吐沫</u>!哈哈!

布里克 你这样说话真叫人恶心。

While <u>眼珠盯着我的奶子，　直咽吐沫</u> (*yanzhu dingzhe wo de naizi zhi yan tumo*) is a close enough translation of "drops his eyes to my boobs an' licks his old chops," 竟然对我动心 (*jingran dui wo dongxin*, touched, moved, attracted) is a bit too polite and wholesome translation of "harbors a little unconscious 'lech' fo' me" (lech, or lecherous—having or showing excessive or offensive sexual desire). A more "faithful" translation would be 色迷迷的(*semimi de*, lustful), which would be much closer to "lech" both denotatively and connotatively.

Below is what Margaret says to Brick about their sex life:[68]

You were a <u>wonderful lover</u> ...

Such a wonderful person to <u>go to bed with</u>, and I think mostly because you were really indifferent to it. Isn't that right? Never had any anxiety about it, did it naturally, easily, slowly, with absolute confidence and perfect calm, <u>more like opening a door for a lady or seating her at a table than giving expression to any longing for her</u>. Your indifference made you <u>wonderful at lovemaking</u>—strange?—but true ... (*underline added*)

你这个人呀, 真是个<u>冤家</u>....

跟你在一块儿<u>过活</u>真舒心。我想这多半是因为你对这种事实在是毫不动心。说得对不对?对这种事根本<u>没半点欲念</u>, 对付起来有自然又从容, 慢悠悠的, 信心十足, 镇静极了, 与其说是对她表白什么<u>爱慕之情</u>, 不如说是

象替位太太小姐开开门，让个座儿。你这种毫不动心的气派使你在跟我同
房这功夫上更招人心疼—奇怪不奇怪?

This translation misses the mark by a wide margin. 冤家 (*yuan jia*) in
Chinese refers to (1) someone one loves; (2) someone one really loves
although appears to hate; (3) someone one hates, literally. Even if we use
the first two possible definitions, it is still off the mark as a translation for
"wonderful lover." Here what Margaret wants to say to Brick is that he is
a great lover in bed—knows how to make love and satisfy her, as she makes
abundantly clear in this speech tinctured with nostalgia and heartfelt longing. Also, translating "go to bed with" in the line "Such a wonderful
person to go to bed with" as 过活 (*guohuo*, to live with) misses the mark
even more. The same is true with translating "wonderful at lovemaking"
in "Your indifference made you wonderful at lovemaking" as 你在跟我同
房这功夫上更招人心疼 (*gen zhaoren xinteng*, filling my heart with aching
tenderness).

One would never know if such mistranslation was caused by miscomprehension or sexual modesty (prudishness?) on the part of the translator.
It was 1982 after all, only a few years after the Cultural Revolution was
over although China had already begun to open up and reform. A more
"faithful" translation would be based on a reading of the text that shows
Margaret speaking tenderly, heartfeltly, and nostalgically, of the joy of
making love with Brick, dizzying and heavenly, exactly because Brick was
indifferent to the whole thing, like a Zen master of sorts (although we
know and Margaret knows too that the real reason for his sexual indifference, despite her "hot" figure, looks, and sensuality, lies elsewhere):

> 你这个人啊真是做爱的高手....
>   和你上床做爱真是爽极了， 我想多半是因为你对这种事漫不经意的原
> 因吧，说得对不对?你做的时候没有任何的心理负担，那么从容自如的，慢
> 悠悠的，绝对地自信，那么镇定自若，感觉不是在宣泄对她的 渴望，
> 而是在替位太太小姐开开门、让个座呢。你这么漫不经意的，跟你做爱反
> 而更爽了 呢—怪吧?

Here, 做爱的高手 (*zuoai de gaoshou*, master of lovemaking) is a more
proper translation for "wonderful lover;" 和你上床做爱真是爽极了 (*he ni
shangchuang zuoai zhen shi shuang ji le*, dizzyingly joyful to go to bed and
make love with you), for "such a wonderful person to go to bed with;" 跟
你做爱反而更爽了呢 (*gen ni zuoai fan'er geng shuang le ne*, even more

dizzyingly joyful to go to bed and make love with you), for "Your indifference made you wonderful at lovemaking."

The same misreading/mistranslation happens with this line by Margaret (said to Brick) later that summer evening on the same topic of their sex life:[69]

> You married me early that summer we graduated out of Ole Miss, and we were happy, weren't we, we were blissful, yes, <u>hit heaven together ev'ry time that we loved</u>! (*underline added*)
> 每回<u>相亲相爱总是乐得什么似</u>的.

相亲相爱 (*xiangqin xiangai*, love each other tenderly) describes an intimate, loving relationship but does not come close to what is meant by "ev'ry time that we loved": every time we made love. So, a more proper translation should be 我们每次做爱都爽极了(*women meici zuoai dou shuang ji le*, every time we made love it was such dizzying joy), or 我们每次做爱都醉仙似的 (*meici zuoai dou shuang de piaopiaoyuxian si de*, every time we made love it was such heavenly joy).

Sex life between Margaret and Brick, on which hinges whether they will get their "fair" share of "th' biggest an' finest plantation in the Delta" if and when Big Daddy dies, is also the topic of a conversation between Big Mama and Margaret (Maggie):[70]

> BIG MAMA: Fair or not fair I want to ask you a question, one question—-<u>D'you make Brick happy in bed</u>?
> MARGARET: Why don't you ask <u>if he makes me happy in bed</u>?
> BIG MAMA: Because I know that—
> MARGARET: <u>It works both ways</u>! (*underline added*)

> 大阿妈公平也罢, 不公平也罢, 我且问你一件事, 一件事:<u>同房你称他心吗</u>?
> 玛格丽特你干吗不问问, <u>同房他称我心吗</u>?
> 大阿妈因为这事我知道....
> 玛格丽特<u>只有两相情愿才大家称心</u>!

称心 (*chenxin*), which literally means to one's heart content, is not too far off from "make someone happy in bed" although it is not as direct and blunt as the way Big Mama and Margaret talk about the subject. However, 只有两相情愿才大家称心 (*zhiyou liangxiangqingyuan cai dajia chenxin*, we both have to put our hearts in it so we both can have it to our heart content) is a far cry from the original both denotatively and connotatively; it is too literary and euphemistic (possibly out of sexual modesty or prudishness) to convey effectively what the mother-in-law and the daughter-in-law talk about. A simple, "literal" translation would get the job done:

> 大阿妈 你床上能满足布里克吗?
> 玛格丽特 你干吗不问问, 床上他能满足我吗?
> 大阿妈 因为我知道....
> 玛格丽特 床上满足是双方面的!

床上能满足 (*chuang shang neng manzu*, can satisfy in bed) and 床上满足是双方面的 (*chuang shang manzu shi shuang fangmian de*, satisfaction in bed works both ways) is not only truer to the original in language, but also truer to the character of Margaret as a more assertive and new kind of southern belle, even in her Chinese reincarnation, a "cat on a hot tin roof" who is not afraid to speak plainly on her own behalf.

Here is another moment between Margaret and Brick, shortly after her tête-à-tête with Big Mama, when Margaret "stands before the long oval mirror, touches her breast and then her hips with her two hands":[71]

> How high my body stays upon me!—Nothing has fallen on me—not a fraction (*underline added*)
> 我身材多高!没出过一点毛病, 一丁点儿都没有....

我身材多高!没出过一点毛病 (*wo shenchai duo gao! mei chu guo yi dian maobing*, my figure is so tall! It has never fallen ill) is an erroneous translation disconnected from the stage description for this moment in dramatic action. What Margaret "brags" about is that her chest, or rather, her breasts, have not sagged a bit despite her age (probably early 30s?): 我的身段还这么挺挺的, 一点儿也没有塔拉 (*wo de shenduan hai zhemo tingting de, yidian'er ye meiyou tala*).

If the heterosexual "sex talk" in the play proved challenging for Chen's translation, when Margaret talks to Brick about what happened between her and Skipper in college, it proved even more challenging:[72]

> —When I came to his room that night, with a little scratch like a shy little mouse at his door, he made that pitiful, ineffectual little attempt to prove that what I had said wasn't true. (*underline added*)
> —当天夜里, 我到他的房间, 象胆怯的小耗子似的, 轻轻在他房门上抓两下, 他就怪可怜的, 勉强跟我好上了, 想要证明我说的不是事实....

他就怪可怜的, 勉强跟我好上了 (*ta jiu guai kelian de, mianqiang gen wo hao shang le*, he was pitiable and reluctantly befriended me) is such a "pitiful, ineffectual" translation of the original disassociated with the context: Margaret has just told Brick how she had confronted Skipper about his feelings for Brick ("SKIPPER! STOP LOVIN' MY HUSBAND OR") and how, when Margaret came to Skipper's hotel room that night, he made a "pitiful, ineffectual little attempt" to prove that he was not gay, that is, he tried to make love to Margaret without success (probably in part because he could not get sexually aroused with a woman). So, what Margaret says to Brick could be translated as follows:

—当天夜里, 我象个怯生生的小耗子似的, 在他房间的门上轻轻敲一下就进去了, 他为了证明我说的不是事实,<u>可怜兮兮地要和我做, 可怎么折腾也做不成</u>。

The underlined part, *kelian xixi de yao he wo zuo, ke zenmo zheteng ye zuo bu cheng* (he tried to make love with me but failed pitiably), blunt as it sounds, is much more accurate and effective in delivering what Margaret says and is truer to her character.

On the same topic of the questionable and guilt-ridden relationship between Brick and Skipper, this is what Brick says to Big Daddy later in the play, when they confront each other and are forced to face their own and each other's demons:[73]

[Maggie] Poured in his mind the dirty, false idea that what we were, him and me, was <u>a frustrated case of that ole pair of sisters</u> that lived in this room, Jack Straw and Peter Ochello!—He, poor Skipper, went to bed with Maggie to prove it wasn't true, and <u>when it didn't work out</u>, he thought it was true!—Skipper <u>broke in two like a rotten stick</u>—nobody ever turned so fast to a lush—or died of it so quick (*underline added*)
　她净往他脑子里灌输那个胡编的下流念头, 说我跟他两人的情况简直就是住在这屋子里<u>搞同性爱的宝货</u>, 杰克·斯特劳和彼得·奥契洛! 可怜的斯基普啊, 他竟跟玛吉睡了觉来证明这种说法是没影儿的事, <u>可是这办法也不成</u>, 连他自己也信以为真了!<u>斯基普就此彻底跨了</u>, 没人象他这么快一下子成了醉鬼, 也没有人象他这么快一下子就死在这上面了....

搞同性爱的宝货 (*gao tongxinglian de baohuo*, treasures who do homosexual love) is an excessive yet incomplete translation of "a frustrated case of that ole pair of sisters that lived in this room" (with "frustrated case" untranslated). 可是这办法也不成 (*keshi zhe banfa ye bu cheng*) is a literal translation of "when it didn't work out" but fails to convey what it really means in this context. 斯基普就此彻底垮了 (*Sijipu jiuci chedi kua le*) is close to the original "Skipper broke in two like a rotten stick" denotatively but the metaphoric power and vividness of the original is lost. What Brick says to Big Daddy could instead be translated as follows:

> 她净往他脑子里灌输那个捕风捉影的下流念头，说我跟他两人和住在这屋子里的<u>那对老不死的二姨娘</u>，杰克·斯特劳和彼得·奥契洛，一模一样，<u>只是没机会在一起而已</u>！可怜的斯基普啊，他竟跟玛吉<u>上床</u>来证明这种说法是没影儿的事，<u>可是做不成</u>，就信以为真了！<u>斯基普就象腐烂了的木棍一断两截，彻底垮了</u>，没人象他这么快一下子成了醉鬼，一下子就死在这上面了....

那对老不死的二姨娘 (*na dui laobusi de eryiniang*, that old pair of sissies) is much closer to the original "that ole pair of sisters"; 只是没机会在一起而已 (*zhi shi meiyou jihui zai yiqi eryi*, only that we didn't have opportunities to live together) relays the idea of Skipper and Brick being "a frustrated case": the two gay men love each other but did not have opportunities to live together like Jack Straw and Peter Ochello; 斯基普就象腐烂了的木棍一断两截，彻底垮了 (*Sijipu jiu xiang fulan le de mugun yi duan liangjie, cedi kua le*) is a literal translation but restores the metaphoric power of "Skipper broke in two like a rotten stick."

One of the "demons" in Big Daddy's life, as he tells it when finally opening up to Brick, is how he feels he has wasted his life on and been bored by Big Mama:[74]

> They say <u>you got just so many and each one is numbered</u>. Well, I got a few left in me, a few, and I'm going to pick me a good one to spend 'em on! (*underline added*)
> 　人家说你精力充沛，可人的精力总有个限。得，我身上还剩下一些精力，就剩下一些，我打算挑个好人儿，花花这点精力！

What Big Daddy alludes to here is probably the old Taoist belief that the amount of a man's energy (including sexual energy) is finite and every time he engages in sex (especially when he ejaculates), the amount of energy is reduced until it is completely spent.[75] Chen's translation 人家说你精力充沛 (*renjia shuo ni jingli chongpei*) for "They say you got just so many" is a mistranslation caused by mistaking the generic "you" as a specific reference to Big Daddy and, reversely, by mistaking the specific reference of sex energy as a generic/general reference of energy; hence the erroneous translation 可人的精力总有个限(*ke ren de jingli zong you ge xian*, a man's energy is limited).a more "faithful" translation would go like this:

人家说你一辈子<u>只能做那么多次，做一次就少一次了</u>。嗯，我还剩下几次，好几次呢，我得挑个可心的人儿好好消受。

Once again, the underlined portion, *renjia shuo ni zhe yibeizi zhineng zuo name duo ci, zuo yici jiu shao yici le* (they say you can make love for only so many times; each time you make love it is deducted from that number), blunt as it sounds, comes closer to what Big Daddy says in this context.

If almost all of the examples from Chen's 1982 rendition of *Cat* discussed above are instances of under-translation due to miscomprehension or sexual modesty or prudishness, this last example is a rare case of over-translation:[76]

> BRICK: Do it!—fo' God's sake, do it …
> MARGARET: Do what?
> BRICK: <u>Take a lover</u>!

> 布里克　干吧!我求求你, 干吧....
> 玛格丽特　干什么?
> 布里克　找个<u>野汉子</u>!

Although 野汉子 (*ye hanzi*, wild man) has almost the same denotation as 情夫 (*qingfu*, lover), connotatively it is quite different and has a much wilder (so to speak) flavor, like "hunk" or "stud," suggesting outlandish and outlawed sexual encounters, which is not implied in the English original.

As alluded to earlier, Chen's 1982 translation of *Cat* was reprinted in a volume of *Foreign Contemporary Plays* (*waiguo dangdai juzuo xuan*, 外国当代剧作选) published by China Drama Press in 1992. In that same volume is a Chinese translation of *The Night of Iguana,* rendered by An Man (安曼). It is a straightforward translation that, unlike Ying Ruocheng's 1963 translation of *Something Unspoken* and several other translations of Williams' works discussed in this chapter, provides no footnotes for the many allusions of paintings, songs, and so on in the play and does not preserve the many instances of Spanish or other language expressions for cultural flavor. In this 1992 rendition, published about 5 years before the decriminalization of homosexual sex in China, sexual innuendos or explicit talk are translated without bothering to repackage and camouflage them with euphemistic or flowery, overly literary Chinese expressions.

Early in *Iguana*, Maxine, ecstatic upon seeing Shannon again, says this to him (followed by An's translation):[77]

> Hah! My spies told me you went through Saltillo last week with a busload of women —a <u>whole busload of females, all females</u>, hah! <u>How many you laid</u> so far? Hah! (*underline added*)
> 哈! 上星期, 我的谍报员向我报告, 你带领一汽车妇女通过了萨尔蒂略—满满的<u>一汽车娘儿们啊, 全是些母货</u>, 哈!<u>你已经搞过几个了?</u>哈!

娘儿们 (*niang'er men*) for "women," 母货 (*mu huo*) for "females," and 搞 (*gao*) for "laid" are both denotatively and connotatively close to the original, with a twist of cultural flavor tinged with vulgarity. Still caught in the excitement of seeing each other, Maxine and Shannon continue to banter:[78]

> MAXINE: Well! Lemme look at you!
> SHANNON: Don't look at me; get dressed!
> MAXINE: Gee, you look like <u>you had it</u>!
> SHANNON: You look like <u>you been having it</u>, too. Get dressed! (*underline added*)

> 玛克辛   喂!让我好好瞧瞧你!
> 香农   先别瞧我, 先把衣服穿上!
> 玛克辛   哎哟, 就好象<u>你刚干过这事</u>似的!
> 香农   你倒好, <u>好像还一直在干着呢</u>。快穿上衣服!

干 (*gan*), like 搞 (*gao*), a vulgar slang expression for having sexual intercourse, almost an equivalent to "fuck" in English, is a proper translation for "had it" and "been having it" but is even more explicit (and "vulgar") than the English original, which is testimonial of how far China had come by this time in terms of sexual mores.

Indeed, by 2018, when Henan University Press put out a Chinese translation of Tennessee Williams's *Memoirs* ("a raw display of private life"[79]), rendered by Feng Qianzhu (冯倩珠), 20 years after homosexual sex was decriminalized, it did not register as much of a cultural shocker at all. Indeed, by 2018, so much had changed, laws, attitudes toward sexual mores and homosexuality, and so many other facets of the sociocultural life that the translator was much freer and therefore more honest and "faithful" in translating the *Memoirs*. By this time, terms referring to homosexuals such as 同志 (*tongzhi*, comrade) and 酷儿 (*ku'er*, queer), and so on were widely used, understood, and accepted, at least on university campuses and amongst those in arts and literature circles. This translation is based on the 1975 edition published by the University of the South Press, including Introduction by John Waters, foreword by Tennessee Williams himself, and Afterword by Allean Hale. There is no dancing around "raw" details—Williams' frank narrations of his awakening sexuality and (reckless) sex escapades, for example, pubescent Tom's innocent sexual experience with Hazel when a high schooler; his first (and perhaps only) full-blown heterosexual encounters with Sally while in college;[80] his first homosexual encounters in college and beyond; his deep, stormy love relationship with Frank Merlo, and so on. The book shocked (and scandalized) America when it was first published in 1972.

Of course, Williams *Memoirs* is so much more than an account of his life, his (homo)sexuality; it is also about his creativity, his growth as a playwright, a theater artist, his many professional relationships, friendships, sweet successes and bitter disappointments and failures. The book, as Williams asserts, is not either "my theatre or my life," but both. In this case, as in the case of so many great artists, it is all but impossible to separate the artist from the person or the person from the artist. It was written as "free association" after all, of "carnal love as well as spiritual love," "a great many moments of joy, both pure and impure," and it was not meant to be merely "entertain[ing]," but illuminating as well.[81]

Since professional book reviews are rare in China, we can use a sampling of ratings and comments gleaned (in the early fall of 2021) from Douban (豆瓣), Chinese equivalent of Goodreads, by way of gauging public sentiments: Out of the 85 readers who reviewed Williams' *Memoirs* (and/or Feng's Chinese rendition), 5 stars: 40%; 4 stars: 45.9%; an overall 86% positive rating.[82] One reader, in a posted comment, says that although Williams had addiction to drugs and alcohol and indulged in sex escapades, he is "a great man and a great friend."[83] Another reader describes Williams as "a fierce sexaholic and lover, an author with self-aware humility, and a man of courage;" his *Memoirs* is a book that "permeates with hormone and overflows with talent." One reader has this to say:

> Honestly, I am not interested in Tennessee Williams' private life, how he indulged in sexual escapades, but the more pages I turned, the more I real-

ized that despite his decadent lifestyle, he is essentially honest and free—his is a life accompanied by fear and anger, suspicion and vanity, desire of the body and the spirit. Williams' desire is several times bigger than that of a typical person, perhaps. Right before the curtain falls on *A Streetcar Named Desire*, Blanche reaches out her hand into the darkness and says: "Whoever you are, I have always depended on the kindness of strangers." Williams *is* every bit like Blanche.

One reader, who had really loved *A Streetcar Named Desire* and *Cat on a Hot Tin Roof*, was "so pleasantly surprised, filled with joy, to find out many years later that the author is such an open and unapologetic homosexual." One reader goes so far as finding himself in the Tennessee Williams as portrayed in the *Memoirs*:

> I love Tennessee Williams' plays, although I had already fallen in love with film adaptation [*Streetcar Named Desire*, starring Vivian Leigh and Marlon Brando, 1953]. Reading his plays somehow resonated with me so much, far more than reading any other writers. That's why I love him. When someone recommended this *Memoirs*, and when I saw the promotional pitch, I knew right away that I'd love this book too. It is bursting with so much sexual desire that it captivates me to the utmost. So, I placed an order for the book.
>
> While reading the book, I loved how he talked about his love affairs, reminding me of mine … If I could return to the South [southern China] to continue my education, my college experiences in the northeast would feel like a big dream in my life and one day, perhaps as a whore, I could perhaps write a memoir to memorialize it, titled *A Fuck Buddy in Northeast China*.

Bringing Williams to Chinese Readers Versus Taking Chinese Readers to Williams: Over/Under/ Mistranslation

In the discussions of the preceding sections, there are a few cases of excessive, over-translations (e.g., translation of Brick telling Margaret to "take a lover") or under-translations (e.g., translations of Tom Wingfield's description of breasts and thighs and Big Daddy's talk about a male's sexual energy being finite, "numbered"), due to misunderstanding or sexual mores or prudishness. This section discusses the issue of over-translation, under-translation, or simply mistranslation, in connection with the tensions between bringing the foreign author/text to the target readers/

culture or taking readers to the source culture of the author/text, that is, the much-discussed issue of foreignization versus domestication. Let us begin with *The Glass Menagerie* again, the first Williams play that saw a Chinese translation shortly after the Cultural Revolution was over.

Here is Williams' character sketch of Amanda Wingfield (followed by Dong Xiu's 1981 translation):[84]

> A little woman of great but confused vitality clinging frantically to another time and place. Her characterization must be carefully created, not copied from type. She is not paranoiac, but her life is paranoia. There is much to admire in Amanda, and as much to love and pity as there is to laugh at. Certainly she has endurance and a kind of heroism, and though her foolishness makes her unwittingly cruel at times, there is tenderness in her slight person.
>
> 她是个身材矮小，充满活力的妇女。她疯狂迷恋于另一个时代和世界。她在舞台上的形象需要细心塑造，而不要按某一典型临摹。她并不疯狂，但她的生活是疯狂的。在许多方面，阿曼达值得称赞，令人爱慕和怜悯，但也又不少地方使人发笑。毫无疑问，她具有忍耐性和英雄气概。虽然他的愚蠢行为有时使她在无意中未免有些残酷，但这位弱小的妇女心地是善良的。

Dong Xiu's translation seems fluent and flows well. However, a careful comparison with the original shows that 充满活力的妇女(*chongman huoli de funü*, a woman full of vitality)is a mistranslation of "confused vitality" because the telling, if not defining, epithet "confused" is lost. A complete and therefore more revealing translation would be 整天瞎忙个不停的女人 (*zhengtian xia mangge butin de nuren*, a woman who is lost yet busy all day). 不要按某一典型临摹 (*buyao an mou yi dianxing linmo*) is a mistranslation of "not copied from type" because 典型 (*dianxing*) as used here is from the Chinese concept 典型人物 (*dianxing renwu*, typical character in typical circumstances). A more accurate translation would be 不要套用某一人物类型 (*buyao taoyong mo yi renwu leixing*, do not copy from a type of characters). 她并不疯狂，但她的生活是疯狂的 (*ta bingbu fengkuang, dan tade shenghuo shi fengkuang de*)is a mistranslation of "She is not paranoiac, but her life is paranoia" because it uses a more generic term of mental illness 疯狂(*fengkuang*, madness) in translating a more specific mental condition, paranoia (the feeling of being threatened, accused, or prosecuted without proof/evidence[85]). Finally, 善良(*shanliang*, kindness) is a rather loose rendition of "tenderness;" a better Chinese "equivalent" would be 温情 (*wenqing*, tender feelings). Lu Jin's 1991 rendition comes much closer to the original in translating "paranoia" as 妄想狂(*wangxiangkuang*) although it also loosely translates "tenderness" into 心地善良 (*xindi shanliang*, kind-heartedness):[86]

> 她不是妄想狂, 不过她的生活是妄想狂。阿曼达身上又许多值得钦佩之处, 可爱、可怜之处和可笑之处同样多。不用说, 她又韧劲, 而且相当英勇, 尽管她愚蠢的行径有时候使得她在不知不觉中变得狠心, 这个身材瘦小的女人是心地善良的。

在不知不觉中变得狠心(*zai buzhibujue zhong bian de henxin*, unwittingly hardens her heart/resolve) is a well-tuned rendition of "makes her unwittingly cruel at times," much better than Dong Xiu's literal translation of "cruel" as 残酷 (*canku*).

The same mistranslation happens with the character sketch of Tom Wingfield:[87]

> And the narrator of the play. A poet with a job in a warehouse. His nature is not remorseless, but to escape from a trap he has to act without pity. (*underline added*)
> 他天性并不残忍, 但为了逃避一个陷阱, 他不得不无情地采取行动。

残忍 (*canren*, cruelty) is an over-translation of "remorseless" (without regret or guilt). A better tuned translation would be无情无义 (*wuqingquyi*, without feeling and sense of responsibility and loyalty).

Various translations of one particular prop in the stage description, "fire-escape," provides a mini-case of the challenges facing Chinese translators of Williams' (or just about any foreign) works:[88]

> The apartment faces an alley and is entered by a fire-escape, structure whose name is a touch of accidental poetic truth, for all of these huge buildings are always burning with the slow and implacable fires of human desperation. (*underline added*)

This fire-escape is an important motif for the play, as explained in this stage description. It reminds of what Henry Thoreau characterizes in *Walden* as "lives of quiet desperation" the mass of men lead:[89]

> What is called resignation is confirmed desperation. From the desperate city you go into the desperate country, and have to console yourself with the bravery of minks and muskrats. A stereotyped but unconscious despair is

concealed even under what are called the games and amusements of man-kind. There is no play in them, for this comes after work. But it is a charac-teristic of wisdom not to do desperate things.

However, Tom, as is portrayed in this play, or in the story told by him-self (as narrator of this "memory play"), driven by this quiet desperation (although his nature is not remorseless), has to act without pity to escape the trap he sees himself in. Here is Dong Xiu's 1981 translation:[90]

> 温菲尔德的住所面对一条巷子，进出靠一架救火梯。救火梯这个名字多少有点诗意，因为所有这些高楼大厦里经常缓慢地燃烧着人们在垂死挣扎中难以扑灭的火焰。

救火梯 (*jiuhuo ti*) means, literally, firefighting ladder, which is not exactly what "fire-escape" signifies as a central motif in this play. 难以扑灭的火焰 (*nanyi pumie de huoyan*, fire that cannot be extinguished) is an over-translation of "implacable fires" probably based on a miscomprehension of "implacable" (unable to be placated) and failure to fully appreciate the fire motif for the play.

Zhao's 1985 translation offers a different take:[91]

> 他们家临街，进出要走太平梯，太平梯这个名字颇有一点偶然而又诗意的真实性， 因为所有这些巨大的建筑物都燃烧着人类绝望挣扎的缓慢而又不灭的火焰。

太平梯 (*taiping ti*) means, literally, heavenly peace ladder, which seems too euphemistic and ornate because for the characters in this play, includ-ing Tom, there is no "heavenly peace" they can escape to. 缓慢而又不灭的火焰(*huanman er you bumie de huayan*)is a much better rendition of "implacable fires" warranted by both the words and the context.

Sensing the significance of the fire motif in the play, Lu's 1991 transla-tion goes out its way to get it right by taking a more direct approach (with a footnote to explain why):[92]

> 这套房间面对一条小巷，出入靠一架避火梯，因为所有这些巨大的建筑物一直燃烧着人类的绝望这股永远熄灭不了的文火。

Of the three translation attempts for fire-escape, 避火梯 (*bihuo ti*) comes closest to the English original although we can go one step further and, to borrow from Lu Xun's idea of硬译 (*yingyi*, hard translation), and translate it as 逃火梯 (*taohuo ti*) so it can serve as a more vivid and accurate over-arching motif for the Chinese rendition of the play: the kind of quiet desperation, existential crisis, or simply, trap, that Tom wants to escape, albeit with much remorse, will never let him go. There is no escaping it, as he realizes toward the end of the play, wherever he is as he drifts in the world, far away from home ("Oh, Laura, Laura, I tried to leave you behind me, but I am more faithful than I intended to be!"[93]).

Here is another instance where Tennessee Williams uses metaphoric language to describe the quiet desperation of the middle class, which, once again, proves rather challenging for Chinese translators:[94]

> the thirties, when the huge middle class of America was matriculating in a school for the blind. Their eyes had failed them, or they had failed their eyes, and so they were having their fingers pressed forcibly down on the fiery Braille alphabet of a dissolving economy.

Here is Dong Xiu's 1981 attempt:[95]

> .... 三十年代, 那时美国广大的中产阶级还刚刚录取进入<u>盲人学校</u>, 不管是眼睛使他们不管用, 还是他们使眼睛不管用, 他们不得不<u>用手指摸索令人恼火的布莱叶盲文</u>, 去<u>解决经济问题</u>。

Dong's translation fails to understand and appreciate the extended meta-phor of "school for the blind" and Braille used by Tom in describing how middle-class Americans struggle in the immediate aftermath of the Great Depression (1929–1933). This failure results in an almost word-for-word translation 用手指摸索令人恼火的布莱叶盲文 (*yong shouzhi mosuo lin-gren naohuo de bulaiye mangwen*) for "having their fingers pressed forcibly down on the fiery Braille alphabet of a dissolving economy," which is nonsensical. Just as perplexing is解决经济问题 (*jiejue jinji wenti*, resolv-ing economic problems), which misreads or mistakes "dissolving" (becom-ing dissipated, decomposed, dispersing, fading away) as "resolving" (settling/finding solutions to a problem).

Zhao's 1985 translation is a slight improvement, yet still fails to capture and relay the full extent of the original:[96]

.... 三十年代, 那时美国庞大的中产阶级<u>正考上盲人学校</u>, 他们的眼睛使他们看不见, 或者说, 他们使他们的眼睛看不见, 所以他们<u>只好用手指来按摩那火辣辣的盲文字母来了解崩溃的经济</u>。

崩溃的经济 (*bengkui de jingji*, a dissolving, collapsing economy) gets the "dissolving" right but 只好用手指来按摩那火辣辣的盲文字母来了解 (*zhihao yong shouzhi lai anmo na huolala de mangwen zimu lai liaojie*) is another almost word-for-word, nonsensical translation.

No enlightenment is gained by the time Lu's 1991 rendition comes along: it once again fails to resolve the metaphoric jigsaw from Tom ("Shakespeare").[97] Indeed, one has to try and unpack Tom's metaphoric jigsaw to bring any clarity for Chinese readers so they understand and appreciate what he tries to say:

.... 三十年代, 那时美国广大的中产阶级<u>两眼一抹黑</u>, 他们的眼睛不好使了, 或者说他们把眼睛弄得不好使了,他们象刚刚在盲人学校注册的新生使劲摸读难懂的布莱叶盲文字母一样, <u>在溃塌的经济中困惑地挣扎着</u>。

两眼一抹黑 (*liang yan yimohei*, being stuck in the dark) and 在溃塌的经济中困惑地挣扎(*zai kuita de jingji zhong kunhuo de zhengzha*, struggling confusedly in the collapsing economy) would come closer in relaying the essence of what Tom tries to say although a perfect equivalent, both in content and in form, is hard to find.

Below is a good example of Chinese translators trying to take the American playwright to the Chinese readers by naturalizing (Sinicizing) a dialogue in *The Night of Iguana* with unmistakable flavor of traditional Chinese culture (followed by the An 1992 rendition):[98]

MISS FELLOWES: It would what?
SHANNON: Shake if not shatter everything left of my faith in <u>essential ... human ...*goodness*!</u>
....
MISS FELLOWES: "<u>Essential human goodness</u>?" Why, just plain human decency is beyond your imagination, Shannon, so lie there, lie there and *lie* there, we're *going*!

费洛斯小姐　　会怎么样?
香农　　即使不说一切破灭的话, 也会动摇, 我还抱有<u>一人之初 ... 性本善</u> ... 的信念。
....

费洛斯小姐   来和我谈谈"<u>人之初, 性本善</u>"的问题吗?哟, 就讲为人正派这一点, 在你已是难以想象的, 所以, 香农, 你就躺在那儿,躺在那儿, 我们可要走了!

人之初, 性本善 is a brilliant translation of "essential human goodness" using the opening lines of *The Three Character Classic* (*sanzijing* 三字经), also translated as Trimetric Classic, one of the Chinese classic texts probably written in the thirteenth century:[99]

人之初	*ren zhi chu*	Humans when born
性本善	*xing ben sha*n	are good natured
性相近	*xing xiang jin*	their characters similar
习相远	*xi xiang yuan*	but develop differently

Upon reading this dialogue, which happens early in the play, a Chinese reader could be put under the impression that Shannon, the defrocked minister-turned-tour guide, is well versed in Chinese classics and can quote "verses and chapters," so to speak, quite handily. He will talk about swimming to China a few times later in the play albeit more as a diversion tactic if anything. Indeed, no one in the play other than Hannah has ever set foot in China.[100]

Although the characters, when "born" (created by Tennessee Williams in his plays) and "reborn" (re-created by Chinese translators) are quite similar, they do "develop" somewhat differently in the latter, assuming certain idiosyncratic traits when they morph into an entirely different, "exotic" language and culture. In one case, Liang's1987 translation of *Streetcar* for staging by the Tianjin People's Art Theatre, the scenes of the play acquire episodic titles typically used in traditional Chinese theatrical practices:[101]

第一幕 投靠 (*toukao*)	Scene One	Seeking Refuge
第二幕 冲突 (*chongtu*)	Scene Two	Conflict
第三幕 扑克牌风波 (*pukepai fengbo*)	Scene Three	Poker Night Storm
第四幕 寻求突破 (*xunqiu tupo*)	Scene Four	Seeking a Way Out
第五幕 玫瑰骑士 (*meigui qishi*)	Scene Five	Knight of Roses
第六幕 爱的隐私 (*ai de yinsi*)	Scene Six	Love Secret
第七幕 谎言 (*huangyan*)	Scene Seven	Lies
第八幕 生日礼物(*shengri liwu*)	Scene Eight	Birthday Gift
第九幕 幸福破灭 (*xingfu pomie*)	Scene Nine	When Happiness Bubble Pops

第十幕 雨打残花 (*yuda canhua*)   Scene Ten   When Rain Hits Wilted Flower

第十一幕 毁灭之路 (*huimie zhilu*)   Scene Eleven   From Here to Perdition

Similarly, names of characters and places can be interesting sites for cultural adaptation. In the same Liang 1987 rendition, Blanche becomes 卜兰姬 (*bu lan ji*) in her Chinese reincarnation. 卜 (*bu*), a real Chinese family name, associated with traditional Chinese astrology, seems an appropriate name for Blanche, given her interest in astrological signs ("What sign were you born under?" she asks Stanley. "I bet you were born under Aries. Aries people are"[102]) and her sense of the pending doom ("The first time I laid eyes on him I thought to myself, that man is my executioner!"[103]). 兰(*lan*), short for 兰花 (*lanhua*, cymbidium), is known in Chinese pop/folk culture as being most princely among the flowers (花中君子,*hua zhong qunzi*), proud, elegant, noble, virtuous, and so on. 姬 (*ji*) is a complimentary reference to a beautiful woman in ancient China. All the cultural elements put together, 卜兰姬suggests a reading of the play that captures so much of the pathos and ethos in association with Blanche who, by nature a flower-like beautiful and kind-hearted (albeit vain, flirtatious, and so on) woman, is doomed to be withered and crushed when caught in such degrading circumstances.

Other translations such as Qi Qing's 1992 rendition use a variation of 卜兰姬 (*bu lan ji*) such as白兰琪 (*bai lan qi*) to give Blanche a more meaningful Chinese identity. 白 (*bai*, white), also a real Chinese family name, is the closest one can get in representing Blanche both in sound and sense; the meaning of 兰*lan* is the same as explained above; and 琪 *qi* is a kind of fine jade. Moreover, 白happens to fit well with the white motif in the play, closely associated with Blanche, both the world she has left behind and the world she finds herself caught in:[104]

The houses are mostly <u>white frame</u>, weathered gray, with rickety outside stairs and galleries and quaintly ornamented gables. This building contains two flats, upstairs and down. Faded <u>white stairs</u> ascend to the entrances of both.

    She is daintily dressed in a <u>white suit</u> with a fluffy bodice, necklace and earrings of pearl, <u>white gloves and hat,</u> looking as if she were arriving at a summer tea or cocktail party in the garden district. She is about five years older than Stella. Her delicate beauty must avoid a strong light. There is something about her uncertain manner, as well as her white clothes, that suggests a moth.

There are also the "white columns" of Belle Reve, the old plantation home in Mississippi, the "small white radio" which Blanche turns on and Stanley, in a fury, snatches and tosses out of the window on the poker night, and "a somewhat soiled and crumpled white satin evening gown" she is in the morning after she was raped by Stanley, and so on.[105] Toward the end of the play, right before the Doctor and the Matron come to take her to the mental institution, when the cathedral chimes sound in the air, Blanche has this to say about herself:[106]

And I'll be buried at sea sewn up in a clean white sack and dropped overboard—at noon—in the blaze of summer—and into an ocean as blue as (*Chimes again*) my first lover's eyes!

The most used Chinese name for Blanche now is 布兰奇 (*bu lan qi: bu,* cloth; *lan,* as explained above; and *qi,* wonder), a phonetic transliteration that is quite prosaic, compared to 卜兰姬 or 白兰琪 discussed above, and does not seem to conjure up any coherent symbolic meaning. The same is true for the names of Stanley (斯坦尼, *si tan ni*), Stella (丝黛拉, *si dai la*), and Mitch (米奇, *mi qi*), phonetic transliterations with no particular significance for Chinese readers other than sounding "foreign" (or exotic).

The name of the Mississippi planation, Belle Reve, has inspired at least two very different Chinese translations: 美梦庄园 (*meimeng zhuangyuan,* beautiful plantation),[107] and 贝尔里夫庄园 (*bei er li fu zhuangyuan*),[108] the latter being a phonetic transliteration that loses all the connotative suggestiveness of the name both as signifier and as signified, and quite a mouthful lacking in both readability and performability.

Similarly, Elysian Fields, the name for the street where the young Kowalskis live, has sparked two translations, 乐土街 (*letu jie*),[109] and 依利恩地段 (*yi li en diduan*),[110] the latter being a phonetic transliteration which, once again, has no particular meaningful cultural association and would prove quite a mouthful for any Chinese actors cast in the roles of Blanche and Eunice in the opening scene of *Streetcar*.[111] 乐土 (*letu,* happy land), which signifies a nirvana-like final resting place, seems a near-perfect equivalent for what the street name means in its source culture, albeit fraught with irony as far as Blanche is concerned. In classical Greek mythology, Elysium, also known as the Elysian Fields, was the paradise reserved for the heroes immortalized by the gods; it was the abode of the blessed after death.[112] Williams uses this mythological abode as the name of the street where Blanche comes and meets her demise, or her "death," figuratively as well as literally (one cannot imagine how she is going to live her life once she is taken to the mental institution, completely at the mercy of strangers, kind and unkind alike). 乐土 (*letu,* happy land) aptly captures the irony embodied in the street name whereas 依利恩地段 (*yi li en diduan*), full of strange sound, signifies very little.

Indeed, death, as a motif, shrouds *Streetcar* from beginning to end and proves quite a challenge to Chinese translators. For example, in one of the conversations between Blanche and Stella early in the play, Blanche explains how hard it was for her to take "the blows in my face and my body" and to take care of all those deaths in the family (followed by Sun's 1991 rendition):[113]

> You just came home in time for the funerals, Stella. And funerals are pretty compared to <u>deaths</u>. Funerals are quiet, but <u>deaths</u>—not always. *(underline added)*
> 你只是在葬礼时才赶回来, 史妲拉。跟<u>送终</u>相比, 参加葬礼要好多得多。葬礼上一切静悄悄的, 而<u>临终</u>时的情况就不一定了。

Here, instead of going for the easy and obvious Chinese equivalent, translating "deaths" as 死亡(*siwang*),[114] Sun's 1991 rendition goes out of its way and, by a stroke of luck or genius (or both), finds 送终(*songzhong*) and 临终(*linzhong*).送终 in Chinese culture means younger members of the family attending upon a dying parent or other senior member of the family and taking care of end-of-life matters, including the funeral, as expected by the virtue of filial piety.[115] 临终 means when one is dying or on the deathbed. So, 送终 and 临终 are the most apt translations of "deaths" as referred to in Blanche's speech, which would give Chinese readers a fuller sense of the sad responsibilities that Blanche had to shoulder alone and of her as an essentially good person—a filial daughter, granddaughter, and niece attending to the dying relatives as they breathed their last. As it happens, Qi Qing's 1992 translation chooses the same two meaningful and apt Chinese terms for "deaths" as referred to in Blanche's conversation with Stella.[116]

As alluded to earlier, upon meeting Stanley for the first time, Blanche senses a mortal danger lurking in the man (although she cannot help feeling drawn to the man, like a moth being drawn to the fire, and flirting with him, or rather, that mortal danger, thanks to the "animal force" he exudes and sometimes exhibits explosively):[117]

> He hates me. Or why would he insult me? The first time I laid eyes on him I thought to myself, that man is <u>my executioner</u>! That man will destroy me, unless—(*underline added*)
> 他是讨厌我，不然为什么要耍着我。我第一见到他，就知道他是我的<u>煞星</u>，他会毁了我，除非—
> 他恨我的，否则他干吗要侮辱我?我第一眼见到他时就自忖，那家伙是我的<u>催命鬼</u>!那个人将会毁了我，除非—
> 他恨我，否则他怎么会辱骂我?我头一次见到他我就想这人将来是<u>杀我的凶手</u>!这人将毁掉我，除非—
> 他恨我。否则他干吗要侮辱我?我看到他的第一眼，我就对自己说，这个人就是我的<u>刽子手</u>!这个人会毁了我，除非—

Of these renditions of "executioner," 杀我的凶手 (*sha wo de xiongshou*, the person who murders me) is a mis- or over-translation based on a misunderstanding of both the word "executioner" and the context in which it is used. An "executioner" is a person who executes people who have been sentenced to death whereas a "murderer" is a person who commits the crime of unlawfully killing a person (especially with malice aforethought): the former enforces the law (albeit in a most violent way) whereas the latter violates the law, also in a most violent and brutal way. In the context of the play, when Blanche arrives at the Kowalskis, a "death sentence" seems to have already been put on her; there is a sense of doom, of the inevitability of tragedy. All of her past, socioeconomic, moral, cultural as well as certain traits in her personality, seem to be conspiring against her ("more sinn'd against than sinning"). Nonetheless, Blanche might still have a chance of escaping "death" if she had not run into Stanley, but in this world of inevitability, or tragedy, there is no such if. Both 煞星 (*shaxing*, bad luck), a term from Chinese astrology, and 催命鬼 (*cuiminggui*, demon that hurries one's death),[118] are under-translations with interesting Chinese cultural twist. Of the four, Feng's 2015 rendition, 刽子手 (*guizishou*, one who carries out a death sentence),[119] is the only one that delivers in full force Blanche's foreboding, which turns out to be true.

Toward the end of the play, when the "executioner" Stanley goes for the kill, more than figuratively, and sexually assaults Blanche, she fights back as fiercely as she can: she smashes a bottle on the table and faces her attacker, clutching the broke top: "I could twist the broken end in your face!" Stanley springs forward, overturns the table between them, and outpowers her:[120]

> Tiger—tiger! Drop the bottle top! Drop it! <u>We've had this date with each other from the beginning</u>! (*underline added*)
> 疯狗!疯狗!把瓶子扔了。从一开始我们的这次<u>约会</u>就订好了。
> 雌老虎—雌老虎!放下瓶子!其实我们俩初次见面就欠下了这笔<u>相思债</u>!
> 母老虎—母老虎!放下那半截破酒瓶!放下!咱们这次<u>约会</u>一开始那我就订好了!
> 母老虎—母老虎!把瓶子头放下!放下!咱们这场<u>约会</u>可是打一起头就订好了的!

Three of the renditions go for the apparent Chinese equivalent for "date": 约会 (*yuehui*). Sun's 1991 rendition, however, goes out of its way and finds a rather interesting expression in the repertoire of traditional Chinese culture and literature: 相思债 (*xiangsi zhai*, debt of mutual longing).[121] At the first glance, 相思债seems an excessive and therefore inappropriate over-translation because it refers to complications between men and women due to romantic entanglements. It seems to conclude the tragic story, the life-and-death fight between two sworn enemies (with Stella caught in the middle) on a romantic note, which is uncalled for, yet when one considers the messy entanglements between the two, how Blanche both despises and feels irresistibly drawn and flirts with him the first time she sets eye on him, this 相思债rendition seems to be onto something (possibly elemental and metaphysical) too, saying what cannot be said with a plain, prosaic约会.

As has been the case since China began to look outside its own territorial boundaries in seeking cultural and spiritual catalyst and stimulus for its own growth, for example, the much storied journey to the west led by Xuanzang (602–664), especially since the late 1800s when a generation of young Chinese undertook the tremendous project of translation for cultural and people renewal to save China in the brave new world, translation has always been much more than technical issues of fidelity versus expressiveness, or as in the case of drama/theater, performability versus literariness. Translating Tennessee Williams, as shown in this chapter, from Ying Ruocheng's 1963 rendition of *Something Unspoken* to the various renditions of *The Glass Menagerie*, *A Streetcar Named Desire*, *Cat on a Hot Tin*

Roof, *The Night of Iguana*, and Williams' *Memoirs* since the 1980s, has been complicated by sociopolitical, cultural, and moral forces at work at the time. Reading these Williams renditions in the context of such sociopolitical, cultural, and moral developments is much more profitable and rewarding than reading them as literary undertakings alone.

NOTES

1. Tennessee Williams, *Tennessee Williams Plays 1937–1955* (New York: The Library of America, 2000), 858. Hereafter, Williams, *1937–1955*.
2. Ibid., 869.
3. See "Xuanzang," https://www.britannica.com/biography/Xuanzang and https://iep.utm.edu/xuanzang/.
4. See Chap. 1, pp. 11–17.
5. This portion of discussion draws from Shouhua Qi, *Western Literature in China and the Translation of a Nation* (New York: Palgrave Macmillan, 2012), 29–86.
6. Briefly, by "domestication" is meant the method of translation that renders the foreign text in fluent, "natural" language of the target culture so the translated text is "transparent" and the translator remains "invisible," whereas by "foreignization" is meant the method of translation that retains a considerable degree of "foreignness" of the source text, for example, the terminology and syntax, without trying to "naturalize" or acculturate it for readers in the target culture. See André Lefevere, "Chinese and Western Thinking on Translation," in Susan Bassnett and André Lefevere, *Constructing Cultures: Essays on Literary Translation* (Bristol, UK: Multicultural Matters, 1998), 12–24; and Lawrence Venuti, *The Translator's Invisibility: A History of Translation* (London and New York: Routledge, 1995).
7. See Pascale Casanova, "Consecration and Accumulation of Literary Capital: Translation as Unequal Exchange," translated by Siobhan Brownlie, in *Critical Readings in Translation Studies*, edited by Mona Baker (London and New York: Routledge, 2010), 286–303.
8. See Susan Bassnett, "The Translator in the Theatre," *Theatre Quarterly* 10.40 (1981): 37–48; and "Translating for the Theatre: The Case Against Performability," *TTR* (*Traduction, Terminologie, Redaction*) 4.1 (1991): 99–111.
9. See Ekaterini Nikolarea, "Performability versus Readability: A Historical Overview of a Theoretical Polarization in Theater Translation," *Translation Journal* 6.4 (October 2002), https://translationjournal. net/journal/22theater.htm.

10. Here is what Ying Ruocheng has to say about his translation of Miller's *Death of A Salesman*:

The original language of the play is very colloquial English. In translating it into Chinse, I tried hard to avoid literary language, because I didn't want it to sound like a stiff translation. Because our cast was from the Beijing People's Art Theatre, my translation is heavily salted with Beijing dialect and slang. I also paid a lot of attention to maintaining the original tempo of the dialogue, because I think that's important to the feeling of the play.

Ying Ruocheng and Claire Conceison, *Voices Carry: Behind Bars and Backstage during China's Revolution and Reform* (New York: Roman and Littlefield, 2009), 162–163.

11. See Chap. 3, pp. 103–124.
12. Ying Ruocheng 英若诚, trans. *Something Unspoken* (*meiyou jiang chulai de hua* 没有讲出来的话) by Tennessee Williams, *World Literature* (*Shijie wenxue* 世界文学) 3 (1963): 44–61. Hereafter Ying, 1963.
13. See Chap. 3, pp. 75–81.
14. Ying and Conceison.
15. See "Peng Dehuai," https://en.wikipedia.org/wiki/Peng_Dehuai. See also Chap. 3, p. 80.
16. Williams, *1937–1955*, 858; Ying, 1963, 44.
17. Ying, 1963, 45.
18. Williams, *1937–1955*, 858; Ying, 1963, 44.
19. See "Gong Guan" (公馆), https://baike.baidu.com/item/%E5%85%AC%E9%A6%86/10410380.
20. Williams, *1937–1955*, 860; Ying 1963, 47.
21. See *"Shengdi"* (圣地 holy land), https://baike.baidu.com/item/%E5%9C%; and *"Zhongguo geming wu da shengdi"* (中国五大革命圣地 five holy lands/seats of Chinese revolution), https://baike.baidu.com/item/%E4%B8%AD%E5%9B%BD%E4%BA%94%E5%A4%A7%E9%9D%A9%E5%91%BD%E5%9C%A3%E5%9C%B0.
22. Williams, *1937–1955*, 860; Ying, 1963, 47.
23. Williams, *1937–1955*, 861; Ying, 1963, 48.
24. Williams, *1937–1955*, 862; Ying, 1963, 49.
25. Williams, *1937–1955*, 863; Ying, 1963, 50.
26. As any Chinese reader of this translated text would know, only someone in a powerful leadership position can speak of himself as 讲民主 (*jiang mingzhu*, being democratic), as a gesture or as a decision-making process, although, in the context of Chinese politics, the unquestionable power is, more often than not, vested in the powerful leader alone.

27. The parallels between what Cornelia describes as her political existential fight, especially when channeled through Ying Ruocheng's capable translations, and how Mao Zedong (毛泽东1893–1976) "rallied his forces" to strike back "cliques," both within the Communist Party and the government and without, who had dared to question his leadership (e.g., his "Great Leap Forward" policies), are too eerily close to miss. See "Anti-Rightist Campaign," https://en.wikipedia.org/wiki/Anti-Rightist_Campaign; "Lu-shan Conference," https://www.britannica.com/topic/Lu-shan-Conference; and "Socialist Education Movement," https://en.wikipedia.org/wiki/Socialist_Education_Movement.

28. Williams, *1937–1955*, 863; Ying, 1963, 49.

29. Williams, *1937–1955*, 870; Ying, 1963, 59.

30. See "Great Leap Forward," https://www.britannica.com/event/Great-Leap-Forward; and Guo Jian, and Yuan Zhou, Yongyi Song, *The A to Z of the Chinese Cultural Revolution* (Lanham, Maryland: Scarecrow Press, 2009), 162.

31. Williams, *1937–1955*, 871–872. See *National Society Daughters of the Barons of Runnemede: Organization, History, Membership* (Athens, GA: McGregor Co., 1937); "Colonial Dames of America," https://en.wikipedia.org/wiki/Colonial_Dames_of_America; and "The Huguenot Society of America," https://en.wikipedia.org/wiki/The_Huguenot_Society_of_America.

32. See Chap. 3, pp. 82–85.

33. Williams, *1937–1955*, 865–866; Ying, 1963, 53.

34. Williams, *1937–1955*, 866; Ying, 1963, 54.

35. Williams, *1937–1955*, 869; Ying, 1963, 57–58.

36. Kwok-sing Li, *A Glossary of Political Terms of the People's Republic of China*, translated by Mary Lok (Hong Kong: The Chinese University of Hong Kong, 1995), 421–422.

37. Dong Xiu东秀, trans., *The Glass Menagerie. The Glass Menagerie (Boli dongwuyuan* 玻璃动物园) by Tennessee Williams, *Contemporary Foreign Literature (Dangdai waiguo wenxue* 当代外国文学) 4 (Oct. 1981): 111–147. Hereafter, Dong, 1981.

38. Lu Xun 鲁迅, "*Guanyu fanyi*" (关于翻译 About translation, 1933), *Contemporary Foreign Literature (Dangdai waiguo wenxue* 当代外国文学) 4 (Oct. 1981): 33; "*Xianjin de xin wenxue de gaiguan*" (现今的新文学的概观 An overview of today's new literature, 1929), ibid., 37; "*Nalai zhuyi*" (拿来主义 On take-ism, 1934,), ibid., 110; and "*Muke jicheng xiaoji*" (木刻纪程小记 Preface of "Woodcut", 1934), ibid.

39. See Chap. 3, pp. 85–93.

40. Zhao Quanzhang 赵全章, trans., *The Glass Menagerie* (*Boli dongwuyuan* 玻璃动物园) by Tennessee Williams, in *Modernist Foreign Literary Works* (*Waiguo xiandaipai zuoping xuan* 外国现代派作品选), vol. 4., edited by Yuan Kejia 袁可嘉 et al. (Shanghai: Shanghai Literature and Art Press 上海文艺出版社), 1985, 594–676. Hereafter, Zhao, 1985.
41. Lu Jin 鹿金, trans., *The Glass Menagerie* (*Boli dongwuyuan* 玻璃动物园) by Tennessee Williams, in *Classic Foreign Tragedies* (*Waiguo zhuming beiju xuan* 外国著名悲剧选), vol. 3, edited by Gao Ruisen 高芮森 (Zhengzhou: Henan People's Press 河南人民出版社, 1991), 233–336, Hereafter, Lu, 1991.

   Apparently, the editor of this volume used a rather broader definition of "tragedy" than theorized by Aristotle, Hegel, or Arthur Miller in his essay "Tragedy and the Common Man." In the preface for the volume, the editor states that the painful existential crisis experienced by the Wingfield family as portrayed in *The Glass Menagerie* shows that "such tragic phenomenon is ubiquitous in America" and that the play is "an indictment of the American society for its injustice." Gao Ruisen 高芮森, "Preface," *Classic Foreign Tragedies*,7.
42. Liang Bolong 梁伯龙, trans., *A Streetcar Named Desire* (*Yuwanghao jieche* 欲望号街车) by Tennessee Williams (Tianjin: Tianjin People's Art Theatre 天津人民艺术院), 1987. Hereafter, Liang, 1987. See Chap. 3, pp. 138–139.
43. Chen Liangting 陈良廷, trans., *Cat on a Hot Tin Roof* (*Re tiepi wuding shang de mao* 热铁皮屋顶上的猫) by Tennessee Williams, in *Cat on a Hot Tin Roof* (*Re tiepi wuding shang de mao* 热铁皮屋顶上的猫) (Beijing: Chinese Social Sciences Press 中国社会科学出版社, 1982), 224–382. Hereafter, Chen, 1982.
44. Sun Baimei 孙白梅, trans., *A Streetcar Named Desire* (*Yuwanghao jieche* 欲望号街车) by Tennessee Williams (Shanghai: Shanghai Translation Press 上海译文出版社), 1991. Hereafter, Sun, 1991.
45. Qi Qing 奇青, trans., *A Streetcar Named Desire* (*Yuwanghao jieche* 欲望号街车) by Tennessee Williams, in *Foreign Contemporary Plays* (*Waiguo dangdai juzuo xuan* 外国当代剧作选) (Beijing: China Drama Press 中国戏剧出版社, 1992), 101–225. Hereafter, Qi Q., 1992.
46. An Man 安曼, trans., *The Night of Iguana* (*Xiyi de yewan* 蜥蜴的夜晚) by Tennessee Williams, in *Foreign Contemporary Plays* (*Waiguo dangdai juzuo xuan* 外国当代剧作选) (Beijing: China Drama Press 中国戏剧出版社, 1992), 363–552. Hereafter, An, 1992.

47. Feng Tao 冯涛, trans., *A Streetcar Named Desire* (*Yuwanghao jieche* 欲望号街车) by Tennessee Williams (Shanghai: Shanghai Translation Press 上海译文出版社), 2015. Hereafter, Feng T., 2015.

48. Feng Qianzhu 冯倩珠, trans., *Memoirs* (*Tiannaxi weiliansi huiyilu* 田纳西·威廉斯回忆录 (Zhengzhou: Henan University Press 河南大学出版社, 2018). Hereafter, Feng Q., 2018. This translation has copyright arrangement with the original publisher, the University of the South based in the US, through proper literary agencies, which doesn't happen often enough when it comes to such matters in China (although there is much more sensitivity and respect in this regard than before).

49. Williams, *1937–1955*, 411.

50. Dong, 1981, 117.

51. See "Romance of the Western Chamber," https://en.wikipedia.org/wiki/Romance_of_the_Western_Chamber.

52. Williams, *1937–1955*, 432.

53. Zhao, 1985, 609.

54. Lu, 1991, 258.

55. Williams, *1937–1955*, 533.

56. Liang, 1987, 76.

57. Sun, 1991, 253.

58. Qi Q., 1992, 186.

59. Feng T., 2015, 148.

60. "Degenerate," https://www.merriam-webster.com/dictionary/degenerate.

61. See "*Xing xinli biantai*" (性心理变态 sexual deviant), https://baike.baidu.com/item/%E6%80%A7%E5%BF%83%E7%90%86%E5%8F%98%E6%80%81/10284613.

62. See Paul de Man, *Allegories of Reading: Figural Language in Rousseau, Nietzsche, Rilke, and Proust* (New Haven: Yale University Press, 1979); and J. Hillis Miller, "Walter Pater: A Partial Portrait," *Daedalus* 105.1 (Winter 1976): 97–113; and "The Critic as Host," *Critical Inquiry* 3.3 (Spring 1977): 439–447.

63. Williams, *1937–1955*, 517.

64. "Put out," https://www.urbandictionary.com/define.php?term=put%20out.

65. Liang, 1987, 5–6; Sun, 1991, 189; Qi Q., 1992, 165; and Feng T., 2015, 112.

66. Williams, *1937–1955*, 880; Chen, 1982, 224.

67. Williams, *1937–1955*, 887; Chen, 1982, 232.

68. Williams, *1937–1955*, 892; Chen, 1982, 238.

69. Williams, *1937–1955*, 910; Chen, 1982, 260.

70. Williams, *1937–1955*, 903; Chen, 1982, 251.
71. Williams, *1937–1955*, 904; Chen, 1982, 252.
72. Williams, *1937–1955*, 911; Chen, 1982, 261.
73. Williams, *1937–1955*, 950; Chen, 1982, 309.
74. Williams, *1937–1955*, 935; Chen, 1982, 289.
75. Shelly Wu, *Chinese Sexual Astrology* (Franklin Lake, NJ: New Page Books, 2007), 132; and Judith Worell, ed., *Encyclopedia of Women and Gender: Sex Similarities and Differences and Impact of Society on Gender* (San Diego, CA: Academic Press, 2001), 298.
76. Williams, *1937–1955*, 897; Chen, 1982, 245.
77. Williams, *1957–1980*, 329; An, 1992, 404.
78. Williams, *1957–1980*, 330; An, 1992, 405.
79. See Jack Richardson, "Unaffected Recollections," *New York Times Book Review*, November 2, 1975, https://www.nytimes.com/1975/11/02/archives/unaffected-recollections-memoirs.html?searchResultPosition=1.
80. Williams, *Memoirs*, 14–29, 42–47.
81. Ibid., xviii, 177.
82. "*Tiannaxi weiliansi huiyilu*" (田纳西·威廉斯回忆录 Tennessee Williams *Memoirs*), accessed September 27, 2021, *Douban Dushu* (豆瓣读书 Douban Books), https://book.douban.com/subject/30295663/.
83. English translations of Douban readers' comments quoted in this section are provided by this author based on the original comments in Chinese gleaned from the Douban website cited in the preceding note.
84. Williams, *1937–1955*, 394; Dong, 1981, 111.
85. "Paranoia," https://www.merriam-webster.com/dictionary/paranoia.
86. Lu, 1991, 236.
87. Williams, *1937–1955*, 394; Dong, 1981, 111.
88. Williams, *1937–1955*, 399.
89. Henry David Thoreau, *Waldon* (London: CRW Publishing Limited, 2004), 12.
90. Dong, 1981, 112.
91. Zhao, 1985, 595.
92. Lu, 1991, 242. Here is the footnote (with English translation provided by this author):

> 避火梯(fire escape): 我国一般称作太平梯, 但是作者在下文中俏皮地说它不但能使人逃避火灾, 还能逃避怒火, 所以直译作避火梯。

> Fire escape: In China, we typically call it heavenly peace ladder (*taiping ti*). However, the author in the subsequent text says humorously that this ladder helps people not only escape from fire disaster, but also escape from fires of anger, hence the literal translation 避火梯 (*bihuo ti*).

93. Williams, *1937–1955*, 465.
94. Ibid., 400.
95. Dong, 1981, 112.
96. Zhao, 1985, 597.
97. Lu, 1991, 244.
98. Williams, *1957–1980*, 432; An, 1992, 423–424.
99. "Three Character Classic: San Zi Jing 三字经," https://www.chinasage.info/three-character-classic.htm#.
100. See Chap. 1, pp.?
101. Liang, 1987, 目录 (*mulu* table of contents); English translations provided by author of this book.
102. Williams, *1937–1955*, 513.
103. Tennessee Williams, *A Streetcar Named Desire*, with an Introduction by Arthur Miller (New York: New Directions, 2004), 111. Hereafter, Williams, 2004. Somehow, this important and oft-quoted line is missing in the version of *Streetcar* included in the anthology published by The Library of America in 2000. See Williams, *1937–1955*, 526.
104. Williams, *1937–1955*, 469, 471.
105. Ibid., 472, 496–500, 548.
106. Ibid., 559.
107. Sun, 1991, 15.
108. Qi Q., 1992, 106.
109. Sun, 1991, 9.
110. Qi Q., 1992, 101.
111. Williams, *1937–1957*, 469, 471.
112. "Elysian," https://www.merriam-webster.com/dictionary/elysian.
113. Williams, *1937–1957*, 479; Sun 1991, 41.
114. Liang, 1987, 1–16; and Feng T., 2015, 26.
115. "*Songzhong*" (送终), https://baike.baidu.com/item/%E9%80%81%E7%BB%88/9185.
116. Qi Q., 1992, 115.
117. Williams, 2004, 111. The quote is followed by Chinese translations: Liang, 1987, 6–7; Sun, 1991, 225; Qi Q., 1992, 177; and Feng T., 2015, 132.
118. See "*Shaxing*" (煞星), https://baike.baidu.com/item/%E7%85%9E%E6%98%9F/70984; and "*Cuiminggui*" (催命鬼), https://baike.baidu.com/item/%E5%82%AC%E5%91%BD%E9%AC%BC/10409305.

119. See "*Gui zi shou*" (刽子手), https://baike.baidu.com/item/%E5%88%B
     D%E5%AD%90%E6%89%8B/5211.
120. Williams, *1937–1955*, 554–555. The quote is followed by Chinese trans-
     lations: Liang 1987, 10–19; Qi Q., 1992, 213; Sun 1991, 339; and Feng
     T., 2015, 213.
121. Sun Baimei 孙白梅 seems to have a knack for culturally flavored and
     therefore evocative renditions of names, places, and terms such as Elysian
     Fields (乐土 *letu*, happy land) and "executioner" (催命鬼 *cuiminggui*,
     demon that hurries one's death)—as discussed earlier.

CHAPTER 3

From Cautious Curiosity to Deep Dive: Interpreting Tennessee Williams

The reception of Tennessee Williams in China has developed with a discernible trajectory, from early rejection and/or cautious curiosity on account of perceived "decadence" and "warped psychology" to gradual acceptance and even full-throated exaltation, overcoming sociocultural and moral barriers to empathize and identify with strangers as ourselves, through literary translation (as discussed in the preceding chapter), critical interpretation (the topic of this chapter), and theatrical adaptation (the topic of the next chapter) in the context of profound changes in China's socioeconomic and cultural life and sex mores during the decades since the beginning of "reform and opening up" in the early 1980s.

USING THE FOREIGN TO SATIRIZE THE DOMESTIC? *SOMETHING UNSPOKEN* THROUGH THE LENS OF 1950s–1960s

As discussed in Chap. 2, the first known Chinese translation of Tennessee Williams is his one-act play *Something Unspoken* (1953) published in a 1963 issue of *World Literature* (*Shijie wenxue* 世界文学). Even though this seems an outlier, a solo act of introducing Williams in China by a single translator, Ying Ruocheng (1929–2003), in the early 1960s, it is fraught with sociopolitical significance. Given the impact of *World*

S. Qi, *Culture, History, and the Reception of Tennessee Williams in China*, Chinese Literature and Culture in the World, https://doi.org/10.1007/978-3-031-16934-2_3

Literature, published by the prestigious People's Literature Press based in Beijing, its readers must have heard it when the proverbial tree fell in the forest, even though no one has ever acknowledged having heard it, at least not publicly by means of published reviews and journal articles. As shown in the preceding chapter, there are simply too many loud and clear and provocative parallels between what is going on in the play, personal and political, and what was unfolding on the sociopolitical stage of China in the late 1950s and early 1960s not to have produced some echoes in the minds of the literary magazine's readers.

The action of the play takes place in the living room of Cornelia Scott, a regal, elderly Southern woman, on the election day of a local chapter of the Confederate Daughters. In this play, Williams "masterfully weaves a brief but poignant tale of unspoken, and seemingly unspeakable, desire and the animosity that arises from it"[1] between Cornelia and Grace, her companion and employee for the last 15 years. The play offers "a glimpse into the private performance rituals" of the two elderly women whose relationship is complicated by "an unnamed, unspoken, presumably lesbian, attraction" between them and by the fact that they come from two different worlds socioeconomically.[2] Cornelia, the "mistress" of the house, wants to vocalize her romantic feelings for her younger female companion/employee, Grace, but is "repeatedly aborted by external circumstances that form an ironic backdrop to the socially dangerous would-be professions."[3] While some reviewers are impressed with Williams' ability to "create tension without action and to give dramatic climax to a lifetime in half-an-hour worth of his sensitively written dialogue," others dismiss the play as "a trite little sketch" that admits "widely contradictory themes, including lesbian desire and bitter contempt in the ladies' relationship."[4] Williams himself describes the play as "a tragicomic one-act"[5] although it is not clear what he means by "tragicomic" in referencing *Something Unspoken*. In the dramatic action of the play as written, there seems not much that is carnivalesquely dark and grotesque that characterize many of his later plays,[6] such as *The Day on Which a Man Dies*, *The Milk Train Doesn't Stop Here Anymore* (1962), and *In the Bar of a Tokyo Hotel* (1969), alluded to in Chap. 1. Whether one can laugh at the tragic elements in the lives of the two elderly women would probably depend on in what frame of mind one reads the play or how the play is staged, for example, whether the two roles are performed with exaggeration. One possible, potentially "profitable" way of reading the play, in its Chinese reincarnation midwifed by Ying Ruocheng, is to see it as a political satire through the lens of the sociopolitical life of the late 1950s to early 1960s.

It is not known how Ying Ruocheng obtained access to this one-act play in the early 1960s of China, where there was limited access to contemporary Western plays such as those written by Williams. It is also interesting, and potentially quite revealing, to wonder why, out of so many dramatic works by Williams, including critically acclaimed *The Glass Menagerie* and *A Streetcar Named Desire*, Ying Ruocheng chose this rather "obscure" one-act play to translate by way of introducing this "American Shakespeare" to China.[7] To understand and appreciate the significance of this translation, let us take a quick review of the larger sociocultural and political contexts of the late 1950s and early 1960s in China and the peritextual elements,[8] as defined by Gérard Genette, framing this published translation.

As indicated earlier, Ying's translation of *Something Unspoken*[9] appears in a 1963 issue of *World Literature*,[10] a bimonthly founded in 1953 by the Foreign Literature Research Institute of the Chinese Academy of Social Science (CASS) and published by the People's Literature Press. For many years it was the only and most authoritative magazine devoted to the introduction, translation, and review of foreign literature—until the Cultural Revolution (1966–1976). It resumed publication in 1977 and is still an important publication today run by the same influential Foreign Literature Research Institute of CASS. Embedded, or rather, featured, in the middle of this issue is Ying's translation of *Something Unspoken*, 20 pages long, the longest piece in an issue of 124-page literary magazine, flanked by translations of revolutionary pieces and thus shielded from possible political censorship and attack: three Cuban writers spearheading the issue with poems chanting anti-American imperialists sentiments and Stefan Zweig (1881–1942) and Giovanni Verga (1840–1922), two popular and politically safe modern Western writers, bringing up the rear with their short stories.

If we turn our gaze beyond the pages of this issue of *World Literature* and travel in time back to 1963, we will find these important developments both in and outside China. Internationally, it was a tense period of Cold War between the US and the Soviet Union. Much of the world was still smarting from the Cuban Missile Crisis (1962) that brought the world to the edge of a full-scale nuclear war. Vietnam War (1955–1975) was escalating with deeper and deeper US involvement.[11] Domestically, China was still suffering the aftermath of the Great Famine (1959–1961), with a death toll possibly in the tens of millions.[12] The famine resulted from policies such as Great Leap Forward (1958–1962) and People's Commune (1958, which lasted till 1983 when it was replaced by township), and so on, campaigns to catapult China into the superspeed of development to catch up and overtake Japan, Europe, and the United States.[13]

As the catastrophic outcomes of such hot-headed policies became obvious, there was a reckoning of sorts in the echelon of the government and the Chinese Communist Party (CCP). One of the sites of such political and ideological maneuvering and jostling was the Lushan Conference[14] held between July and August 1959. The major topic of the conference was the Great Leap Forward, which resulted in the purge of the Defense Minister, Marshal Peng Dehuai (彭德怀 1898–1974), who had had the courage (or audacity) to question the Great Leap Forward policies based on his first-hand investigations of the realities, in a "letter of opinion" sent to Mao Zedong (毛泽东 1893–1976), the supreme leader of the CCP. Mao saw such expressions of opinion as a personal affront, rallied his forces to strike back, and purged Peng (and a "clique" of other top cadres sympathetic to and supportive of Peng) from the echelon of power. Parallel to this development was the Anti-Rightist Campaign (1957–1959),[15] a nation-wide campaign to crack down on those, both within and outside the CCP, especially intellectuals, who dared to speak up and criticize the CCP, its monopoly on power and its hot-headed policies. Barely a few years later, as the Great Famine eased up somewhat, Mao launched the Socialist Education Movement (aka the Four Cleanups Movement),[16] which proved to be a precursor of the ordeal of the Cultural Revolution.

Once again, it would be impossible to know today why and how exactly Ying Ruocheng chose this particular one-act play to translate and even how he had gotten hold of a copy of the play, given that the play was written in 1953 and had only a few performances in the US, with far less publicity than that received by *The Glass Menagerie*, *A Streetcar Named Desire*, or *Cat on a Hot Tin Roof*, and why *World Literature*, based in Beijing, chose or decided to publish the translation, having it flanked by politically correct or safe and innocuous pieces of foreign literature in the same issue.[17] If the lesbian theme embodied in *Something Unspoken* is more than latent, albeit not spoken of explicitly, it would not be something readily visible to Chinese readers of the Ying's translation because the issue of homosexuality, topical as it was in the West then and as it is in China today, would not be on their radar simply because there were so many other more essential existential challenges and hardships they were dealing with, both physical (such as food or famine) and political. The political topical-ness of the play was simply too apparent and in-your-face, so to speak, for the Chinese readers to have missed. Indeed, they would be bombarded with the volley of evocative descriptions and fiery exchanges loaded with fiery political resonances, as shown in the preceding chapter, for example:

帝王般的威严 (*diwang ban de weiyan*, imperial majesty), 阴谋 (*yinmou*, plotting in the dark), 两面三刀 (*liang mian san dao*, two faces and three daggers), 讲民主 (*jiang minzhu*, being democratic), 敌视我的小集团 (*dishi wo de xiao jituan*, a clique hostile to me), 一个派系 (*yige paixi*, a clique), 反对我的运动 (*fandui wo de yundong*, a movement against me), 有组织的运动 (*you zuzhi de yundong*, an organized movement), 粉碎这个反对我的运动 (*fensui zhege fandui wo de yundong*, to blast into powder this movement against me,), 把我的队伍动员起来了(*ba wo de duiwu dongyuan qilai*, rally my forces), 洁身引退，完全退出 (*jieshen yintui, wanquan tuichu*, retreat/ resign with a clean, impeccable reputation), 除了—最高位置以外—什么— 也不接受! (*chule zui gao weizhi yiwai shenmo ye bu jieshou*, will accept no office except the highest), 皇帝的长袍 (*huangdi de changpao*, imperial gota), 不可战胜的样子 (*buke zhansheng de yangzi*, invinsible looking), 都有点说不出来的—恐惧 (*dou youdian shuobuchu lai de kongju*, all somehow frightened of you), 智慧的泉源 (*zhihui de quanyuan*, fountain of wisdom), and 皇帝一样的威严 (*huangdi yiyang de weiyan*, imperial grandeur).

Readers of *World Literature*, mostly teachers, artists, writers, scholars/ intellectuals, as well as college students, who had just lived through the Anti-Rightest campaign, some having paid a dear price for having spoken out, must have heard of the Lushan Conference. They were now being caught in another round of political campaign, the Socialist Education Movement (the Four Cleanups Movement) to purge their minds of politically incorrect thoughts and to purge "reactionary elements" from the ranks of party, government, and educational and cultural institutions.

Ying Ruocheng, the translator of *Something Unspoken*, must have known only too well the price one would have to pay for speaking out and criticizing the Party. This is what Ying had to say in his memoir *Voices Carry* about what happened during the Anti-Rightest campaign:[18]

After the early, heady days of the new republic, China's intellectuals embarked on a terrifying roller-coaster ride. Our leaders initially exhorted us to speak our minds during the 1957 Hundred Flowers Movement, but then, almost overnight, the leadership counterattacked, and those who had made the most scathing comments were singled out and labeled Rightists. During the nationwide movement, at least 300,000 people suffered this disgrace—my brother Ying Ruocong was one of them.

Ying himself would be arrested in 1968, two years into the Cultural Revolution, and imprisoned for no specific crimes other than being who he was—his pedigree (his grandfather founded Fu Jen Catholic University in Beijing in 1928, among other things[19]) and his line of work; he was not released or "liberated" until 1971.[20]

In his two-paragraph "Postface" tagged onto his translation of Williams' play, Ying Ruocheng gives a quick bio of the American playwright, describing him as "having drifted rootlessly in the US and Mexico" and worked at many odd jobs during his youth (meaning, he was one of *us* working class people) and then gives a mixed assessment:[21]

> Tennessee Williams is heavily influenced by psychoanalytic studies and pessimistic philosophies. His plays, especially recent plays, include excessive depictions of sexual abnormalities, sometimes with brutality. The characters coming from his pen are, typically, fallen and degenerated.

This negative assessment would be the view of Williams in China for a long time to come. However, Ying sees something positive in Williams, too, which would fit more comfortably with the dominant "socialist realism" ideology of arts and literature, especially when it comes to exposing the not-so-pretty realities of the "old society" (before 1949) and of the capitalist West:

> Nonetheless, some of his works truthfully reflect some realities in America today. *Something Unspoken* is one of such works, which was first staged in January 1958. In this short play that lasts only for 30 or 40 minutes, the author shows us, through a cast of only two characters and minimal stagecraft, the spiritual world of an upper-class woman in the deep South—her bull-headed arrogance, indulgences, and spiritual nihilism and lethargy, exposing the dishonesty, hypocrisy, and betrayal underneath the façade of culture and decorum of the bourgeoisie.

One gets a sense that by "fallen and degenerated" and "indulgences, and spiritual nihilism" Ying was referring to the homosexual theme embodied in the play. Did he have something else in mind? Or rather, did he intend the translation as a political satire of sort, to voice the unspoken or the unspeakable, "using the foreign to satirize the domestic" (*jie wai feng nei*借外讽内), or rather, "doing one thing under the cover/façade of another (*ming xiu zhan dao, an du chen cang*明修栈道, 暗度陈仓)? One can never know with any degree of certainty. However, as shown in pertinent discussions above and in Chap. 2, the text of Ying's translation of *Something Unspoken*, its paratextual environment, and more importantly, its sociopolitical context—momentous events unfolding in the late 1950s and early 1960s—warrant and even invite such a reading.

CAUTIOUS CURIOSITY IN THE EARLY 1980s

Ying Ruocheng's apparent ambivalence about Tennessee Williams, seeing both the negative and positive in this American writer, would be shared by Chinese scholars 20 years later, in the early 1980s.

When the Cultural Revolution ended and China began to reopen to the outside world, all things Western—ideas, ideologies, fads, as well as new and not-so-new science and technology—gushed in and have since transformed China in every facet of its socioeconomic, cultural, and technological life. As it was the case in the decades of the late nineteenth century and the early twentieth century, there was a tidal wave of revival of learning, in the form of reprints of classics that had been condemned as poisonous weeds and hence banned during the Cultural Revolution, both Chinese and Western classics—mostly reprints of earlier translations. With the blessings of the Communist Party's Propaganda Department and spearheaded by the Literature Research Institute of the Chinese Academy of Social Sciences, national flagship publishing houses People's Literature Press and Shanghai Translation Press resumed the ambitious Foreign Literature Classics project, which included 200 titles, covering epics, lyrics, drama, and fictional works from ancient and medieval times all the way to the nineteenth century. In 1981, these two flagship presses joined hands to push the envelope and test the hitherto rarely touched, potentially treacherous territory of modern and contemporary Western literature. Their first bold, ambitious translation and publication endeavor was Twentieth-Century Foreign Literature Series, which included Ernest Hemingway's *For Whom the Bell Tolls*, William Faulkner's *Sound and Fury*, D. H. Lawrence's *Sons and Lovers*, and Gabriel García Márquez's *Hundred Years of Solitude*.[22]

It was around this time, in 1980, that *Contemporary Foreign Literature* (*dangdai waiguo wenxue* 当代外国文学), a journal devoted to the introduction and translation of contemporary foreign literature, came into being. It began as a semi-annual and became a quarterly the following year. As alluded to in Chap. 2, in the fourth issue of the magazine in 1981 appeared a full-text translation of Tennessee Williams' *The Glass Menagerie*, followed by a relatively long essay (5 two-column pages) on Tennessee Williams by Zuo Yi (左宜), probably the first extended critical review of the American playwright by a Chinese scholar and therefore deserves some attention here.[23]

The essay begins by giving a brief biography of Tennessee Williams as one of the most notable post-World War II American playwrights, noting his successes with *The Glass Menagerie, A Streetcar Named Desire, Cat on a Hot Tin Roof,* and *The Night of Iguana*. It characterizes his characters as mostly lonely, overtly sensitive, eccentric, and unlucky small people (*xiao renwu* 小人物): homeless and drifting artists, such as Hannah of *Night* and Val of *Orpheus Descending*, those who want to escape from reality, such as Tom of *Glass*; handicapped people such as Laura of *Glass*; and sexaholic and homosexual such as Blanchet of *Streetcar* and Brick of *Cat*. They are mostly of the middle and lower rungs of the society and therefore do not fit in and remain outsiders; they fight against the hostility around them but always fail and are crushed, spiritually, and sometimes physically too. The author attributes this to the influence on Williams by Freudian psychoanalysis, which places human unconscious and biological instincts as the dominant force of human behavior, and the influence of D. H. Lawrence and his views of sexual liberation.

Then, the essay gives a more detailed discussion of *Glass*: it being a "memory play" based on Williams' own family and situated in the post-Great Depression America, written as "plastic theatre" as opposed to the exhausted realist theatre. As to the play's main characters, Tom plays the dual role of both narrator and character; Amanda is a typical southern belle who is lost; and Laura, as fragile as her glass menagerie collection, is the central figure of the play, her "reunion" with the gentleman caller Jim, albeit short-lived, being the climax of the play, and so on. Then, the essay moves onto *Streetcar*, with a more "nuanced" take on Blanche DuBois than dismissing her as a "sexaholic" two pages earlier: after the death of her husband by suicide, the loss of her family plantation, and so on, she feels lost spiritually and materially so she indulges in promiscuity and prostitutes herself to fill the void inside her. Having nowhere to go, Blanche comes to her sister's place in New Orleans, but due to her bad reputation she is crushed and ends up in a mental institution—another example of a southern belle lost in the past and crushed by the present. The essay is not without sympathy to Blanche, seeing her as a victim of societal violence and cruelty. It mentions her accidental discovery of her husband being a homosexual (which leads to his suicide) as a cause of her demise without "denouncing" homosexuality as a decadent lifestyle (as implied in Ying's two-paragraph Postface although he did not come out and say so explicitly). At the end of the essay the author points out that although Williams did not achieve the same success in the 1960s–1970s as he had done with his earlier plays, his place in American drama and in the world is secured.

One can see that written in 1981, barely a few years after China opened its door to the outside world, Zuo Yi's essay was as informed as could be expected under the circumstances. In 1985, another translation of *The Glass Menagerie*, rendered by Zhao Quanzhang (赵全章), was published in a volume of *Selections from Foreign Modernist Literature* (*Waiguo xiandai pai zuopin xuan*, 外国现代派作品选) published by Shanghai Art and Literature Press. Included in this volume are translations of poems by William Carlos Williams, Robert Lowell, Philip Larkin, Ted Hughes, and short stories by Joyce Carol Oats, and *The Good Person of Szechuan* by Bertolt Brecht. In the Preface for the volume, Yuan Kejia (袁可嘉 1921–2008), a well-known Chinese Academy of Social Sciences scholar based in Beijing, explains the rationale for publishing four volumes of such foreign modernist works, including selections of ten sub-genres, from late Symbolism to black humor, arranged chronologically, from the modernist/early twentieth century through the two world wars to the contemporary. Volume 4, in which Zhao Quanzhang's translation of *The Glass Menagerie* appears, is devoted to the 1950s–1960s, the so-called "postmodernism" period. Below is the conclusion of Yuan's preface:[24]

Western modernist literature is bourgeois in nature. With the exception of a small few, it reflects the worldview, life philosophy, and aesthetics of the bourgeois ideology. Its propagation of anarchism, ego-centralism, human-nature-ism (人性主义), humanism (人道主义), pessimism, pornography-ism (色情主义), and subjective idealist aesthetics can have grave corrupting effect. We have to be wary lest we absorb its ideology without subjecting it to criticism; and lest we indiscriminately promote its aesthetic principles and artistic methods and praise its creativity and "self-expression" without upholding our own principles. It will lead to grave damages.

This note of caution (Readers of these foreign modernist works: consider yourselves forewarned!) could have come from an honest assessment of Western modernist works as a whole, or from a self-protection instinct, learned from lessons of the not-too-distant past, to hedge against criticism or condemnation if the political wind changed (again),[25] or both. In the appended essay "Western Modernist Literature as I Understand it" (*Wo suo renshi de xifang xiandai pai wenxue*, 我所认识的西方现代派文学), Yuan gives a more extended and somewhat nuanced version of his views of Western modernist literature (summarized here to give a fuller sense of his views, which are not only personal, but also representative).[26]

An important thing we have to consider as we implement the more open cultural policies is how to correctly treat Western modernist literature. It is an important, complicated issue that needs earnest, in-depth discussion, from a historical, materialist, and dialectic perspective. Without a comprehensive and correct understanding, we will not have any basis to assess and adapt. Such a comprehensive and correct understanding has to be holistic, covering four important aspects/characteristics: political ideological leaning, reflection of reality, literary assumptions, and techniques. Politically, Western modernism is bourgeois, but it is neither champions of bourgeois monopoly nor avant-gardes of bourgeois revolution; rather, it is the mouthpiece of middle and petty-bourgeois discontent.

Most Western modernist writers are lower- middle-class intellectuals, oppressed and exploited, having no political power or influence; they are contemptuous of bourgeois monopoly and their political ideology is typically self-centered anarchy and democracy-ism (民主主义的). However, they are "avant-gardes" only in the sense of their literary practice, not in the sense of revolutionary social changes.

Their reflection of reality has its duality. It is particularly pungent in exposing four kinds of primary, essential relationships: individual and society, interpersonal, human and nature, and individual and self, and how these relationships are twisted and disjointed; how humans are alienated from society, from each other, and from oneself, which lead to psychic wounds and degeneration, spiritual nihilism, and pessimistic despair. This is where modernist literature has its inestimable social significance because it helps understand how human nature is twisted under the enormous pressure of capitalist system, how one loses oneself, one's dignity, and one's humanness in the existential struggle. However, modernist literature's reflection of reality is limited and personal; it does not reflect the thoughts and feelings of the broad masses who are struggling to make do and earn a living; it does not reflect the resistance and struggle of the working class and other democratic forces. Eugene O'Neil's *Hairy Ape* is such a negative example which ends with Yank, a working-class man, going to the zoo to seek recognition from a hairy ape; his is a story of retrogression instead of progression, devolution instead of evolution. Modernist literature does not expose the deep-rooted social problems and tends to over-generalize, universalize, and describe problems rooted in the social system/structure as "misery of being." Therefore, it tends to indulge in nihilism, individualism, pessimism, pacifism, and so on.

So, the correct way is to extrapolate Western modernist literature from its subjective idealism and absorb what is valid and useful, such as how it dives into the human psyche and how it uses psychological realism, blending/coupling psychological realism with social realism to give fuller description of human existence and relations, as is done in Faulkner's *Sound and Fury*. Western modernist techniques such as "interior monologue" have received so much attention lately. Using "interior monologue" can help deepen portrayal of characters; however, using it nonstop in a story, beginning to end, would not help create a fully developed character. The same is true for other techniques such as scrambled time and space, multi-layered and multiple-point-of-view narration, and so on. The lessons we learn from Western modernist literature, both positive and negative, are that artistic method has to fit the demand of content and subject to the constraints of laws of art. When introduced to any technique coming from the outside world, we have to carefully study where it works (or not), digest, and adapt it for our use; we should neither accept and adopt it as it is or nor flat-out reject it.

Yuan Kejia's ambivalence toward Western modernist literature, both curious and cautious, seeing it as both positive and negative, useful and valuable and potentially damaging (when introduced, accepted, and adopted without subjecting it to careful examination and criticism), and so on, would be shared by many Chinese scholars well into the 1990s. If there is any hedging in the positioning of Yuan and many other scholars, the need for self-protection is real rather than hyped, imaginary, or paranoiac, because the debates between those for keeping the door open or opening it even wider and those for shutting it have never stopped since the late 1970s and early 1980s; such debates are feverish at times and always consequential, albeit one can never predict with certainty which camp will have the upper hand (for the time being), resulting in real policy changes.

New Chapters in the Early 1990s

The first full-blown scholarly attention to Tennessee Williams came in the form of chapters in two books on American drama, the first known book-length study on the subject: *Contemporary American Drama* (*dangdai meiguo xiju* 当代美国戏剧) by Wang Yiqun (汪义群), published by Shanghai Foreign Language Education Press in 1992 and *History of American Drama* (*meiguo xiju shi* 美国戏剧史) by Guo Jide (郭继德) published by Henan People's Press in 1993.

Although Guo Jide's *History of American Drama* was published in 1993, its manuscript had been completed in 1991. Guo (1941–2020)[27] graduated from college in 1965, on the cusp of the Cultural Revolution and had been a visiting scholar at Canadian and American universities five times since the 1980s, having opportunities to meet and have extensive conversations with Arthur Miller. *History of American Drama* was a work-in-progress for ten years since his first visit to Canadian Queens University in 1979. During those years he published *Dictionary of American Literature* (*Dangdai meiguo wenxue cidian* 当代美国文学词典) (1987) and *Arthur Miller on Drama* (*Ase mile lun xiju* 阿瑟·密勒论戏剧) (1988), followed by *Selections from American Drama* (*Meiguo xiju xuandu* 美国戏剧选读) (1994), *Studies in American Literature* (*Meiguo wenxue yanjiu* 美国文学研究) (2002), *Essays on Dramatic Works of Eugene O'Neill* (*Youjin ao'ni'er xiju lunwen ji* 尤金·奥尼尔戏剧研究论文集) (2004) and *Dream and Reality: Twentieth Century American Literature* (*Ershi shiji meiguo wenxue: mengxiang yu xianshi* 20 世纪美国文学:梦想与现实) (2004), and so on. As Guo acknowledged in the preface to *History of American Drama*,[28] this first significant introduction of American drama/theatre, from a historical perspective, was based on a number of important publications on pertinent subjects in the United States and elsewhere in the West, for example, Walter J. Meserve's *An Outline History of American Drama* (1965), Ruby Cohn's *New American Dramatists:1960–1980* (1982), Christopher William Edgar Bigsby's *A Critical Introduction to Twentieth-Century American Drama* (1985), Gerald Martin Bordman's *The Concise Oxford Companion to American Theatre* (1987), Philip C. Kolin's *American Playwrights Since 1945: A Guide to Scholarship* (1989), James David Hart's *The Oxford Companion to American Literature* (1980), and Emory Elliott's *The Columbia Literary History of the United States* (1988).

Guo Jide's *History of American Drama* has 20 chapters. The first four chapters give an overview of the contour of the historical development of American drama, from the early colonial period to the early days of the United States to the realist drama of the late nineteenth century and then onto modern American drama in the early decades of the twentieth century. The remaining chapters are devoted, respectively, to Eugene O'Neill (1888–1953), Elmer Rice (1892–1967) and Clifford Odets (1906–1963), Lillian Hellman (1905–1984) and Thornton Wilder (1897–1975), African American drama, post-war American drama, Tennessee Williams (1911–1983), Arthur Miller (1915–2005), Edward Albee (1928–2016), Theatre of the Absurd, women playwrights, minority playwrights, and so on. It is in this critical discursive context that we should see Guo Jide's chapter on Tennessee Williams.

Compared to the space Guo devoted to O'Neill (80 pages out of a book of 510 pages, about 15%) and to Arthur Miller (50 pages, about 10%) respectively, the space he gave Tennessee Williams was only 13 pages (less than 3%). Although we cannot measure the importance of an author by the space assigned him alone, it is a good indication, nonetheless. O'Neill rightly claims the lion's share not only because of his importance in the history of American drama, or American literature, for that matter, but more importantly, because of his connection with the Chinese culture.[29] As noted by Guo in the chapter on O'Neill, quoting Arthur Miller, O'Neill was drawn to the East, especially China,[30] and although his 1929 trip to China turned out to be somewhat disappointing, he remained keenly interested in ancient Chinese culture, especially Chinese philosophies.[31] By the time Guo set out to Canada for his first trip abroad as a young visiting scholar (1979–1980), Arthur Miller had just visited China in the fall of 1978, right before the establishment of US–China diplomatic relationship, the first important contemporary American dramatist to visit China. The story of Arthur Miller and his *Death of a Salesman* in Beijing was well told by Miller himself in his 1983 book *Salesman in Beijing*.[32]

Guo's chapter on Williams begins with a few pages going over some salient biographical facts and career highlights of the American playwright, praising him as "the most representative playwright amongst Southern writers."[33] This dubious honor seems to put Williams in the pigeonhole of "regional" or "local color" status, with which Williams himself might not be too pleased. Guo's reading of Williams' plays seems shaky at times. For example, concerning *Cat*, Guo makes quite a few assertions unwarranted by the text of the play as written by Williams: Margaret tried to sleep with

Skip, instead of Brick, her husband, in order to get pregnant and produce an heir; she forced Skip into alcoholism, which soon ruined him; Brick, out of revenge and desire to crush him, told Big Daddy that he had been diagnosed with terminal cancer; and so on.[34] Although Guo has a rather positive view of Williams' "courage to break into 'taboo topics' such as violence, rape, castration, homosexual love, drug addiction, and alcoholism to boldly expose various sick and ugly phenomena of American society," he cautions, as Yuan Kejia did when introducing Western modernist literature (alluded to earlier), the social significance of his works is weakened because Williams, under the heavy influence of Freudian psychoanalysis and D. H. Lawrence, believes in the creative and destructive power of biological instincts, or rather, libido, while overlooking the decisive root cause of tragedies: society.[35] Guo concludes his chapter on Williams with a "both and" verdict:[36]

> Controversies over Williams existed before and will continue. However, no matter how big the differences are, no one can deny the radiance he added to the post-war American drama with his glorious artistic achievements; similarly, no one can deny that unhealthy spiritual tendencies in Williams's works, which, if we introduce them (to China) wholesale, without subjecting them to proper criticism, would inevitably produce negative influence.

Such sociological or sociopolitical approach was typical of Guo and literary criticism in general even 10 years after China began the policy and daunting task of "reform and opening up." To help put Guo's cautious ambivalence toward Tennessee Williams in proper context, here is what he has to say about the achievements of Eugene O'Neill:[37]

> Inspired and caught in the wave of modernist literature, O'Neill broke away from the confines of the traditions of realist drama and forged a multi-faceted, multi-level probe into the depths of human existence, which resulted in a number of expressionist tragedies, psychoanalytic tragedies, and faith tragedies (*xinyang beiju* 信仰悲剧). He was particularly apt in catching the spirit of the times as well as going ahead of times; both the thought content and technical craft of these plays were so innovative that they will not feel outdated or passé even half a century later (today).

Nonetheless, when commenting on plays such as *Desire under the Elms*, *Strange Interlude*, and *Mourning Becomes Electra*, Guo took the time to point out that while the plays, under the heavy influence of German philosophers such as Schopenhauer and Freudian psychoanalysis, showed depths in exposing the ills of Western society, their overemphasis on sexual desire and so on weakened or diluted the social significance of these plays:[38]

> His tragedies mostly do not write about important social problems directly and therefore their content sometimes feels rather opaque (*huise* 晦涩). Of course, by pointing this out doesn't mean that these plays are completely without social significance; rather, it is meant to say that O'Neill uses a new angle to probe deep into human existence.

It is not clear what Guo meant by O'Neill not writing about important social problems directly. At the end of his discussion on *Mourning Becomes Electra*, Guo had this to say:[39]

> *Mourning Becomes Electra* was written in 1929–1931, when America was deep in an existential crisis. It is a pity that O'Neill did not write about such social problems directly. However, it does reflect, albeit indirectly, the social ills and misery of American society at the time: the heart-chilling reality of coldness in human relations and willingness to resort to violence out of sexual desires.

Could he have accorded Williams the same treatment instead of cautioning against wholesale introduction without subjecting his plays to proper criticism? Does this have more to do with the playwright, or rather, the biography of the playwright (i.e., Williams was a professed and practicing homosexual)? Perhaps one would have to wait for a decade or so for Chinese scholars to fully acknowledge Williams without such cautionary note.

As to Arthur Miller, Guo celebrated him as a "universally acknowledged playwright of social problems." Miller told him in person in 1981 that "plays should express the aspirations of the entire society and have noble and uplifting impact on the existence of humanity."[40] Guo's preference for realist theatre revealed itself once again in his comment on Miller's use of expressionistic techniques in plays such as *Death of a Salesman*. According to Guo, the fluidity of time and space, which deepens and complicates the dramatic action of the play and is effective in showing the inner worlds of characters such as Willy Loman, also caused confusion on the part of some audiences about past and present, illusion and reality, and so on, which would not have happened with a pure realist play (*chun xian-shi zhuyi xiju* 纯现实主义戏剧).[41]

As can be expected, Guo saved his most unreserved praises to Elmer Rice (1892–1967), "a gifted realist playwright who persisted unfalteringly in writing about important social problems and exposing the ugly ills of society with a sharp-edged knife,"[42] and Clifford Odets (1906–1963), a famed "proletarian," "progressive," and "Ibsen-esque" serious playwright on the American theatre scene who focused on social problems":[43]

> Most of his plays, especially those published in the 1930s during the Great Depression, are filled with substantive thought content—writing about important social problems of the times, having the courage to probe sensitive social problems, and boldly exposing flaws and injustice of contemporary society.

Perhaps unbeknownst to Guo as he was working on his *History of American Drama* book, another book project on American drama was progressing at the same time, undertaken by Wang Yiqun (汪义群) of Shanghai International Studies University, who had also taught at Shanghai Theatre Academy.[44] In addition to *Contemporary American Drama* (*Dangdai meiguo xiju* 当代美国戏剧),[45] the subject for this segment of the discussion, Wang was the author of book-length studies of Eugene O'Neill and was editor of anthologies of Western modernist drama. His *Contemporary American Drama* project (published around the same time as Guo's book) began as an assignment, a key project for the Ministry of Education, originally titled *Post-War American Drama*, which shows the attention given to American drama from government agencies to scholars. The book is structured chronologically, with a historical overview from the colonial period to the end of the 1940s, and then devotes a chapter each to the American drama in the 1950s, 1960s, and 1970s respectively and thereafter. This chronological organization inevitably leads to Williams, O'Neill, and Miller being discussed fragmentarily in several chapters because their careers, especially that of Williams and Miller, stretched across multiple decades covered by the book. In the section on American drama 1945–1950, Wang, like Guo Jide in his *History of American Drama*, praises Miller for his sense of the moral obligations of an author: literature, including modern drama, should posit "the idea of value, of right and wrong, good and bad, high and low, not so much by setting forth these values as such, but by showing, so to speak, the wages of sin."[46] Miller's idea would resonate well with both traditional Chinese idea of "literature as vehicle for *dao*" (*wen yi zai dao* 文以载道) and the emphasis on the sociopolitical role and function of literature in the dominant art and literature discourse in China. Like Guo Jide, Yuan Kejia, and other scholars of Western (modernist) literature, Wang finds himself obligated to point out that although Miller was well-intended, his solutions to the problems were outdated, his methods for dramatic development relied too much on coincidences and plot gimmicks, or *deus ex machina* (e.g., a fabricated letter from Larry Keller, an unseen but important character in the 1947 play *All My Sons*).[47]

In the same 1945–1950 section, Wang spends three paragraphs on Tennessee Williams's *The Glass Menagerie* (1945), praising it as an extraordinary work because it has nothing to do with the war that had just ended although it is a "memory play." The play, Wang enthuses, signifies the dawning of a new age of American drama/theatre in both subject matter and style and with this achievement, Williams joins the ranks of the greatest American playwrights.[48] In the ensuing chapter on the 1950s, Wang celebrates William as one of the twin-stars (the other being Arthur Miller) on the American drama/theatre scene, based on his successes with *Rose Tattoo* (1951), *Cat on a Hot Tin Roof* (1955), *Orpheus Descending* (1957), *Sweet Bird of Youth* (1959), and *Period of Adjustment* (1960).[49] This chapter devotes 19 pages to Williams, the longest discussion on him in this book,[50] characterizing him as a southern author having kinship with William Faulkner (1897–1962), Carson McCullers (1917–1967), and Thomas Wolfe (1900–1938) both in subject matter and in portrayal of southern life, people, and experiences. After a brief overview of Williams life and career, Wang chooses two of his most celebrated plays since *The Glass Menagerie* to discuss, *A Streetcar Named Desire* and *Cat on a Hot Tin Roof*. Like *The Glass Menagerie*, Wang says, *Streetcar* focuses on the women question through the portrayal of Blanche Dubois who, elegant, sensitive, and affectionate, dwells too much in an imaginary world, and ends up being crushed like a fragile work of art.[51] She rejects the kind of crudity she sees in Stanley, yet couldn't help being drawn to it too, which helps spell her tragic demise. In Williams' plays, Wang goes on to say, the southern belles such as Amanda, Laura, Blanche, are portrayed as lonely, twisted, "the last aristocrats" (*zuihou de guizu* 最后的贵族) of the deep south, lost in a strange world of brutal competition, and Alma of *Summer and Smoke*, a strung minister's daughter, is portrayed as torn between her puritanical upbringing and her desire for physical and sexual love as embodied in the wild young doctor who grew up next door.

In the 1960s chapter, Wang describes Williams, along with Miller, as a pair of dimmed or dimming stars (*shuang xing de shuaiwei* 双星的衰微),[52] with perhaps only *The Night of the Iguana* (1961) and *The Milk Train Doesn't Stop Here Anymore* (1962) as worth mentioning. Williams' dramatic works in the later phase of his career, Wang observes, echoing the dismissive, negative assessment that haunted Williams well into the 1990s, are marred by excessive use of symbolism, as exemplified in *Kingdom of Earth* (1968) and *In the Bar of a Tokyo Hotel* (1969).[53] Occupying the center stage of this chapter, so to speak, are a generation of rising stars, Jack Gelber (1932–2003), Arthur Kopit (1937–2021), Jack Richardson (1934–2012), and Edward Albee (1928–2016). It is worth noting that this chapter has a section devoted to Black Theatre, plays of black experiences by black playwrights, excluding plays about black experiences by white playwrights such Eugene O'Neill (*The Emperor Jones*, 1920), Paul Green (*In Abraham's Bosom*, 1926), and Clifford Odets (*Golden Boy*, 1937). One of the black playwrights included in this section is Lorraine Hansberry (1930–1965). Her play *A Raisin in the Sun* (1959) was translated into Chinese in the 1960s, but did not see a stage production until 2020, about half a century later.[54]

Tennessee Williams, along with Miller, all but disappears in the chapter on 1970s and thereafter, the vacated space being filled by another group of rising stars, for example, Paul Zindel 1936–2003), John Guare (1938–), David Rabe (1940–), Sam Shepard (1943–2017), Lanford Wilson (1937–2011), David Mamet (1947–), and Michael Weller (1942–). In the concluding pages of the book Wang mentions August Wilson (1945–2005) as a rising star on the American drama/theatre scene, his plays *Ma Rainey's Black Bottom* (1984) and *Fences* (1985) having received accolades such as New York Drama Critics' Circle award, Tony Award for Best Play, Pulitzer Prize for Drama, and so on.

Deep Dive in the Early Twenty-First-Century

By one measure, Tennessee Williams had finally arrived, so to speak, as far as his reception in China is concerned, when a 1981 issue of *Contemporary Foreign Literature* (*dangdai waiguo wenxue* 当代外国文学) not only featured a full-text translation of *The Glass Menagerie*, but also a picture of him (taken in a bar in Turkey in 1948) in the cover art. By another measure, Williams had finally begun to command the kind of scholarly attention he deserved, at last, when, at the dawning of the twenty-first century, PhD students in American and/or comparative literature programs found him intriguing, promising, and safe enough to bet their budding academic career on by choosing his dramatic works as proper subject for their doctoral dissertations.[55] As a matter of fact, by the end of 2020, no less than 10 books/monographs, mostly based on the authors' PhD dissertations on Williams, had been published, some in English as they were originally written, some translated or rewritten into Chinese. One would go out on a limb and say that the number of master's thesis projects, let alone that of undergraduate senior theses/papers, would be many times more. Numerous journal articles on Williams, many focusing on the topics and themes of gender, sexuality, and homosexuality as portrayed in his dramatic works, have been published too.

One of the first of these Chinese PhD candidates who were adventurous and enterprising enough to try and stake out a career path with a Williams dissertation project was Li Li (李莉), which she completed in 2002 at Nankai University. She then published a monograph based on the dissertation in 2004, titled *Woman's Growth: Feminist Approach to Tennessee Williams' Works* (*Nüren de chengzhang licheng: Tiannaxi weiliansi zuopin de nüxing zhuyi jiedu* 女人成长历程:田纳西·威廉斯作品的女性主义解读).[56]

Li Li sets out to study Tennessee Williams from a feminist perspective by focusing on his six major plays, arranged chronologically, tracing four stages of growth and development, that is, from "the traditional stereotypes to new women, who strive for their desired respect, their own identities, and finally for love" by defying male domination: the passive and victimized women; the awakening women; the aggressive women; and the mature women. Li puts Laura of *The Glass Menagerie* (a "passive and victimized virgin") and Blanche of *A Streetcar Named Desire* (a "misled and mistreated prostitute-image heroine") in the first category. As time progresses, Li explains, Williams begins to "offer his female characters more strength to violate and defy traditional roles, hence the category of "awakening women." Li puts Alma of *Summer and Smoke* and Serafina in *The Rose Tattoo* in this category, women who dare to resist their "objectified placement within the patriarchal society" and "strive for their own identity." For the category of "aggressive women" there seems no better example than Margaret of *Cat on a Hot Tin Roof*, who fights "to win control over her marriage and the family inheritance, which is essential for women's equality," and "to become the victor over men at home and in society eventually." As if on cue, Hannah and Maxine, the two women of *The Night of The Iguana* (about 17 years had lapsed since *Glass* and six years since *Cat*), have enough time to grow and become "the mature women" who are in a position to "offer spiritual and physical guidance and support to their opposite sex." This "Utopian" society envisioned by Williams, according to Li, "coincides with the theory of liberal feminists: to establish an ideal world in which men and women enjoy equal opportunities, and have respect, compassion, and love for one another."[57]

Li justifies her "feministic approach" to Williams' dramatic works because, she asserts, although Williams did not acknowledge any influence of feminist theories, he could not help but reflect the kind of experiences and observations he had accumulated over the years, from his sister, mother, female friends, writers, directors, managers, critics, and actresses, who supplied inspiration and raw material for his dramatic works:[58]

> His knowledge and unique insights enabled him to probe into such social issues as women's suffering, women's movement, and women's voice as a whole. He sought to find the verbal equivalents for his female characters' tortured inner selves, a search that led him closer to the realistic portrayal of women in his plays.

Citing Helene Cixous' view that one should not confuse the sex of the authors with the sex of the characters they create, Li posits that one does not have to be female in order to have important feminist themes in one's creative works although she falls short of calling Williams a feminist writer. Williams, according to Li, "used feminism subconsciously."[59] Although not all female characters would fit nicely into the categories or labels Li has assigned them, for example, Amanda and Blanche are more than passive victims in the dramatic worlds they each find themselves, as a first PhD dissertation and indeed as a first monograph on Williams in China, it was bold enough.

In the same year that Li Li's monograph was published, another PhD student at Beijing Normal University, Xu Huaijing (徐怀静), had just completed her dissertation project on Williams. A monograph based on the dissertation titled *Masculinity Crises: Troubled Men in Tennessee Williams' Major Plays* (*Tie beixin: Tiannaxi weiliansi juzuo zhong kunhuo de nanren men* 铁背心:田纳西·威廉斯剧作中困惑的男人们)[60] would be rewritten in Chinese and published three years later in 2007. As a matter of fact, three other PhD projects on Williams, also focusing on the issues of gender and (homo)sexuality, were in the works around the same time and before the first decade of the new century was over, they would all be revised and/or expanded into monographs and published.

The Chinese title of Xu Huaijing's monograph, 铁背心 (*Tie beixin Iron Vest*), suggested by the editor for the book,[61] seems to work as a trope to show that underneath the ironclad surface of masculinity is a vulnerable human body, a being in crisis, as the English title suggests. Indeed, in this study Xu turns her attention, full blast, to the male characters in Williams' plays. As Xu explained, she began to be interested in Tennessee Williams in 2000, which she further pursued when she studied as a postdoctoral student at Yale University (2005–2006). For quite a while she had felt that there was a gap in the half-a-century of scholarship on Tennessee Williams in the English-speaking world and it took her eight years to finally find her own angle, her own voice in the discourse of Williams studies: male characters in Williams (major) plays who had been neglected by scholars. Williams, according to Xu, portrays his female characters as victims of the patriarchy: they are weak, nervous, and stranded in reality. However, his male characters are caught in the same predicament, albeit in different ways: despair, insecurity, and frailty. In other words, men in Williams' major plays all show various degrees of identity crisis, which is rooted in the pressure and anxiety put on them by the patriarchal society and culture.[62]

Xu's study on the male characters in Williams' major plays draws from a broad range of primary and secondary sources as well as critical perspectives on sexuality, gender, more particularly masculinity, which she could have access to during her postdoctoral year at Yale. Among these sources and perspectives which help situate her own study in proper cultural and critical contexts are: Roger Horrocks, *Masculinity in Crisis: Myths, Fantasies and Realities* (1994); David Morgan, *Discovering Men* (1992); Robert Stoller, *Masculin ou Féminine* (1989); Christopher T. Kilmartin, *The Masculine Self* (2000); Larry May, *Masculinity & Morality* (1998); Guy Corneau, *Absent Fathers, Lost Sons*, translated by Larry Shouldice (1991); Clyde W. Franklin, *The Changing Definition of Masculinity* (1984); Mark E. Kann, *A Republic of Men: The American Founders, Gendered Language and Patriarchal Politics* (1998); Alan Sinfield, *Out on Stage: Lesbian and Gay Theatre in the 20th Century* (1999); Bryne Fone, *Homophobia: A History* (2000); K.J. Dover, *Greek Homosexuality* (1980); Eve Kosofsky Sedgwick, *Between Men, English Literature and Male*

Homosocial Desire (1985); Albert Ellis, *The Homosexual in America: A Subject Approach* (1951); John M. Clum, *Still Acting Gay: Male Sexuality in Modern Drama* (2000); David Savran, *Communists, Cowboys, and Queers: The Politics of Masculinity in the Works of Arthur Miller and Tennessee Williams* (1992); Dennis Altman, *Homosexuality Oppression and Liberation* (1971); Susan Brownmiller, *Against Our Will: Men, Women and Rape* (1975); Holly Devor, ed., *Gender Blending: Confronting the Limits of Duality* (1989); Tim Edwards, *Exotics and Politics: Gale Male Sexuality, Masculinity and Feminism* (1994); and John MacInne, *The End of Masculinity: The Confusion of Sexual Genesis and Sexual Differences in Modern Society* (1998).

The book is divided into five chapters:

Chapter One Mama's Boy (*mama de erzi* 妈妈的儿子)
Chapter Two Absent Fathers, Runaway Sons (*quewei de fuqin, taowang de erzi* 缺位的父亲, 逃亡的儿子)
Chapter Three Violent Men (*baoli de nanren* 暴力的男人)
Chapter Four Frail Men (*cuiruo de nanren* 脆弱的男人)
Chapter Five Homosexuality and Homophobia (*tongxinglian he tongxinglian konjuzheng* 同性恋和同性恋恐惧症)

Below is a brief summary (with occasional comments) of each of the chapters to give a fuller sense of the arguments Xu pursues in her study.[63]

Chapter One Mama's Boy studies the first group of troubled men undergoing masculinity crises. They are good looking yet somewhat clumsy when pursuing women, and appear to be more feminine than "manly," not the kind of "hunters" expected in the American culture; they are still attached to their mothers like babies. Their mothers, on the other hand, like Amanda Wingfield of *The Glass Menagerie* and Violet Venable of *Suddenly Last Summer*, overindulgent, narcissistic, frustrated in their failed marriages, transfer or invest all their tenderness in their sons. Such overprotection and indulgences would stunt the growth of the sons and leave them stuck in the "womb stage" of development. It is interesting to note though that in this chapter Xu spends considerable time discussing Amanda and Violet as overindulgent and narcissistic mothers whereas there is little discussion of Tom and Sebastian as their respective mama's boy—a challenging case to prove, perhaps. Instead, considerable time and space is given to a lengthy discussion of Lot of *Kingdom of Earth* (*The Seven Descents of Myrtle*), a sickly young man who is excessively attached to the memory of his late mother, and Mitch of *A Streetcar Named Desire* as their respective mama's boy.[64]

Chapter 2 Absent Fathers, Lost Sons is a study of the phenomenon of father's absence in modern society and its psychological damage to the growth and development of the sons. As the agrarian society of the Old South became industrialized, the sons of affluent families became lost: they struggled in confusion and suffered from depression. Tom Wingfield seems to fit the bill perfectly: he has to assume the dual role of being his mother's son and being the provider of the family. Tom's decision to escape, according to Xu, results from his desire to follow the footsteps of his father, or rather, to search for his father who had long escaped and had been absent (present only as a "larger-than-life-size photograph over the mantel"[65]) and establish his own sexual identity. The same is true of Shannon of *The Night of the Iguana*, whose search for God is search for his father in disguise.

Chapter 3 Violent Men studies how American culture appreciates and encourages men to be dominant, aggressive, and powerful, as evidenced in the themes of plays such as *A Streetcar Named Desire*, *Cat on a Hot Tin Roof*, and *Sweet Bird of Youth*. In a patriarchal society, power, especially economic power, is the core in defining a male's masculinity, as embodied in the characters of Big Daddy, "Boss" Finley, and Stanley. One of the sites where men exercise their power and expresses their masculinity, sometimes violently, is sex, as is the case of Stanley. Although on the surface Stanley seems least likely to experience crisis in masculinity, underneath the facade of aggressive masculinity is a pseudo-identity and a rather frail man.

Chapter 4 Frail Men is a study of four good-looking, sensitive men who, under the pressure of the American society on masculinity, show themselves to be frailer than they can help: George Haverstick and Ralph Baitz of *Period of Adjustment*, Chance Wayne of *Sweet Bird of Youth*, and Val of *Orpheus Descending*. While George, a newlywed, fails in the marriage bed due to performance anxiety, Ralph, who married his wife Dorothea for her money only, does not find her sexually attractive. To realize his American Dream, a construct of the socioeconomic component of masculinity in American culture, he allows himself to be a male prostitute to del Lago, whose Hollywood stardom has faded. Feeling threatened by Val, a modern Orpheus figure endowed with the power of imagination, poetry, and sexuality, patriarchal men eventually murder him out of insecurity, jealousy, fear, and hatred.

Chapter 5 Homosexuality and Homophobia studies the homosexual themes in Williams' plays. Living in a society filled with homophobia, the first and foremost thing in a male identity is his masculinity and therefore he has no choice but to deny being a homosexual and reject any suspicion or suggestion of him being so. Such is the case of Brick of *Cat on a Hot Tin Roof*, who experiences the identity crisis because he has absorbed and internalized homophobia prevalent in American society. Thanks to intense bias against homosexuals in society when Tennessee Williams was writing most of his plays, he had to keep the homosexual themes in the background and homosexual characters off the stage or in the backstory that has already happened before the curtain rises, for example, Sebastian of *Suddenly Last Summer* and Allan of *A Streetcar Named Desire*.

As if Xu Huaijing had undertaken her dissertation project as a counterpoint of sort to Li Li's feminist approach about two years prior, she thus sums up the rationale, relevance, and importance of her study:[66]

> As feminist movement develops and accumulates momentum, oppression of women under patriarchal system and culture has received broad attention. However, the confusion and misery of men under the same pressure have been neglected. Through portrayal of this group of male characters suffering from crises in masculinity, Williams exposes the damage inflicted on men by the traditional definition of manhood and masculinity and subverts the discourse of male identity. To a large degree these portrayals spring from Williams' own life, the confusion and crises he himself had suffered throughout his life.

Although *Iron Vest* (铁背心), or rather *Masculinity Crises*, is the work of an early-career Chinese scholar (Xu calls this book her "youth work" or juvenilia, "少作"[67]), it shows considerable promise and opens up new possibilities for further research by other PhD students and early-career scholars, despite the problems that almost all such studies suffer when one tries to create a neat system and fit all the characters in: there is so much complexity in the male characters as portrayed by Williams that none of the labels (Mama's Boy; Absent Fathers, Runaway Sons; Violent Men; Frail Men; Homosexuals and Homophobes) alone can do justice to anyone of them.

Xu Huaijing's monograph on Williams was followed by another, at the same pace of publication two years after the completion of PhD dissertation: Li Ying (李英)'s *A Psychoanalytic Critique of Desire in Tennessee*

Williams Plays (Tiannaxi weiliansi xiju zhong yuwang de xinli toushi 田纳
西·威廉斯戏剧中欲望的心理透视)in 2008, based on her PhD dissertation
completed in 2006 at Shandong University, directed by Guo Jide, author
of the book *History of American Drama* discussed earlier.[68] The book is in
English, with foreword (by Guo Jide), preface, and afterword in Chinese.
Li Ying notes in the preface that despite the surge of interest (in China) in
Tennessee Williams since the 1990s, scholarly attention has been limited
to his major plays *A Streetcar Named Desire, The Glass Menagerie,* and *Cat
on a Hot Tin Roof*; little attention has been paid to the other works in his
dramatic oeuvre, especially his later works. Also, for quite some time, with
a few exceptions (e.g., the two monographs discussed above), Chinese
scholarship on Williams is not much more than overviews of his biography, career highlights, and plot synopses. This is what Li sets out to correct with her PhD dissertation project by expanding to include Williams'
later dark comedies with a thematic focus on desire as embodied and
expressed in intimate connection with other important sociomoral and
psychological dimensions: desire and insanity; desire in sexual violence and
homoeroticism; desire and fugitive artists; desire and death wish; and
desire in the schizophrenic subject.[69]

In the first chapter of the monograph Li Ying gives an overview of psychoanalytic criticism informed by Sigmund Freud, Jacques Lacan ("Desire
and the Interpretation of Desire in *Hamlet*"), Peter Brooks ("Freud's
Masterplot"), Harold Bloom (*The Anxiety of Influence*), Gilles Deleuze
and Felix Guattari (*Anti-Oedipus: Capitalism and Schizophrenia*), and several PhD dissertations completed in the US that include Williams in their
studies: Daniel Jon Friedman's *Pedagogies of Resistance* (Yale University,
2004), Cecilia R. Petit's *Trauma on Stage: Psychoanalytic Readings of
Contemporary American Drama* (New York University, 2002), and Little
Gray's *A Disease of the Spirit: The Identification and Examination of Shame
in Selected Works of Modern American Literature* (Ohio State
University, 1999).

In the chapter on desire and insanity Li Ying presents a mini-case study
of three of Williams characters, Blanche of *A Streetcar Named Desire,*
Catherine Holly of *Suddenly Last Summer,* and Serafina of *The Rose Tattoo.*
Streetcar, according to Li, is a tragedy of desire, or rather, a tragedy of
Blanche whose repression springs from her sense of guilt over her husband's death and her repressed desire caused by the deprived phallus
(deprived by her homosexual husband). This repressed desire, ironically, is
fulfilled by the masculine power of Stanley who also turns out to be her

"executioner," or rather, "the avenger of Blanche's homosexual husband."[70] All of this, in turn, leads to her loss of subjectivity and insanity.[71] Catherine of *Suddenly Last Summer* knows the secret truth of the death of Sebastian, the object of her desire who, however, does not reciprocate because he is a homosexual (whose goal is to sacrifice himself to God). This rejection, which often takes rather aggressive and humiliating forms, drives Catherine into insanity, yet, ironically, makes her "a keener eye for the truth than others who are not melancholiac,"[72] especially under psychological therapy by Dr. Cukrowicz. Although both Blanche and Catherine are "mourner-protagonists," they end up differently: the former is doomed into melancholia for the rest of her life while the latter has a chance of getting well through releasing her repressed desire and regaining her subjectivity.[73] Serafina of *The Rose Tattoo* is another mourner-protagonist who is caught between the tensions of order and death on the one hand and passionate disorder and life on the other, which causes her deep melancholia. However, her interest in life is rekindled and her sexuality reawakens eventually when she knows the truth of her husband's infidelity and when the persistent seduction of Alvaro, a truck driver of well-built torso and brimming vitality, finally disarms her and breaks the resistance she has put up.

Li Ying's chapter on desire in sexual violence and homoeroticism is an attempt to revisit a topic that has been well studied, that is, the influence of D. H. Lawrence on Tennessee Williams,[74] through the lens of Harold Bloom's theory of "anxiety of influence": how Williams ("ephebe," poetic son-figure) transforms the redemptive power of heterosexual love as portrayed by Lawrence ("precursor," poetic father-figure) in his novels such as *Lady Chatterley's Lover* (1928) into its corruptive, destructive, and even violent opposite in heterosexual or homosexual love in his plays such as *Kingdom of Earth, Suddenly Last Summer,* and *Sweet Bird of Youth.*[75] Her next chapter on desire and fugitive artists studies "outcasts" (sexual, religious, and/or fugitive) in Williams plays. Mostly autobiographical, these "artist-protagonists," such as Tom of *The Glass Menagerie* and Val of *Orpheus Descending,* "retreat into a fantasy space beyond social confinement where they can create a new role of life, a new identity to redefine themselves," for whom art "is a disguised fulfilment of repressed desire."[76] In the chapter on desire and death wish, Li tackles Williams' obsession with the subject of death which undergoes three psychological transformations in his lifelong artistic creations: initiating death in *Cat on a Hot*

Tin Roof, learning to accept death in *The Milk Train Doesn't Stop Here Anymore* and wishing to die for rebirth in *The Two-Character Play*.[77] It is noteworthy that Li Ying includes in her study *The Milk Train Doesn't Stop Here Anymore* (1963) which "hails the beginning of Williams later period."[78] Apparently, *The Two-Character Play* (aka *Out Cry*, 1966) also falls into the "late plays" category. Indeed, the last chapter of Li's monograph does what she has promised to do at the outset of her dissertation project: to try and fill a gap in Chinese scholarship on Tennessee Williams by giving a discussion of his later plays, those wild, grotesque "black comedies," such as *Slapstick Tragedy* (1965), *The Seven Descents of Myrtle* (1968), and *In the Bar of a Tokyo Hotel* (1969). Williams wrote these plays, after having experienced "the dreadful period of almost clinical depression," by way of breaking out of the conventionality of his earlier plays that brought him his success and fame, and more importantly, by way of expressing his schizophrenia self:[79]

> Though he experimented to display his later plays in the form of black comedies, the motif was always centered on the human psyche and the truth of man's being. He emphasizes a kind of survival, a resigned acceptance or grim endurance of life's ills. The sense of catastrophe is seldom absent from his plays; indeed, an aura of catastrophe hangs over all his major plays. This is Williams' weakness but also a strength.

This overall positive view of Williams' late plays is a far cry from that of both Guo Jide, Li's dissertation advisor, and Wang Yiqun who, in their respective books on American drama in the early 1990s, cautioned against the unhealthy spiritual tendencies in Williams's works or dismissed Williams' late plays supposedly marred by excessive use of symbolism. After all, much had happened in the short span of about ten years, from the early 1990s to the early 2000s when Li was conducting research for her dissertation project, including the decriminalization of homosexual love in China. Not so incidentally, during the same period of time, the rehabilitation of Williams' reputation, re-reading and reassessing his late plays as bold artistic experiments through the theoretical lenses of Mikhail Bakhtin, Antonin Artaud, Julia Kristeva, and so on,[80] was in full steam in the US through the endeavors of many scholars and artists. Li benefited from such pioneering work, as duly noted in her review of literature for the monograph and pertinent chapters. At the very end of her monograph, Li acknowledges the challenge of writing the dissertation in English, having to try and "balance Western Styles of criticism and Eastern analysis. The former is more analytic, specific, and evidence based, while the latter is more poetic, sensitive and speculative." She tried to have her own "[E]astern way of plotting settled within a [W]estern theoretical framework,"[81] which may not have always worked and which may account for the repetitiveness and redundancies within sections and between individual chapters. Nonetheless, based on and drawing from a tremendous amount of primary texts, secondary sources, including critical theories and studies of Williams plays, especially his late plays, Li Ying accomplishes what she sets out to do for this dissertation project and the monograph that grows out of it.

In 2010, two more monographs would be published, *The Homosexual Subtext in Tennessee Williams* (*Tiannaxi weiliansi xinlun* 田纳西·威廉斯新论) by Li Shanghong (李尚宏),[82] based on his PhD dissertation completed in 2005 at Shanghai International Studies University and revised/rewritten into Chinese, and *Presence and Absence of the Father in Tennessee Williams' Theatre* (*Tiannaxi weiliansi xiju zhong fuqin de zaichang yu quex*, 田纳西·威廉斯戏剧中父亲的在场与缺席) by Liang Chaoqun (梁超群),[83] based on his PhD dissertation completed in 2008 at East China Normal University. Both monographs, as indicated by their respective titles, can be seen as further expansion of and inquiry into topics and issues, especially gender and (homo)sexuality, addressed in the monographs by Li Li (李莉, 2004), Xu Huaijing (徐怀静,2007), and Li Ying (李英, 2008) discussed above although all five authors began and completed their PhD studies within just a few years of each other.

Although the Chinese and English (or any other two languages) titles of the same monograph/book do not have to be literal, "faithful" translations of each other, the disconnect or dissonance between Li Shanghong's 田纳西威廉斯新论 (*Tiannaxi weiliansi xinlun*, New Perspectives on Tennessee Williams) and *The Homosexual Subtext in Tennessee Williams* is so conspicuous that it calls attention to itself. Despite the "newness" claim in the Chinese title, 田纳西·威廉斯新论 is vague and generic, shortchanging both the English title[84] and, more importantly, the content of the monograph. Indeed, any prospective reader has to pay particular attention to the English (sub)title to get a sense of what the book is about. It is not clear whether this Chinese title was a choice of the author, of the publisher, or both, due to concerns about the sensitive subject matter. It would seem "safer" to announce the subject of the monograph 同性恋 (*tongxinglian* homosexual) in the English (sub)title, under the cover of an innocuous Chinese (main) title, so as not to attract any unwanted attention. Although there has been no explicit religious or legal prohibition or denunciation of homosexuality in China as has been the case in the West, Li states in the introduction of the monograph that this topic is still a considerable taboo for the broad masses (despite the decriminalization of homosexuality in 1997).[85] As a matter of fact, Li finds it necessary to declare, at the outset, the heterosexual identity of the author (to differentiate himself from many Western scholars who have studied the same topic) and state where he stands on the still sensitive topic/issue:

This author is not a homosexual. The discussions throughout this book follow these two principles:

1. The principle of fair scholarly inquiries. The sole purpose of this book is to study the dramatist's creativities to deepen readers' understanding of his dramatic works. This author does his utmost to avoid any homosexuality-related propaganda outside the dramatic works under discussion.

2. The principle of sympathetic understanding for Williams the playwright and homosexual characters in his dramatic works. Extended research and controversies have led to this consensus based on modern science: homosexuality "is caused by a complex interplay of genetic, hormonal, and environmental influences."[86] For many people (homosexuals), homosexuality is not a psychological or pathological problem, nor a result of immoral choices; rather, it is something innate. During Williams times the homosexual community suffered immensely due to social prejudice and discrimination. This author believes that society should treat this community humanely and give them sympathetic understanding.

With the grounds safely covered, Li Shanghong takes a deep dive, so to speak, into the homosexual (sub)text in Williams' works with a level of cogency not often seen among the monographs under discussion in this chapter. Using the title of Williams' autobiographical play *Something Cloudy, Something Clear* (which dramatizes his experiences in Cape Cod during the pivotal summer of 1940, when he met his first love Kip Kiernan) as the overarching trope for the inquiry, Li tries to unpack the six techniques, or rather, stratagems Williams employs to camouflage the homosexual (sub)text or themes in his plays:

1. Dead homosexual characters occupying the central stage
2. Feigned denunciation of homosexuality
3. Male body as object of desire
4. White as "dress code" for homosexual characters
5. "Doing one thing under cover of another" (*ming xiu zhan dao, an du chen cang* 明修栈道,暗渡陈仓)
6. Male homosexuals, female bodies

Of the six, "dead homosexual characters occupying the central stage" is perhaps the most "conspicuous" stratagem employed by Williams and the most studied by scholars: Homosexual characters, though dead before the curtain rises, occupy a central place in the development and dramatic action of the play, for example, Allan Gray, Blanche's young husband in *A Streetcar Named Desire*; at least four dead or offstage homosexuals in *Cat on a Hot Tin Roof*: Jack Straw and Peter Ochello, original owners of "th' biggest an' finest plantation in the Delta,"[87] Skip, and a friend of Brick and Skip at Ole Miss ("a pledge" of theirs to their fraternity who "*attempted to do an unnatural thing*" so they "dropped him like a hot rock!" and "told him to git off the campus"[88]); and Sabastian of *Suddenly Last Summer*. These homosexual characters, though dead (or vanished) before the curtain rises, still "haunt" the play in the fourth dimension; they are often the center of the story. For example, although Allan never appears on stage in person and although Blanche seems to be the central character of *Streetcar*, the tragic action unfolding on the stage is to trace the root cause of tragedy: the death of Allan by suicide. It is even more so with *Suddenly Last Summer*: the tension between Catherine and her aunt Mrs. Violet Venable throughout the play surrounds the mysterious death of Sebastian—his (homo)sexual exploitation and his bizarre violent and cannibalistic death.[89]

The stratagem of "feigned denunciation of homosexuality" sounds like a page taken from *Thirty-Six Stratagems (sanshi liu ji* 三十六计), a classical Chinese text that describes the stratagems for winning battles and dealing with the enemies, and so on. Before homosexuality was decriminalized in the US, Li Shanghong explains, Williams feigned denunciation of homosexuality, as was the case in one of his early one-act plays, *Auto-da-Fé* (1941).[90] The plot of this play concerns a young postal worker, Eloi, whose sexuality is repressed by a rigidly moralistic mother. On its surface, the play is about a young postal worker setting himself on fire by way of denouncing the ugly rottenness in the society surrounding him; at a deeper level it is also a last act of protest lodged by a closet homosexual who has internalized the societal prejudice of homosexuality. Also, Williams sometimes associates homosexual characters with disease, a popular trope in literature, which, in the eyes of censors and audiences, could be seen as a way of "denouncing" or punishing them, but Williams invests much understanding and sympathy in the portrayal of such characters. The typical disease Williams uses, such as tuberculosis and colon cancer, much like AIDS, is an identifier (albeit opaque to most people) for homosexuals. By having positive characters, such as Pablo Gonzales of *The Mysteries of the Joy Rio* (1941), possibly his first homosexual protagonist, or Big Daddy of *Cat on a Hot Tin Roof* suffering from such diseases, Williams calls for society to understand and accept homosexuality.[91] Although this is a rather intriguing way of looking at Williams' portrayal of homosexual characters in his plays, it would be unlikely for any censors or audiences to see a closet homosexual character burning himself in protest as an "denunciation," feigned or real, of homosexuality rather than the cankerous social prejudices. Similarly, one would be hard put to make a case for Big Daddy being another closet homosexual (besides Brick, his son) in *Cat*, as Li claims without presenting compelling (if not exactly convincing) evidence to support it.

"Male body as object of desire" is another stratagem used by Williams, a male homosexual playwright, to give expression to homosexual themes in his plays. Contrary to what is typically done in art and popular culture, Li Shanghong explains, which presents the female body as object of sexual desire and fantasy, Williams' dramatic works often depict the male body as "beautiful" and charming, which is often the focal attention and object of sexual desire and fantasy through the gaze of female characters. Such is the case of Stanley in *A Streetcar Named Desire*. Despite his "animal's habits" and "ape-like" crudeness which she despises, Blanche could not resist his physical charm (the "animal force" which Stanley "gave a wonderful exhibition of") and could not help flirting with him (Williams even arranges to have Stanley remove his shirt in Blanche's presence—to be "comfortable" and to show off his wonderful physique).[92] There is a degree of truth, unsettling as it is, in what Stanley says as he rapes her near the end of the play: "We've had this date with each other from the beginning!"[93] In *Cat on a Hot Tin Roof*, Williams goes one step further in shining the spotlight on the beautiful body of Brick, the object of Margaret's desire. She talks dreamily and hungrily of "what a wonderful lover" Brick used to be, "a wonderful person to go to bed with": how they "hit heaven together ev'ry time that we loved!"[94] despite his indifference to her, an attractive woman who can still catch the eye of so many other men, including Big Daddy— at least Margaret thinks so ("I sometimes suspect that Big Daddy harbors a little unconscious 'lech' fo' me ... Way he always drops his eyes down my body."[95]).[96]

If one person or character dresses in white (often enough, if not all the time), that is probably a personal choice, a fashion statement of sort, and an expression of one's unique personality, attitudes, and so on. When many people or characters (across different plays) do so, it becomes a pattern, and the sign (white clothing as both signifier and signified) calls attention to itself and acquires unusual significance. As Li Shanghong explains, it is not accidental that many of the male characters in Williams' plays are dressed in white, for example, Sebastian in *Suddenly Last Summer* ("Sebastian was white as the weather. He had on a spotless white silk Shantung suit and a white silk tie and a white panama and white shoes, white—white lizard skin—pumps!" Catherine tells Dr Cukrowicz.[97] As a matter of fact, white is quite a motif throughout the play: white wicker table and white wicker chair, white street, white hill, white blazing days, white bone, and more. Our first glimpse of Brick in *Cat on a Hot Tin Roof,* when he finally steps out of the shower, is a man wrapped in a "white towel-cloth robe;"[98] he remains thus clothed for much of Act One as dramatic action of the play unfolds and gains intensity.

Indeed, white clothing in Williams' plays means more than meets the eye because, as Williams describes in his novella *The Knightly Quest* (1965): white silk scarf is the signature prop Gewinner brings with him as he goes out and "hunt[s]," which will be used as blanket for homosexual encounters too.[99] Even Dr Cukrowicz of *Suddenly Last Summer* is dressed in white too ("all in white, glacially brilliant, very, very good-looking"[100]). Perhaps this "very young blond" doctor is an unwitting closet homosexual, too. Just as interestingly, Blanche Dubois of *Streetcar* is often dressed in white, which is typically understood as signifying her desire to cover her soiled past, but can also be construed to mean that she is potentially a male homosexual trapped or masqueraded in a female body.[101] Intriguing as the question of whether Big Daddy, Dr Cukrowicz, and Blanche are also closet homosexuals is, there is enough white clothing in Williams' plays to make the case without trying to stretch it a bit too far, seeing everyone or anyone (dressed in white or not) as a closet homosexual.

A strong case can certainly be made for Williams' use of "doing one thing under cover of another" (*ming xiu zhan dao an du chen cang* 明修

栈道,暗渡陈仓) stratagem by way of representing homosexual issues and themes, so much so that by now (if not by the time Li Shanghong was undertaking his dissertation project in the early 2000s) it has become all but an open book (so to speak). On the surface, Tom struggles with the responsibility of having to support his mother and sister in a fatherless family (father having abandoned the family to chase his long-distance dream). However, at a deeper level, Tom may also be struggling with his sexuality, which explains his going to the movies every night and staying till midnight (movie theaters having been one of the public spots for homosexuals to meet for quite some time[102]) and his finally deciding to leave and find himself. At one level, *A Streetcar Named Desire* is a story of how Blanche is caught between the agrarian culture of the south and the newly industrialized culture, seeks shelter with her sister but ends up being raped by her brother-in-law, and sent to the mental institution. Underneath it all, albeit told as a backstory, the play is about Blanche's accidental discovery of her husband's homosexuality and exposing him publicly, which leads to his death and her own tragic demise. The same is true of *Cat on a Hot Tin Roof*: a two-strand story of a familial fight over the inheritance as a result of Big Daddy's terminal illness diagnosis and Brick's struggle with his (homo)sexuality and the pain that brings on himself, Margaret, and Big Daddy.[103] In the case of both *Streetcar* and *Cat*, the homosexual theme, though seemingly secondary and mostly told as backstory, is so visible, without much camouflaging, that it would be hard to imagine any audiences or theatre reviewers to have missed it or mistaken it for anything else even in Williams' own days.

Is Blanche a male homosexual trapped in a female body? And Alma of *Summer and Smoke*? Blanche is such an intriguing and complicated, multi-layered character, perhaps the most fascinating character created by Williams and one of the most fascinating characters in American drama (or literature), that she invites many "profitable" readings from a variety of lenses. For example, she is seen as possibly a closet homosexual (lesbian) because of her penchant for being dressed in white. In his discussion of the sixth stratagem deployed by Williams to represent homosexual themes, Li cites Blanche again as a possible example of a male homosexual trapped in a female body: although she appears to be a typical woman character in the eyes of lay audiences, she could come across as a male homosexual in the eyes of homosexual community because of her quirky, telltale behaviors, for example, her preference for dim and avoidance of light, her indulgence in long baths, and her interest in young men (such as high school students and the young collector). Alma in *Summer and Smoke* is offered as another example because she suffers from sexual oppression as Williams did during his youth and because Williams professed a particular connection with her ("*Alma* of *Summer and Smoke* is my favorite—because I *came out* so *late* and so did *Alma*, and she had the greatest struggle"[104]). It is questionable, though, whether that is enough to make the case of Alma being a female alter-ego of Williams himself in terms of being a male homosexual. After all, Williams had a strong connection, at a deep sociocultural, psychological, and emotive level, with all the important characters he created. For example, in a conversation with Terkel, he said:[105]

> You must remember that you're now talking to a man who has gone through what Blanche went through. I've been in the asylum, and I've been survived. (*Laughs*). I came out. (*Laughs*).

In a way, one can go out on a limb to say, borrowing the famous "Madame Bovary, *c'est moi*" line from Gustave Flaubert, that every one of the important characters, Blanche, Stanley, Tom, Alma, Brick, and so on, is Williams, their creator, in one shape, form, or another. That, however, does not necessarily make each of them Williams' alter-ego as a male homosexual. Sometimes, when one is so bent on, so obsessed with looking for something anywhere, one will likely see its specter popping up just about everywhere, real or phantastic. To his credit, Li is fully aware that there are exceptions to all generalizations and there is a huge difference between "real" life (where there are as many different behaviors as homosexual individuals) and "stylized" performance on the stage.[106]

In Xu Huaijing's 2007 book on the male characters in Williams major plays discussed earlier, there is a chapter on absent fathers and runaway sons. Half of that equation, fathers, is the focal attention of another monograph also published in 2010, *Presence and Absence of the Father in Tennessee Williams' Theatre* (*Tiannaxi weiliansi xiju zhong fuqin de zaichang yu quexi*, 田纳西·威廉斯戏剧中父亲的在场与缺席) by Liang Chaoqun (梁超群) based on his doctoral dissertation at East China Normal University. This study narrows the scope of research and zooms in on the fathers, their presence and absence, in four "old" classics of Williams: *The Glass Menagerie, A Streetcar Named Desire, Cat on a Hot Tin Roof,* and *The Night of the Iguana*. As Liang sees it, "The presence or absence of the father in these both critically acclaimed and commercially successful Broadway plays is particularly revelatory about the dramatist's psychological make-up and the American culture of his time":[107]

The absence of the father from the menagerie-like Winfield household represents the Godless existential human condition. The dead father that haunts Blanche is a toxic legacy that drives the female protagonist to destruction as the streetcar named desire takes her to the scene of her tragic downfall. The coarse, imposing, verbally abusive, and critically ill but still powerful and benevolent Big Daddy is the dramatist's tribute to American pragmatism, which is believed to have potential to save human beings from existential despondency now that Dionysian redemption is also found to be delusional. The powerless father figure in *Iguana* testifies to the futility of the quest for father-saviors, but his sensitivity and dignity enable him to become an eloquent attorney in defense of humanity, which is capable of communicative rationality where the hope of redemption seems to reside.

The topic of the "father-figure" in Williams plays, present or absent, seems a well-trodden path that may not lead one to many insights and new discoveries. The value of such a study in the twenty-first century is probably more in the process than in the product: how one conducts the research and mounts a cogent analysis. Liang begins by (re)establishing the biographical source and inspiration of the "father-figure" in his plays: Williams' well-known "hate-love" relationship with his biological father, Cornelius Coffin Williams, his changing visions of his father "interplayed with his religious, social, cultural, and political attitudes which underwent important modifications over his two decades of artistic and commercial success from the mid-1940s through the early 1960s." Williams' portrayal of the father-figure in his major plays and the audience's enthusiastic responses also "reflect Americans' complicated and delicate involvement with the patriarch at every institution of every sort in the few middle decades of the 20th century" and keep pace with the psyche of the nation.[108]

For any study of the father-figure in Williams' dramatic works, his first successful play *The Glass Menagerie* would offer itself as the first promising site to visit. The father-figure in this play, Liang posits, which is absent physically yet present all the time, in the form of the picture and his ghostly spirit, expresses two of Williams "unconscious drives simultaneously: his latent patricidal fantasy and his wish to be his father's son instead of his mamma's boy." The fatherlessness of the family, according to Liang, constitutes an "effective metaphor for the existential conditions from which God has been excused by Nietzsche" and such philosophers; the play amounts to an outburst of "creative violence triggered by the Nietzschean discovery of the irrational power that defines an important part of the existential conditions of humankind. It presents a picture of the disjointed world in the aftermath of the absence of the father," which stands for "the violation of the social promises that American society has made."[109] This is a rather intriguing take on the play, centering on the question of the father-figure, but how could Liang, or just about anyone, gain access to Williams' "unconscious drives," especially his "latent patricidal fantasy," is anyone's guess. Nonetheless, the parallels Liang draws between Hamlet and Tom, as "oedipal revolts," are compelling enough (although it would seem fallacious to follow the logic pursued here and conclude that Shakespeare created the character of Hamlet out of his own latent patricidal fantasy).[110]

Liang continues the quest for biographical parallels in *A Streetcar Named Desire*. Here, he sees the character of Stanley as "Williams' manifesto to his father declaring his success and his attainment of manhood and independence." Now that he has achieved success and recognition, Liang says, Williams has "the guts to arrange for the father to be dead rather than just absent"—a literal, or figurative fulfillment of his latent patricidal fantasy. On the other hand, Blanche DuBois' dead father symbolizes "the toxic legacy of the institutionalized Christianity as the most prevalent Apollonian illusion that has dominated the Western mind." Here, Liang sets Stanley and Blanche up as soldiers of the Dionysian and the Apollonian, respectively; in the battle between the two, Stanley wins because he represents both the old Dionysian and the new frontier spirit whereas Blanche loses because she embodies the "depriving and self-defeating Apollonian self-denial" and the spiritless past.[111] Once again, intriguing as this reading is, in trying to fit what happens between Stanley and Blanche into the neat dichotomy of the Dionysian and the Apollonian, it would have to conveniently bypass and overlook so many other important strands in the dramatic world as envisioned in *Streetcar*, including Stanley's shrewdness, for example, in the way he finds out about Blanche's soiled past in Laurel and weaponizes it against her, and the apparently Dionysian streaks in Blanche's character and desire-driven behavior, for example, her reckless pursuit of physical pleasure and her addictive cravings for the booze (helping herself to Stanley's alcohol), albeit both prove to be self-destructive and fail to help her escape from reality and fill the emotive and spiritual void. Her last-ditch attempt to defend herself, when cornered by her cunning and ape-like "executioner," out of mortal fear and despair, by using a (Dionysian) bottle of Stanley's, which she has smashed broken on the table between them, is pathetic, sad, and fraught with irony.

In contrast to his reading of both *Menagerie* and *Streetcar*, Liang does not see the father–son bond of love between Big Daddy and Brick in *Cat* as a representation of the messy relationship between Williams and his father; rather, "it reveals the dramatist's desire and fantasy" for them to become better versions of their respective selves if they communicate better. Further, Liang sees Big Daddy, powerful, benevolent, though gravely ill, as "the father's glorious comeback after his exile" from *Menagerie* and *Streetcar*, which reflects Williams' "conversion to American pragmatism" and "the mid-20th century appeal in America to 'national greatness.'" Williams probably would not be amused at all if he were told that he had converted to American pragmatism and his play, or his portrayal of Big Daddy as a father-figure, was his way of joining the choir and singing America the Great, or he had somehow turned right, like his country in the 1950s, thanks to his personal success. As for Brick, his "melancholia and existentialist rejection of the world are dragging down not only himself but also largely innocent people like Maggie," who, according to Liang, functions as an "eloquent spokesperson of pragmatism, which reconciles the conflicts between Brick-type innocence and Big Daddy-like success."[112] One would be hard put to try and reconcile Brick's "melancholia and existentialist rejection of the world" and his supposed innocence, which he had long lost back in Ole Miss when Skip died because of their unspeakable, socially unsanctioned feelings for each other. That dark secret, a gnawing sense of shame and guilt, has haunted him ever since and he has never recovered (which explains why he limps around with a crutch, literally and metaphorically).

Williams' saga with the father-figure culminates with *Iguana*, which, according to Liang, signifies the dramatist's "conversion from creative violence typical of Nietzschean philosophy to constructive communication," through which process the dramatist "liquidates his old self obsessed with 'religion of sex' and escapism." In this play, "the proud but fragile and vulnerable father is at once charming and disconcerting. He himself turns out to be one of the reptilian, hopeless creatures that human beings typically are, like the iguana at the end of its rope. The father-figure reveals the dramatist's tentative conclusion about the futility of the quest for any father-life saviors in life." The solution, instead, is to reach out and communicate, as Nonno exemplifies, who has a sensitive soul and "is eager to tell and listen, and communicate."[113]

Scanning the landscape of Williams' scholarship in China when the second decade of the twenty-first century swings around, one could feel the "anxiety" (to borrow from Harold Bloom) of scholars who try to find new things to say about the American playwright or new ways to say the "old things"—variations of the same themes, for example, gender, southern belles, fathers and sons, (homo)sexuality—hoping to shed some new light, if possible. It is the same challenge for scholars, up-and-coming or late-comers, just about anywhere when they embark on a path that seems to have been well trodden by scholars before them. The second decade of the twenty-first century is not disappointing in this regard, however, with the publication of another five monographs mostly based on the authors' PhD dissertations, with varying degrees of achievement.

The first of these is *The Thematic Study of Margin in Tennessee Williams' Plays* (*Tiannaxi weiliansi juzuo de bianyuan zhuti yanjiu* 田纳西·威廉斯剧作的边缘主题研究) by Zhang Xinying (张新颖), published in 2011. It is based on her dissertation completed in 2009 at East China Normal University, advised by the same professor, Fei Chunfang (费春放), as Liang Chaoqun's on the father-figure in Williams' four major plays that have just been discussed (one could only imagine the kind of sharing of insights and resources and/or quiet competition between Zhang and Liang as they were conducting high-stake research on the same author albeit there is no mentioning of each other in the prefaces for their respective monographs). Zhang Xinying's monograph takes a look at Williams' dramatic works at both personal (psychological) and cultural levels through the lens of Freudian psychoanalysis and other critical perspectives informed by Erich Fromm, Carl Jung, and Jacques Lacan.[114] She acknowledges the work of two other PhD dissertations before hers, Li Shanghong's *The Homosexual Text and Subtext in Tennessee Williams Works* (2005), and Li Ying's *A Psychological Critique of Desire in Tennessee Williams Plays* (2006), both having been discussed in the preceding segments, and finds both valuable yet somewhat lacking—Li Shanghong's study being limited to Williams "pre-Stonewall plays" and amiss in overlooking "the social and political significance of Williams' plays," and Li Ying's work on homosexuality not comprehensive enough because it is only one of "five marginal subjects."[115] Therefore, Zhang sets out to remedy the perceived deficiencies in Chinese scholarship on Williams, as can be seen in some of the content covered by the four core chapters in her monograph: Tennessee Williams' Self-Portrait as a Homosexual Artist; Living on the Social Margin; Envisioning an Ideal World; and Braving Mainstream Discourse.

The chapter "Tennessee Williams' Self-Portrait as a Homosexual Artist" pursues the topic in three sections: (1) Female Characters as Williams' Emotional Root (e.g., Laura of *The Glass Menagerie*: a poetic, fragile, otherworldly beauty; Blanche of *A Streetcar Named Desire*: a surrealistic sexually perverted spirit; Alma of *Summer and Smoke*: an allegorical figure struggling to "come out"); (2) Mythical Figures on the Sacred Mission (Valentine of *Orpheus Descending*: Williams' first attempt to save the world; Sebastian of *Suddenly Last Summer*: Williams' conversion to the cruel God; Shannon of *The Night of Iguana*: Williams seeking for his all-loving God); and (3) Younger Personae on the Journal of Self-pursuit (Felice of *The Two-Character Play*: the last effort to regain his artistic identity; Writer of *Vieux Carré*: Williams revisiting his lost muses; August of *Something Cloudy, Something Clear*: Williams recalling his old love).[116] If this chapter, like Liang Chaoqun's study of the father-figure in Williams' major plays, adopts an essentially biographical and psychoanalytic reading of Williams plays, Zhang's next chapter, titled "Living on the Margin," shifts to a sociological approach, citing (appropriately or not) T. S. Eliot's idea of "depersonalization" of art.[117] This chapter discusses the theme of characters being ostracized in a society of homophobia (largely internalized) and trying to escape (by way of writing and death) without much success. Like Li Shanghong before her, Zhang asserts, without citing any substantive text evidence, that Big Daddy is a "closet homosexual" and goes on to say, even more problematically, that Big Daddy "not only passes on his homosexual genes to Brick but also infuses his prostrated principle into Brick."[118] In the chapter titled "Envisioning an Ideal World," Zhang tries to unpack the spirit/flesh dichotomy (communion, split, battle, and reconciliation), the socially imposed binary of gender boundaries; and the disjointed Humankind/Nature relationship.[119] The last chapter, titled "Braving Mainstream Discourse," returns to the biographical and psychoanalytic approach used in the first chapter, drawing parallels between the characters and their creator, but adds an important sociopolitical perspective to situate the discussion in the context of his times and see his portrayal of marginalized homosexuals, mostly opaque and camouflaged, as a conscious or unconscious counterargument against the mainstream discourse.[120] Zhang's study, as she promises at the outset, does encompasses many more of Williams' plays and tries to see his characters through biographic, psychoanalytic, and sociopolitical lenses—yet it sometimes tries too hard to fit everything into neat categories and rushes to draw conclusions unwarranted by the text and subtext of a play.

The year 2013 saw the publication of two books on Williams: *Reimagining the Past: Southern Belles in Tennessee Williams' Plays* (*Chong xin xiangxiang guoqu: Tiannaxi weiliansi juzhuo zhong de nanfang shunü*, 重新想象过去:田纳西·威廉斯剧作中的南方淑女) by Jiang Xianping (蒋

贤萍)[121] and *Broadway Troubadour: Tennessee Williams* (*Bailaohui de xin-gyin shiren*百老汇的行吟诗人) by Han Xi (韩曦).[122] Despite its title, which suggests a rehashing of a well-studied topic, Jiang Xianping's monograph, based on her PhD dissertation completed at Nanjing University, approaches it from an interesting and potentially rewarding angle: southern belles as "performers," as they attempt to reimagine the past, to preserve and continue the old traditions and reconstruct their new identities.[123]

The conceptual framing of this approach is in part informed by C. W. E. Bigsby's "Tennessee Williams: The Theatricalizing Self." Tennessee Williams once stated that he had created "imaginary worlds into which I can retreat from the real world because … I have never made any kind of adjustment to the real world," which, Bigsby thinks, is true of Williams' characters, too. Such failure of adjustment could lead to neurosis and psychosis in one direction and art in the other, which forms the base of both Williams and the characters created by him.[124] Also informing Jiang's study is Judith Butler's theory of "gender performativity," the idea of identity as free and flexible and gender as a performance, not an essence.[125] Butler further clarifies the idea of performativity:[126]

> Performativity cannot be understood outside of a process of iterability, a regularized and constrained repetition of norms. And this repetition is not performed by a subject; this repetition is what enables a subject and constitutes the temporal condition for the subject. This iterability implies that 'performance' is not a singular 'act' or event, but a ritualized production, a ritual reiterated under and through constraint, under and through the force of prohibition and taboo, with the threat of ostracism and even death controlling and compelling the shape of the production, but not, I will insist, determining it fully in advance.

No less directly relevant to Jiang Xiangping's study is Roger Boxill's idea that Williams' southern belle characters are "performers:"[127]

> There is usually something theatrical about the belle, a something whose day is passed, or that comes to naught, or that was never much to begin with … (they) are, or were, all performers … The production Amanda Wingfield makes of the evening Jim O'Connor calls is a flop. Nor does the eloquent Blanche Dubois, English teacher and poet's widow, make a hit with the groundling, Kowalski, by playing the lady.

As a matter of fact, the idea of the southern belles as performers forms at least part of Maher Moussa's 2001 PhD dissertation completed at Michigan State University, titled *The Re-Invention of the Self: Performativity and Liberation in Selected Plays by Tennessee Williams*. Mooussa argues that:[128]

> the self is not a fixed, stable, and coherent entity, but rather a performative self that plays different roles, wears different masks, and presents itself in different scripts. Most of the critics who have tackled Williams's plays have argued that his characters are tom between such dichotomies as flesh and spirit, and body and soul. In my study, I re-examine such claims, reassess Williams's characters' identity, and revisit the tensions and clashes that haunt these characters. I argue that the notion of identity Williams dramatizes is more complex and multidimensional than the clear-cut binary dichotomies through which these characters are often perceived. The alternative notion I present, in lieu of these readings, is that the self Williams constructs is performative with a multiplicity of faces and facets. I re-examine the self by applying different theories to come to a fuller understanding of Williams's notion of identity.

According to Moussa, Blanche of *Streetcar* recreates "a new image of herself to cope with her loss of social status, prestige, and respect;" the identity of Brick of *Cat* is constructed via the masks and façades and "is ultimately a result of negotiation between his private desires on the one hand, and the public resistance to the legitimacy of such desires on the other hand;" and that the liberated self is a myth and theatricality is impasse because it is impossible for the self "to be liberated from this performativity" and that "the self can be captured in its totality and open-endedness only through its own performativity which prevents the self from becoming an essentialized entity that feeds on clearly defined stereotypes and prejudices."[129]

Jiang Xiangpin takes a departure from Moussa, however, and contends that such performativity is liberating because these southern belles have a choice of the roles they play in constructing their identity in accordance with their moral values.[130] Jiang contends that Williams' southern belles are marked by their ritualized performativity, both linguistically and physically: Amanda and Laura of *The Glass Menagerie*, to re-create the glory of a romanticized past or to escape into a mythologized world; del Lago (travelling incognito as Princess Kosmonopolis) of *Sweet Bird of Youth*, to overcome and transcend an alienated self and to rejuvenate that self;

Blanche of *A Streetcar Named Desire*, to pursue her ideals and to cope
with reality and dreams; and Alma of *Summer Smoke*, to free herself from
dogmas for enlightenment and joy of life.[131] However, in the modern
world these southern belles are forever lost and their attempts to escape
reality through indulgences in nostalgia and fantasies are bound to fail;
and they cannot escape from destruction and tragedy.[132] In this conclusion
that Jiang draws for her study, there is no substantive difference from the
argument that Moussa makes in his study. Indeed, if there is any freedom
of choice to speak of in the cases of Amanda, Blanche, and so on, it has to
be a kind of "condemned" freedom in the Sartrean sense, given the
"extreme situation" and indeed the existential predicament in which they
find themselves.[133] Nonetheless, in this Sartrean sense of freedom of
choice, there is something "heroic" on the part of Amanda, Blanche, and
many other characters and underneath it all there is dogged "optimism"
on the part of their creator, Williams, as embodied in Sartre's play *Morts
sans sépulture* (The Victors).[134]

Hang Xi's *Broadway Troubadour: Tennessee Williams* reads more like a
companion to Tennessee Williams than a monograph with a well-focused
and in-depth study of a topic although the author completed her PhD dissertation on Williams at Nanjing University in early 2000s. The book
includes chapters devoted to Williams' life, career as a playwright, influences on Williams, characters created by Williams, artistic world of the
"poet laureate," and a chronology. As a "companion"—a comprehensive
introduction and overview of Williams, this book should prove valuable,
especially to college students who have burgeoning interest in this
American playwright. Chapter 3 of the book, for example, covers influences on Williams, from classical mythologies, religions, to Anton
Chekhov, D. H. Lawrence, and Hart Crane, that have been well studied
and documented. The chapter on Williams' characters includes southern
belles on the margins and men who escape or self-exile.

One thing noteworthy is what Zhou Weipei (周维培) says in his foreword for the book, outlining the sociocultural context for the rediscovered interest in and relevance of Tennessee Williams in the twenty-first
century:[135]

The 1980s was the most open period in Chinese art and literature. On the
stage and screen alone, all kinds of isms and styles came tumbling in from
outside, with both good and bad and proved an eye-opening experience for
Chinese audiences of Western theatre and films development in the last hun-

dred years. Chinese audiences, who are familiar with and appreciative of critical realism and grand narratives have no time or appreciation of playwrights such as Tennessee Williams who seemingly were writing for themselves and appealed to only a small "elite" audience. Today, as our country has catapulted to being the second biggest GDP economy in the world, salesmanship is not an enviable job. We suddenly find ourselves deeply ensnared in the same social predicaments described by Williams: tensions between city and country, individual and community, emotional loneliness and despair of spiritual redemption, and struggles for women, women's rights, and sexual orientations. Now, when we reopen the dramatic works by Williams and such overlooked playwrights, we may find many scenes and characters that feel so familiar and descriptions and analyses of problems that have reference value; we now understand and appreciate the attitudes of American people toward such problems which we are experiencing now; we can now more accurately grasp and assess such American playwrights as they try to capture and represent the times, spirit, and soul of their society.

Indeed, other than a heterosexuality disclaimer in one case alluded to earlier, none of the authors of the monographs published in the twenty-first century feels "apologetic" for choosing Williams for their dissertation projects or to find it necessary to add a note of caution or prewarning against the negative and potentially corrupting aspects of his dramatic works, as Guo Jide and Wang Yiqun did 10 years before them. Hang Xi ends her introduction thus, in a full-throated celebratory mode:[136]

> Tennessee Williams is a rebel of his times, a revolutionary of artistic forms, and more importantly, a courageous and unfaltering fighter against all injustices in the world. Therefore, his dramatic works have everlasting life and appeal on the stage.

The end of the second decade of the twenty-first century saw two more monographs on Tennessee Williams based on the authors' PhD dissertations: *The Legend of Encouragement and Decadence: The Study of Tennessee Williams and His Drama* (*Lizhi yu tuifei de chuanqi: Tiannaxi weiliansi jiqi xiju yanjiu* 励志与颓废的传奇:田纳西·威廉斯及其戏剧研究) by Gao Xianhua (高鲜花), published in 2019,[137] and *The Study on Tennessee Williams from the Perspective of "Heterology"* (*Linglei rensheng: yizhi shiyu xia de Tiannaxi weiliansi yanjiu* 另类人生: 异质视域下的田纳西·威廉斯研究) by Liang Zhen (梁真), published in 2020,[138] each noteworthy in its own way. The main title of Gao Xianhua's monograph, *The Legend of*

Encouragement and Decadence (励志与颓废的传奇) is interesting because it seems a promise to tell the legendary story of Williams (as an inspiration of sort to the readers) rather than an indication of the topical focus of a scholarly study. What separates this monograph, based on Gao's dissertation completed at Shanxi Normal University, from almost all the other PhD dissertation-based monographs under discussion in this chapter, is that it is the first and only one that has a chapter on Williams and China, that is, the China image (*zhongguo xingxiang* 中国形象) as portrayed in Williams' dramatic works and the supposed Chinese influence on the American playwright.

This aspect of Gao's monograph is singled out by Meng Zhaoyi (孟昭毅) for praise in his foreword.[139] Her PhD dissertation advisor, Kang Ximin (亢西民), in his foreword for the monograph, also enthuses about Gao's attention on how Williams drew from traditional Chinese *xiqu*, among other things, in his dramatic creation and what China meant for Williams:[140]

> Tennessee Williams has a deep connection with China. Although he never visited mainland China, the image of China appears in his plays every now and then. During the years of McCarthyism, China seemed a nirvana he so longed for but could never reach.

The same is true, according to Kang, for the characters created by Williams:

> Many of the marginal characters and people struggling at the bottom of society—whether they suffer spiritual misery, emotional loneliness, or feel lost and therefore are indulgent in sensual pleasures, or drift alone in life—cherish a deep longing for love and desire to escape, and China, due to its "utopian-ness," would inevitably appeal to them as their ideal nirvana or oasis. Therefore, the "image of China" would embody, both for his dramatic works and in his own life, a metaphysical and ontological be-all and end-all significance.

Kang acknowledges that "thanks to his plays filled with homosexuality, heterosexuality, and violence (slaughter, cannibalism, alcoholism, drug addiction) and such social phenomena, they proved to be hard for Chinese audiences to accept and appreciate. Therefore, Tennessee Williams' dramatic works and their relationship with contemporary Chinese drama/theatre have not received adequate attention and study." This, Kang goes on to state, is incompatible with the once-in-a-hundred-year profound changes we are undergoing, China as a big country/nation/power [大国] status and our responsibilities in today's world, the "Road and Belt" strategies we are implementing, and our long-cherished goals to introduce and promote Chinese culture, including Chinese scholarship to the world. Therefore, further and more systematical study of Tennessee Williams' dramatic works and their influence and reception in China is not only very important, but also very necessary.

This claim of high-stake importance for more Williams scholarship, closely associated with China's "Road and Belt" strategic vision and program to rebuild and reclaim the nation's place and role on the world stage, seems such a far cry from the mixed reception Williams received in the 1980s and even early 1990s. Williams himself would probably be surprised (if not shocked) or amused by the momentous role he had been assigned; indeed he would probably be perplexed when told of the China (as nirvana) wish cherished by him and his characters, albeit latently.

Gao Xianhua herself seems a bit more judicious or unsure, wavering between being unreservedly celebratory and somewhat cautious when assessing or ascribing such significance to the China image that emerges from Williams' dramatic works:[141]

> Tennessee Williams and the characters in his dramatic works sing during their life's journeys and search while drifting, trying to assuage their anxiety of being homeless, to seek freedom and safety while being rudderless. There seems an ideal place of respite in the heart of Williams, i.e., faraway, infinitely multifarious China. Reading Williams dramatic works carefully, we will encounter frequent appearances of "China," "Shanghai," "Chinese philosophy," "Chinese paper lantern," "Chinese sayings," "Chinese lotus," "lantern," and such China related images. Given the fact that Williams never visited Chinese mainland his entire life, what do all those China images really mean? How did he construct them?

Gao is fully aware that the China image as perceived by people from the outside world is "constructed not based on an objective and comprehensive knowledge of China but based on China-utopia inspired ideology and imaginings, and therefore is 'blind man and elephant' kind of partial image or mirror-image which reflects more of the imaginer than China."[142] Indeed, to her credit, Gao situates her discussions of the China image in Williams' dramatic works in the historical context of China images in the

West, including the United States, from the eighteenth century onward, both good and bad, from idealizing China as a Shangri-La to dismissing it as a backward place left behind by modernity (Western civilization). She also properly places Williams' China image in the context of US–China relations in the 1940s–1960s, especially McCarthyism, which prosecuted homosexuals and Communists alike. However, awareness of the historical, contextual complexity surrounding "China image" fails to caution her against the "leap" she takes in the conclusion she draws:[143]

> As a member of the homosexual community, Williams longed for escape in his heart. Based on signs and cues in his dramatic works, he chose China as his first choice of destination. China, as portrayed by him, is not perfect, but is materially abundant, culturally tranquil, morally tolerant, and therefore is an ideal sanctuary.

It is even more perplexing that Gao draws this conclusion with clear knowledge of Williams' three trips to Asia, his special friendship with Yukio Mishima, and the scarcity of direct China references in Williams works.[144] Gao is also aware of the negative references about Chinese philosophy made by Blanche when trying to talk her sister Stella into leaving Stanley, yet she is convinced that Williams' China image is dominantly "positive" and that "he places his ultimate hope on the faraway and beautiful China as his final destination:" Through a series of references to Chinese artifacts, philosophical attitudes, and cultural tropes, Williams constructed his own "ideal republic" (*lixiang guo* 理想国)—China.[145]

Gao's discussion of Williams' "borrowing" of symbolic representation from traditional Chinese *xiqu* is just as perplexing. It is based on a quick reference to a 2014 adaptation of *Streetcar* jointly staged by Chinese and American theatre artists, Beijing TinHouse Productions (*Beijing tiepi wu jushe* 北京铁皮屋剧社[146]) and Theatre Movement Bazaar, and directed by the latter's artistic director Tina Kronis.[147] It was a physical theatre production that incorporated some elements of traditional Chinese *xiqu*, a theatrical fusion of energies and talents of artists from two very different cultural and theatrical traditions.[148] Using this latter day bold production as the basis upon which to draw the conclusion that Williams was influenced by traditional Chinese *xiqu*[149] is, to put it mildly, stretching it a bit too far.

In contrast, a journal article published in 2017 on the same topic is much more judicious and nuanced in assessing the significance of "Chinese elements" (*zhongguo yuansu* 中国元素) in Williams' dramatic work. It breaks such elements into two groups, material (lanterns, slippers, tea, cooks and restaurants) and immaterial (Chinese ideas and philosophy), and then assigns three different functions to them as used in *The Night of Iguana*; random and irrelevant (e.g., the question of the price of rice in China when Hannah draws Shannon); as an excuse to escape and avoid facing reality (e.g., Shannon wanting to "take the long swim to China); and as "another painless atonement" (e.g., Hannah believing this is why Shannon wants to swim out to China). The author concludes that Williams' understanding of Chinese culture and philosophy is fragmented, hazy, and even schizophrenic, and not more than that of an average American (which, of course, does not mean it is unworthy of critical studies).[150]

True to its title, Liang Zhen's 2020 monograph *The Study on Tennessee Williams from the Perspective of "Heterology,"* the last to be discussed in this chapter, gathers a heterogeneous assortment of Williams' related topics and tries to see them through the lens of "heterology," for example, Williams as a southern "bohemian" both in his life experiences and as an artist; as a questioner of the American myth; and as an admirer of the faraway and exotic. Liang defines Williams' "heterological style" by drawing from the concept as understood by Georges Bataille (1897–1962) that deals with the existence of the Other or 'unknowable being,' the unassimilable, or the excessive, and the concept of "heresy" powerfully presented in *The Right to Heresy: Castellio Against Calvin* by Stefan Zweig (1881–1942):[151]

> The "heterological" in Tennessee Williams is more like a blending of the two (Bataille and Zweig). Williams characters are all "heteros", whether they are rich or poor, fit or handicapped, beautiful or ugly; they do not fit in with their world; such misfit has nothing to do with his/her own volitions. Whether they voluntarily reject being conformed, as described by Bataille, or they have different views about something, as described by Zweig, their common denominator is that they are not accepted (by others).

What really stands out in Liang's monograph is the chapter titled "Admirer of the Faraway and Exotic," which includes a section titled

"Fragrant Cherry Blossom" (*piao xiang de shan yinghua* 飄香的山樱花)
that discusses the influence of Japanese culture and theatre, especially the
noh theatre and Yukio Mishima. Limited as it is, it is the only "extensive"
study on this topic by a Chinese scholar. Liang's discussions benefit considerably from known sources on the topic, especially Sarah Elizabeth
Johnson's MFA thesis completed in 2014 at University of Iowa titled *The
Influence of Japanese Traditional Performing Arts on Tennessee Williams
Late Plays*.[152] What makes Johnson's study particularly valuable is that
with funding support from the university she got to travel to Japan to
experience Japanese traditional performing arts of *noh* and *kabuki*, as a
westerner, from outside, much as Tennessee Williams had done during his
trips to Japan. Her "insights" into the Japanese traditional performing arts
may not be expertly, but are relevant and of reference value, especially her
analyses of three of Williams late plays, *The Day on Which the Man Dies*, *In
the Bar of a Tokyo Hotel*, and *The Milk Train Doesn't Stop Here Anymore*.
Liang's discussion of Williams' fascination with the idea of death (and
sexual desire) both in life and in his dramatic works is quite intriguing.
Her conclusion is that both Williams' "hetero" life and the "hetero" characters in his dramatic works are, in the end, expressions of Williams' guid-
ing spirit of "art for life"[153]—life in its full biological, ontological, and
sociomoral sense.[154]

From the cautioning note Ying Ruocheng wrote for his 1963 rendition
of *Something Unspoken*, the first known published Chinese translation of
Williams works, to the serious yet still cautious interest shown by scholars
such as Guo Jide and Wang Yiqun in the early 1990s, to the enthusiastic
deep dive undertaken by aspiring scholars in the first two decades of the
twenty-first century, equipped with various critical lenses, for example,
psychology, psychoanalysis, gender and politics, and so on, Chinese reception of Tennessee Williams has come a long way. This decades-long journey, from the early 1960s to the early twenty-first century, has to be viewed
in the context of dramatic developments in the politics, culture, and sexual
mores in the country to see its full significance. The achievement, on the
whole, is remarkable despite the occasional overzealous and/or unsubstantiated claims and faulty notes in the scholarship. However, where will
this journey go from here, not just in terms of the reception of Williams,
but more importantly, in terms of the reception of all things Western,
including arts and literature, seems uncertain at this time, given recent
developments in China.[155]

NOTES

1. Greta Heintzelman and Alycia Smith-Howard, *Critical Companion to Tennessee Williams, A Literary Reference to His Life and Work* (New York: Infobase Publishing, 2014), 253.
2. Neal A. Lester, "27 Wagons Full of Cotton and Other One-Act Plays," in *Tennessee Williams: A Guide to Research and Performance*, edited by Phillip C. Kolin (Westport, CT: Greenwood Press, 1998), 6–7.
3. Ibid., 7.
4. Ibid., 4 and 8.
5. Tennessee Williams, *Memoirs*, with an Introduction by John Walters (New York: New Directions, 2006), 174–175.
6. See Annette J. Saddik, *Tennessee Williams and The Theatre of Excess: The Strange, The Crazed, The Queer* (Cambridge, UK: Cambridge University Press, 2015).
7. See Matthew Biberman, "Tennessee Williams: The American Shakespeare," *Huffington Post*, March 26, 2011, https://www.huffpost.com/entry/tennessee-williams-the-am_b_838552.
8. Grahm Allen, *Intertextuality* (New York: Routledge, 2000), 103–107.
9. Ying Ruocheng 英若诚, trans., *Something Unspoken* (*Meiyou jiang chulai de hua* 没有讲出来的话) by Tennessee Williams, *World Literature* (*Shijie wenxue* 世界文学) 3 (1963): 44–62.
10. See "*Shijie wenxue*" (世界文学 World Literature), https://baike.baidu.com/item/%E4%B8%96%E7%95%8C%E6%96%87%E5%AD%A6/6256191.
11. See "Cold War," https://www.britannica.com/event/Cold-War; "Cuban Missile Crisis," https://www.britannica.com/event/Cuban-missile-crisis;" and "Vietnam War," https://www.britannica.com/event/Vietnam-War.
12. See Xun Zhou, *The Great Famine in China, 1958–1962: A Documentary History* (New Haven, CT: Yale University Press, 2012).
13. See "Great Leap Forward," https://www.britannica.com/event/Great-Leap-Forward; and "Commune," https://www.britannica.com/topic/commune-Chinese-agriculture.
14. See "Lu-shan Conference," https://www.britannica.com/topic/Lu-shan-Conference.
15. See "Anti-Rightist Campaign," https://en.wikipedia.org/wiki/Anti-Rightist_Campaign; and Zhu Zheng 朱正, *Fan youpai douzheng quan shi* (反右派斗争全史 *Anti-Rightest Movement*) (Taibei: ShowWe Press, 2014).
16. See "Socialist Education Movement," https://www.britannica.com/topic/Socialist-Education-Movement.

17. For consequences of speaking out directly, see Xi Lian, *Blood Letters* (New York: Hachette Book, 2018).
18. Ying Ruocheng and Claire Conceison, *Voices Carry: Behind Bars and Backstage during China's Revolution and Reform* (New York: Roman and Littlefield, 2009), 136. See also "Hundred Flowers Campaign," https://www.britannica.com/event/Hundred-Flowers-Campaign.
19. See "Ying Ruocheng," https://en.wikipedia.org/wiki/Ying_Ruocheng.
20. Ying and Conceison, 3–58.
21. Ying Ruocheng 英若诚, "Postface" (*houji* 后记), *World Literature* (*Shijie wenxue* 世界文学) 3 (1963), 61–62.
22. See Shouhua Qi, *Western Literature in China and the Translation of a Nation* (New York: Palgrave Macmillan, 2012), 142–155.
23. Zuo Yi 左宜, "Tennessee Williams' Early Works" (*Tiannaxi weiliansi de zaoqi zuopin* 田纳西·威廉斯的早期作品), *Contemporary Foreign Literature* (*Dangdai waiguo wenxue* 当代外国文学) 4 (Oct. 1981):143–147.
24. Yuan Kejia 袁可嘉, "Preface" (*Yinyan* 引言), *Selections from Foreign Modernist Literature* (*Waiguo xiandai pai zuopin xuan* 外国现代派作品选), vol. 4-1 (Shanghai: Shanghai Literature and Arts Press 上海文艺出版社, 1985), 4.
25. For heated debates on questions of "modernism" and "modernity" in the 1980s, see Qi, *Western Literature*, 163–170.
26. Yuan Kejia 袁可嘉, "Western Modernist Literature as I Understand it" (*Wo suo renshi de xifang xiandai pai wenxue* 我所认识的西方现代派文学), *Selections from Foreign Modernist Literature* (*Waiguo xiandai pai zuopin xuan* 外国现代派作品选), vol. 4-2 (Shanghai: Shanghai Literature and Arts Press 上海文艺出版社, 1985), 1136–1142.
27. See "Guo Jide" (郭继德), https://baike.baidu.com/item/%E9%83%AD%E7%BB%A7%E5%BE%B7/3509093?fr=aladdin.
28. Guo Jide 郭继德, *History of American Drama* (*Meiguo xiju shi* 美国戏剧史) (Zhengzhou: Henan People's Press 河南人民出版, 1993).
29. An international centenary celebration of Eugene O'Neill took place in China around the time the two books on American drama by Guo Jiide and Wang Yiqun respectively were being published. See Liu Haiping and Lowell Swortzell, eds. *Eugene O'Neill in China: An International Centenary Celebration* (Westport, CT: Praeger, 1992).
30. Guo, J., 106.
31. By the time his ship sailed into the Shanghai harbor in 1929, as part of his world tour, O'Neill had already read as much about Chinese philosophy, especially Taoism (Daoism), as any major Western writer, such as Oscar Wilde and Bertolt Brecht. He came to recharge his battery, so to speak, to be inspired on the native soil that had given birth to Laozi (604–531

BC), who seemed so different from Arthur Schopenhauer, Friedrich Nietzsche, and Sigmund Freud, the troika that had influenced his world-view immensely.

Hating "idiotic publicity" and not wanting to be bothered by the snooping Nationalist government's secret police, O'Neill, along with his wife Carlotta Monterey, mostly stayed within the walls of Astor House Hotel (*Licha fandian*, known today as *Pujiang fandian*). Although his plan to write a play featuring Qinshi Huangdi, the first emperor of China, did not come to fruition, O'Neill did in1936 build the famed Tao House ("the right way of life") in Danville, California, using the Nobel Prize award of $40,000 he received that year. It is at this home of perfect *fengshui* (wind and water), surrounded and protected by the Las Trampas hills on three sides, far away from the madding crowd, that O'Neill wrote, among other things, *The Iceman Cometh* (1939) and *Long Day's Journey into Night* (1941–1942), as he struggled with nagging mental and physical health challenges.

See Frederic Wakeman Jr., *Policing Shanghai*, 1927–1937 (Oakland, CA: University of California Press, 1995), 64; Beverly Lane, "History of Tao House," http://www.eugeneoneill.org/about-tao-house/; and Robert M. Dowling, *Eugene O'Neill, A Life in Four Acts* (New Haven, CT: Yale University Press, 2016), 365.
32. See Arthur Miller, "In China," *The Atlantic Monthly*, March 1979, 90–117; *Salesman in Beijing* (New York: Viking, 1983); and Arthur Miller and Inge Morath, *Chinese Encounters*. *Chinese Encounters* (New York: Farrar Straus Giroux, 1979).
33. Guo, J., 270.
34. Ibid., 277.
35. Ibid., 278.
36. Ibid., 280.
37. Ibid., 110–111.
38. Ibid., 152.
39. Ibid., 158.
40. Ibid., 285.
41. Ibid., 311. Interesting enough, Guo did not say a word of the staging of *Death of A Salesman* in Beijing (directed by Arthur Miller) in the spring of 1983, a noteworthy event in the history of contemporary Chinese cultural life and in the history of Chinese reception of Western arts and literature, especially modernist works.
42. Guo, J., 186.
43. Ibid., 194.
44. See "Wang Yiqun" (汪义群), https://www.sta.edu.cn/7f/3a/c1562a32570/page.htm.

45. Wang Yiqun 汪义群, *Contemporary American Drama* (*Dangdai meiguo xiju* 当代美国戏剧) (Shanghai: Shanghai Foreign Language Education Press 上海外语教育出版社, 1993).
46. Arthur Miller and Phillip Gelb, "Morality and Modern Drama," *Educational Theatre Journal* 10–13 (Oct.,1958), 190.
47. Wang, Y., 37.
48. Ibid., 37–38.
49. Ibid., 42–43.
50. Ibid., 70–89.
51. Ibid., 77.
52. Ibid., 32.
53. It is interesting to note that for a long time, Wang's *Contemporary American Drama* was the only book-length study on Williams that mentions *In the Bar of a Tokyo Hotel* and other "late plays" of his—until Li Ying's monograph *A Psychoanalytic Critique of Desire in Tennessee Williams Plays* (2008), which includes a chapter devoted to Williams' late plays and Liang Zhen's *The Study on Tennessee Williams from the Perspective of "Heterology,"* which gives considerable attention to Williams' interest in Japanese culture and literature, more particularly, traditional Japanese theatrical art forms. See discussions in the next section of this chapter.
54. Wang, Y., 197–204. See Emily Feng, "First Chinese-Language Production of *A Raisin In The Sun* is Staged in Beijing," *NPR*, September 3, 2020, https://www.npr.org/2020/09/03/908274058/first-chinese-language-production-of-a-raisin-in-the-sun-is-staged-in-beijing; and Shouhua Qi, "Pushing the Boundaries: Staging Western Modern(ist) Drama in Contemporary China," in *The Edinburgh Companion to Modernism in Contemporary Theatre*, edited by Adrian Curtin, et al. (Edinburgh, Scotland: Edinburgh University Press, 2022).
55. According to Annette Saddik, author of *Tennessee Williams and the Theatre of Excess: The Strange, The Crazed, The Queer* (Cambridge, UK: Cambridge University Press, 2015), *The Politics of Reputation: The Critical Reception of Tennessee Williams' Later Plays* (Plainsboro, NJ: Associated University Press, 1999), and editor of *Tennessee Williams: The Traveling Companion and Other Plays* (New York: New Directions, 2008), when she considered taking on Williams for her PhD dissertation in the early 1990s, she was earnestly discouraged from doing so because, she was told, she would be ruining her budding academic career thanks to the overall negative, dismissive reception of Williams in the US at the time. Annette Saddik, "From Broadway Darling to Outrageous Outlaw: Tennessee Williams and the American Theatre," Invited Faculty Lecture (via WebEx), October 8, 2020, Western Connecticut State University, Danbury, CT.

56. Li Li 李莉, *Woman's Growth: Feminist Approach to Tennessee Williams' Works* (*Nüren de chengzhang licheng: tiannaxi weiliansi zuopin de nüxing zhuyi jiedu* 女人成长历程:田纳西·威廉斯作品的女性主义解读) (Tianjin: Tianjin People's Press 天津人民出版社, 2004).
57. Li, L., Introduction, 1–2.
58. Ibid., 3.
59. Li, L., 3–4.
60. Xu Huaijing 徐怀静, *Masculinity Crises: Troubled Men in Tennessee Williams' Major Plays* (*Tie beixin: Tiannaxi weiliansi juzuo zhong kunhuo de nanren men* 铁背心: 田纳西·威廉斯剧作中困惑的男人们) (Beijing: Tongxin Press 同心出版社, 2007).
61. Ibid., 287.
62. Xu, H., Introduction, 1–2.
63. Ibid., 12–19.
64. Xu, H., 2–8, 20–29.
65. Tennessee Williams, *Tennessee Williams Plays 1937–1955* (New York: The Library of America, 2000), 401.
66. Xu, H., 19.
67. Ibid., 286.
68. Li Ying 李英, *A Psychoanalytic Critique of Desire in Tennessee Williams Plays* (*Tiannaxi weiliansi xiju zhong yuwang de xinli toushi* 田纳西·威廉斯戏剧中欲望的心理透视) (Beijing: Modern Education Press 现代教育出版社, 2008).
69. Ibid., 3–9.
70. Quoted in Li, Y., 79. See Arthur Gantz, "A Desperate Morality," in *TW: A Collection of Critical Essays*, edited by Stephen S. Stanton (Englewood Cliffs, NJ: Prentice-Hall, 1977), 128.
71. Li, Y., 79
72. Quoted in Li, Y., 96. See Sigmund Freud, "Mourning and Melancholia" (1917), in *General Psychological Theory*, edited by Philip Rieff (New York: Macmillan Publishing Co., Inc., 1978), 167.
73. Li, Y., 100.
74. See for example, Norman J. Fedder, *The Influence of D. H. Lawrence on Tennessee Williams* (Berkely, CA: University of California Press, 1966); and Gilbert Debusscher, "Creative Rewriting: European and American Influences on the Dramas of Tennessee Williams," in *The Cambridge Companion to Tennessee Williams*, edited by Matthew C. Roudane (Cambridge, UK: Cambridge University Press, 1997), 167–188.
75. Li, Y., 126–127.
76. Ibid., 144.
77. Ibid., 175
78. Saddik, *The Politics of Reputation*, 111.

79. Li., Y., 33–34, 201–235.
80. Saddik, *Tennessee Williams*, 3–5.
81. Li, Y., 240.
82. Li Shanghong 李尚宏, *The Homosexual Subtext in Tennessee Williams* (*Tiannaxi weiliansi xinlun* 田纳西·威廉斯新论) (Shanghai: Shanghai Foreign Language Education Press 上海外语教育出版社, 2010).
83. Liang Chaoqun 梁超群, *Presence and Absence of the Father in Tennessee Williams' Theatre* (*Tiannaxi weiliansi xiju zhong fuqin de zaichang yu quexi* 田纳西·威廉斯戏剧中父亲的在场与缺席) (Shanghai: Shanghai Sanlian Books 上海三联出版社, 2010).
84. The English title for Li's PhD dissertation, completed in 2005, is *The Homosexual Text and Subtext in Tennessee Williams Works*, which seems to be more accurate and appropriate as far as the content of the dissertation and indeed the monograph is concerned. See Zhang Xinying 张新颖, *The Thematic Study of Margin in Tennessee Williams' Plays* (*Tiannaxi weiliansi juzuo de bianyuan zhuti yanjiu* 田纳西·威廉斯剧作的边缘主题研究) (Beijing: Science Press 科学出版社, 2011), 10.
85. Li, S., 11.
86. See "Sexual Orientation & Homosexuality," https://www.apa.org/topics/lgbtq/orientation.
87. Williams, *1937–1955*, 907.
88. Ibid., 948.
89. Li, S., 17–18, 76–87.
90. See "Auto-da-fé" (Public Ceremony), https://www.britannica.com/topic/auto-da-fe; and https://en.wikipedia.org/wiki/Auto-da-f%C3%A9.
91. Li, S., 60–75.
92. Williams, *1937–1955*, 482, 508–510.
93. Ibid., 555.
94. Ibid., 892, 910.
95. Ibid., 892, 910.
96. Li, S., 20–22.
97. Tennessee Williams, *Tennessee Williams Plays 1957–1980* (New York: The Library of America, 2000), 141–142.
98. Williams, *1937–1955*, 893.
99. Tennessee Williams, *The Knightly Quest*, in Tennessee Williams, *Collected Stories* (New York: New Directions, 1994), 439–441.
100. Williams, *1957–1980*, 101.
101. Li, S., 23–24.
102. Margaret Cruikshank, *The Gay and Lesbian Liberation Movement* (New York: Routledge, 1992), 127. See also Scott McKinnon, *Gay Men at the Movies: Cinema, Memory, and the History of a Gay Male Community* (Fishponds, Bristol: Intellect, 2016).
103. Li, S., 24–26.

104. Albert J. Devlin, ed., *Conversations with Tennessee Williams* (Jackson, MI: University Press of Mississippi, 1986), 228.
105. Quoted in Bert Cardullo, ed., *Conversations with Stanley Kauffmann* (Jackson, MI: University Press of Mississippi, 2003), 112.
106. Li, S., 24–26.
107. Liang, C., I.
108. Ibid., II–III.
109. Ibid., III–V.
110. Many scholars, though, have gone through this path in search of new interpretive possibilities. See Julia Reinhard Lupton, et al., *After Oedipus: Shakespeare in Psychoanalysis.* (Ithaca, NY: Cornell University Press, 1993).
111. Liang., C., III-V, 78–119.
112. Ibid., V–VI, 120–152.
113. Ibid., VI–VIII, 171–225.
114. Zhang, X., 17.
115. Ibid., 11.
116. Ibid., 18–66.
117. T.S. Eliot, "Tradition and Individual Talent," in *The Sacred Wood: Essays on Poetry and Criticism* (New York: Alfred A. Knopf, 1921), 47.
118. Zhang, X., 92, 94.
119. Ibid., 106–160.
120. Ibid., 161–207.
121. Jiang Xianping 蒋贤萍, *Reimagining the Past: Southern Belles in Tennessee Williams' Plays* (*Chong xin xiangxiang guoqu: Tiannaxi weiliansi juzhuo zhong de nanfang shunü* 重新想象过去：田纳西·威廉斯剧作中的南方淑女) (Beijing: Guangming Daily Publishing House 光明日报出版社, 2013).
122. Han Xi 韩曦, *Broadway Troubadour: Tennessee Williams* (*Bailaohui de xingyin shiren* 百老汇的行吟诗人) (Beijing: Qunyan Press 群言出版社, 2013).
123. Jiang, X., 10.
124. C. W. E. Bigsby, "Tennessee Williams: the Theatricalising Self," in *Modern American Drama*, 1945–2000 (Cambridge, UK: Cambridge University Press, 2000), 31–68.
125. See Judith Butler, *Gender Trouble: Feminism and the Subversion of Identity* (New York: Routledge, 2006) and *Bodies That Matter: On the Discursive Limits of "Sex"* (New York: Routledge: 1993).
126. Butler, *Bodies That Matter*, 29.
127. Roger Boxill, *Tennessee Williams* (London and Basingstoke, New York: Macmillan Education, 1987), 36.

128. Maher Moussa, *The Re-Invention of the Self: Performativity and Liberation in Selected Plays by Tennessee Williams*. PhD dissertation (Ann Arbor: Michigan State University, 2001), ii–iii.
129. Ibid.
130. See Jean-Paul Sartre, *Existentialism Is a Humanism*, translated by Carol Macomber (Yale University Press, 2007).
131. Jiang, X, 13–14.
132. Ibid., 241–244.
133. Ibid, 12.
134. See Shouhua Qi and Wei Zhang, "Total Heroism: Reinterpreting Sartre's *Morts sans sépulture* (The Victors) for the Chinese Stage," *Theatre Research International* 44.2 (2019): 171–188.
135. Zhou Weipei 周维培, "Foreword" (*Xuyan* 序言). Han Xi 韩曦, *Broadway Troubadour*, 2.
136. Hang, X., 7.
137. Gao Xianhua 高鲜花, *The Legend of Encouragement and Decadence: The Study of Tennessee Williams and His Drama* (*Lizhi yu tuifei de chuanqi: tiannaxi weiliansi jiqi xiju yanjiu* 励志与颓废的传奇: 田纳西·威廉斯及其戏剧研究) (Beijing: China Theatre Press 中国戏剧出版社, 2019).
138. Liang Zhen 梁真, *The Study on Tennessee Williams from the Perspective of "Heterology"* (*Linglei rensheng: yizhi shiyu xia de Tiannaxi weiliansi yanjiu* 另类人生:异质视域下的田纳西·威廉斯研究) (Ningbo, Zhejiang: Ningbo Publishing House 宁波出版社, 2020).
139. Meng Zhaoyi 孟昭毅, "Foreword 1" (*xuyi* 序一), Gao Xianhua 高鲜花, *The Legend*, 1–3.
140. Kang Ximin 亢西民, "Foreword 2" (*xuer* 序二), Gao Xianhua 高鲜花, *The Legend*, 5–8.
141. Gao, X., 84.
142. Ibid., 85.
143. Ibid., 94.
144. Ibid., 95,
145. Ibid., 105.
146. See TinHouse productions (*Tiepiwu jushe* 铁皮屋剧社), http://www.tinhouseprod.com/index.php?m=content&c=index&a=lists&catid=8.
147. See "Theatre Movement Bazaar," https://theatremovementbazaar.org.
148. For more discussion of this production, see Chap. 4, pp.?
149. Gao, X., 7, 131.
150. Huo Xincun 霍新村, "Chinese Elements in Tennessee Williams Dramatic Works" (*Tiannaxi weiliansi zuopin zhong de zhongguo yuansu* 田纳西·威廉斯作品中的的中国元素), *Northeast Asia Forum* (东北亚外语论坛) 6 (2018): 27–31.
151. Liang, Z., 24.

152. Sarah Elizabeth Johnson, *The Influence of Japanese Traditional Performing Arts on Tennessee Williams Late Plays*, MFA (Master of Fine Arts) thesis (University of Iowa, 2014).
153. Liang, Z., 195.
154. The bibliography section of Liang Zhen's monograph is also a heterogeneous assortment of Williams related primary and secondary sources that appears to be hastily put together and would benefit from at least another round of careful editing/proofreading.
155. See Chap. 6 Conclusion of this book.

CHAPTER 4

Becoming Blanche Dubois: Adapting Tennessee Williams for the Chinese Stage

In 2016, after more than two decades of absence on the Chinese stage, a production of *A Streetcar Named Desire* was mounted in Shanghai by the Shanghai Dramatic Arts Centre. Wang Huan (王欢), translator and director of this production, enthuses that a classic like Williams' *Streetcar* transcends time and space and that it is particularly resonant with China today. In a country that is undergoing dramatic changes, Wang says, where "old social rules are declining and new commercial civilization is in the making," one can find many migrants and misfits in big metropolises such as Shanghai and Beijing, both in the socioeconomic and psychological senses, very much like the main characters in the Williams play.[1] This sentiment, recognizing Williams' characters such as Balance Dubois as amongst "us," if not exactly "us," is such a far cry from the dismissive attitude of some important theatre artists such as Huang Zuolin (黄佐临) in the early 1980s, rejecting them as sick, twisted, faraway American "other."[2] This recognition, long in coming, and Chinese theatrical adaptation of Williams under discussion in this chapter, have to be seen through the lens of the convoluted history of modern Chinese drama/theatre, especially its adaptation and appropriation of Western classics for its cultural and artistic renewal.

S. Qi, *Culture, History, and the Reception of Tennessee Williams in China*, Chinese Literature and Culture in the World, https://doi.org/10.1007/978-3-031-16934-2_4

THEATRICAL ADAPTATION FOR CULTURAL RENEWAL

In some ways, the history of modern Chinese drama/theatre is a history of how Chinese theatre artists adapt and appropriate Western classics for their sociopolitical and cultural needs, from the late 1800s to the twenty-first century, for example, what to adapt and how to adapt, and so on. This is the context in which we should view and assess Chinese adaptation (as well as translation and interpretation, discussed in Chaps. 2 and 3) endeavors with regard to Tennessee Williams.[3]

Chinese early exposure to and encounters with Western drama/theatre began in the decades following the Opium War (1839–1842), as China was forced to open its doors for Westerners to come in and trade and proselytize and for the Chinese—albeit only a small handful, mostly imperial envoys and diplomats sent to Western countries to represent the Qing interest abroad—to go and see the outside world for themselves. Even from outside, looking in, scratching no more than the physically observable surface, these early experiences of Western drama—the differences as compared to traditional Chinese *xiqu*, from the imposing physical structures of theaters to the breathtaking verisimilitude ambience to the perplexingly respectable social status of actors, would register a level of responses that can only be described as cultural shock. Early Chinese encounters with Western drama also took the form of "West cometh to East" through the agency of newspapers, Western expatriates in China, visiting drama troupes, and campus productions at mission colleges in Shanghai and elsewhere.

However, a truly remarkable, momentous development in the history of Chinese drama would be the 1907 adaptations of *La Dame aux Camélias* and *Uncle Tom's Cabin* by young members of the Spring Willow Society in Tokyo, by way of saving China from its perceived moribund fate, awakening the spirit of its people, and renewing its ancient culture, for example, its drama/theatre. This, adapting Western drama for China's national and cultural renewal, was the inspiration for the 1918 special issue of the *New Youth* magazine that gave a full-throated introduction of Henrik Ibsen and "Ibsenism" as (mis)read by Hu Shi and like-minded contemporaries, which harbingered an era, and indeed a movement that appropriated the Western playwright as a champion of sorts, and Nora, the heroine of *A Doll's House*, as a rallying cry, for the cause of women's liberation. It was the same quest for enlightenment and cultural renewal that took a new generation of intellectuals and artists to Western classics as represented by Brecht, Beckett, and Miller in the years immediately after the Cultural Revolution (1966–1976). Experimenting with expressionism, the Epic Theatre, the Theatre of the Absurd, and other ideas and ways of modern and postmodern Western drama/theatre has profoundly changed both the *what* and the *how* in the contemporary Chinese theatre scene. Indeed, although scholars disagree as to whether those bold performances by young Chinese students in Tokyo in 1907 should be credited as the birth cry of *huaju* (spoken drama), and by extension, modern Chinese drama, over a century of reimagining Western classics since then—to reinterpret, to relocate, and to re-create transnationally, transculturally, as well as translingually, mostly through adaptation endeavors—for the Chinese stage bespeaks a history of uneasy convergence of East and West complicated by tensions between divergent sociopolitical forces and cultural proclivities.

Typically, adaptation endeavors assume one of the four modes: fidelity (faithful to the original play in story, structure, and production), indigenization (appropriating the original play as inspiration and raw material to make a new Chinese play, especially in a traditional *xiqu* genre), hybridization (interfusing two distinctive dramatic traditions into the same theatrical event), and experimentation (experimental in story, structure, and production, whether it takes the form of *xiqu*, *huaju*, or a mishmash of the two). In practice, however, there is considerable fluidity among the four modes. As discussed in earlier chapters, Tennessee Williams came to China rather belatedly, in comparison to Eugene O'Neill, Arthur Miller, and other Western contemporaries of his. He remained a stranger, or rather, absent on the Chinese stage for decades until the late 1980s. Of Williams' major plays, Chinese theatre artists have been particularly fascinated with *A Streetcar Named Desire*, a play, despite its "problematic" characters, that seems to have enough dramatic action and tensions, a clear arc of development from exposition to climax to denouement to draw and hold the interest of prospective theatergoers. Its share of star power, especially powerful performances of Marlon Brando and Vivian Leigh in the 1951 film directed by Elia Kazan (a film so well-known in China that almost all Chinese actors portraying Blanche and Stanley would have to try and measure up to), helps too. *The Glass Menagerie* and *Cat on a Hot Tin Roof* have also seen a few productions, but mostly on college campuses.

Indeed, there have been no known professional productions of *Cat on a Hot Tin Roof*. Given the sensitive and challenging subject matter of *Cat*, which has seen only one published translation,[4] and the difference between reading such plays and staging them, one can perhaps speculate why. However, the 2015 Chinese production of Paula Vogel's 1997 play *How I Learned to Drive* should have pushed enough boundaries for plays such as *Cat*. Like Williams' *The Glass Menagerie*, Vogel's *How I Learned to Drive* is also a memory play but features a scrambled chronology that follows Li'l Bit, now in her early 30s, as she revisits memories of her complicated and troubling relationship with Uncle Peck (husband of her maternal aunt), from pre-adolescence through teenage and college years to adulthood, to make sense of what happened during those years: sexual abuse, sexual coming of age, and guilt.[5] It seems that portraying homosexuality on the stage, both opaque and explicit, as in the case of *Cat*, remains a challenge for the Chinese theatre artists.

Compared to the explosion of scholarly interest in the last two decades or so, as discussed in Chap. 3, Williams is somewhat underrepresented on the Chinese stage. However, one cannot say with any degree of certainty that any Western playwright, even Shakespeare,[6] is fully represented on the Chinese stage (or any world stage, for that matter) for the simple reason that Chinese theatre artists have to be highly selective and deliberate when deciding which play to mount for production out of sociocultural, moral, artistic, funding, and box office concerns.

BECOMING BLANCHE DUBOIS: *A STREETCAR NAMED DESIRE*

Tianjin People's Art Theatre Production, 1988[7]

The 1988 production of *A Streetcar Named Desire* by Tianjin People's Art Theatre signified the first major step taken by the Chinese toward understanding and embracing Tennessee Williams on the stage. It was a partnership of strangers, so to speak, that is, a British director and Chinese cast and crew mounting a play created by an American playwright about people the Chinese had a hard time relating to.

In spring 1986, while visiting London, Liang Bolong (梁伯龙), a Central Academy of Drama (Beijing) professor of acting, had a chance to see a production of Chekhov's *Three Sisters* directed by Mike Alfreds (1934–). Impressed with the production and the best director award Alfreds would receive later that year (for directing Chekhov's *Cherry Orchard*), Liang, through the Sino-British Cultural Association, extended an invitation to the British director on behalf of Tianjin People's Art Theatre and would serve as his interpreter during his stay in China in

1988. It is not clear though whether Liang's invitation was also inspired by the recent successful production of *Death of a Salesman* in Beijing directed by Arthur Miller (1983), which was followed by a successful production of Eugene O'Neill's *Anna Christie* directed by George C. White (1984).[8] What is clear is that 1988, right on the eve of dramatic events on Tiananmen Square that would rock the country and shape the direction it would be going for decades to come, was a year when all kinds of ideas were being voiced and different movements, artistic as well sociopolitical, were fermenting restlessly. For Mike Alfreds, the invitation from China would provide an opportunity to realize a lifetime dream of his: to direct a production of *A Streetcar Named Desire*, a play intimately associated with names such as Elia Kazan, Laurence Olivier, Jessica Tandy, Marlon Brando, Vivien Leigh, among others. All the stars seemed perfectly aligned for Alfreds to pursue an artistic "new continent," as he would put it during an interview with Liang Bolong, who also provided a Chinese translation of the play for the production[9]—an interesting joint cultural venture of an American playwright, a British director, and Chinese cast and crew.[10]

In a way, Tianjin, a major port city in northeastern China (opened up as a treaty port not long after the First Opium War, 1839–1842), about 80 miles southeast of Beijing, seemed a perfect setting for *A Streetcar Named Desire* originally set in the port city of New Orleans. In its days Tianjin saw the establishment of foreign concessions (by the British, Americans, Russians, Japanese, Germans, etc.), destruction of wars (e.g., the battle of Tianjin during the 1900 Boxer Rebellion), and its share of the wretched—migrants, transients, and prostitutes struggling for existence although the "scarred" history of the city might not have been on the mind of Alfreds, Liang, and Tianjin People's Art Theatre as they set their sight on *A Streetcar named Desire* for their joint cultural venture.

By this time in China, "reform and opening up" had been going on for more than ten years. Although the realist mode, a blend of the nineteenth-century realism associated with Ibsen and Stanislavski, was still the dominant mode on the theatre scene, Chinese theatre artists had begun to explore and experiment with other forms of theatrical representation. They had already staged, among other things, Brecht's *Life of Galileo* (1979), *The Caucasian Chalk Circle* (1985), Sartre's *Dirty Hands* (1981), Ibsen's *Peer Gynt* (1983), and Miller's *The Crucible* (1981) and *Death of a Salesman* (1983) and (re)introduced the Theatre of the Absurd as associated with Beckett and Ionesco.[11] Artistically, however, this 1988 production was not as venturous as one might have expected. It was very much in the "fidelity" mode, taking no bold creative license to reinterpret Williams' play or to remake it to appeal to the Chinese audiences. The challenge, as Alfreds saw it, was how to help the Chinese actors, such as Chang Ruyan (an accomplished actor cast for the role of Blanche DuBois) and Lü Yi (an actor with a "muscular and sinewy" physique not unlike that of Marlon Brando, cast for the role of Stanley Kowalski) to fully under-stand the complex socioeconomics and psychologies of the main charac-ters and give authentic, full-throated representations on the stage.[12]

Under Alfreds' guidance, Chang Ruyan eventually came to a fuller appreciation of Blanche as a complex, colorful, many-faceted character instead of being either good or bad, heroine or victim as the Chinese had been accustomed to representing and seeing on the stage: Blanche is well cultured, sensitive, vulnerable, snobbish, manipulative, hypocritical—all of these and perhaps more. Chang took on the challenge of putting "all these Blanches together" into "one real Blanche" on the stage and by all accounts succeeded. Chang's Blanche, dressed in white hat, white coat, and white gloves, "gossamer and dainty, vulnerable, yet dangerous," flut-ters in the home of her sister Stella and brother-in-law Stanley, all fur-nished in white, too, her white fragility brutally exposed under intense stage lighting. Lü Yi's Stanley, dressed in red silk pajamas, exuding palpa-ble animal vitality, proves "a worthy rival to Brando as Blanche's sexually hungry predator" and executioner. As reported by the *Tianjin Workers Daily*, when the play ended on the opening night, enthusiastic applauding lasted for more than nine minutes; the audience was reluctant to leave even after the actors had received three curtain calls. The show traveled to Beijing later that year to perform during the First Chinese Drama Festival and was equally warmly received there.

The 1980s amounted to a heyday of Chinese adaptations of Western classics, heralded by the 1979 adaptation of Brecht's *Life of Galileo* and followed by Shakespeare's *Merchant of Venice* (1980–1982), Sartre's *Dirty Hands* (1981), Miller's *Death of a Salesman* (1983), Brecht's *The Caucasian Chalk Circle* (1985); Sophocles' *Oedipus the King* (1986); Beckett's *Waiting for Godot* (1987); Euripides' *Medea* (1989), and rounded up by Shakespeare's *Hamlet* (1990, directed by Lin Zhaohua (林兆华), a production loaded with explicit and opaque sociopolitical signifi-cance[13]). In contrast, the 1990s, at least according to some Chinese schol-ars, represented a lull in this regard, with no significant, noteworthy adaptation endeavors, partly due to complicated sociopolitical, cultural, and economic reasons. This seems particularly the case with Williams. For the entire decade, there was only one known production of *The Glass Menagerie* staged by Shenyang Spoken Drama Troupe in 1994, of which there is no known media coverage or reviews. There seems a big gap or disconnect between Tennessee Williams' scholarship and theatrical productions.[14]

With the decriminalization of homosexual sex in 1997 and its removal from the list of mental disorders in 2001 by the Chinese Society of Psychiatry, there was an explosion of scholarly interest in Williams. Many journal articles and graduate theses began to pay attention to homosexual themes in Williams plays too, including that of *A Streetcar Named Desire*.[15] This would pave the way for more notable productions in the twenty-first century, for example, campus production at Shanghai Theatre Academy (2002, to be discussed in the next segment), physical theatre production (2014), and productions by Shanghai Dramatic Arts Centre (2016–).

Poker Night Blues: *A Physical Theatre Production 2014*

In 2014, after more than two decades of absence on the Chinese stage via professional productions, *Poker Night Blues* (*Zhipai ye bulusi* 纸牌夜布鲁斯), a physical theatre adaptation of *Streetcar*, was staged by Beijing TinHouse Productions (*Beijing tiepi wu jushe*北京铁皮屋剧社),[16] a young company founded in 2013, and the Theatre Movement Bazaar[17] based in Los Angeles. This was a joint, intercultural endeavor: director/choreographer, Tina Kronis; playwright, Richard Alger; producers, Li Yanda and Pan Yi, featuring an all-Chinese cast/ensemble: Chen Haihua as Blanche, Yang Bin as Stanley, Xu Jingqian as Stella, Fang Yiheng as Mitch, performed in Chinese with English supertitles.[18]

According to Tina Kronis, artistic director of the Theatre Movement Bazaar and director/choreographer of the 2014 production, she has been keenly interested in reinterpreting and deconstructing classics using cadence, humor, and feelings that we can resonate with today, exploring and tapping potential physical theatre elements to appeal to audiences today. She is not interested in replicating the original Broadway production or the 1952 film production directed by Elia Kazan. As a physical theatre production with minimal dialogue, this 2014 production can be said to be both faithful and subversive to Williams' play in trying to create something new, even with the choice of its title, *Poker Night Blues*, resurrecting Williams' original title for the play but adding a rich twist of "blues," a quintessential American music to give the production a motif that recurs and ambience that permeates the production. The production also interjects humor, both verbal and nonverbal, into the performance to surprise and entertain the audiences not only because there are comic elements in the classic text, but also because in real life comedy and tragedy come hand in hand; there is tragedy in comedy and comedy in tragedy.[19]

With Salsa-Latino music setting the rhythm, the stage set evokes the period with vintage radio and telephone, dresses, jackets, hats (although actors do not have on wigs and makeup to look more American/Western, a problem Chinese theatre artists sometimes have to wrestle with even today, as is the case of the production of *Raisin in the Sun* in 2020[20]) and the performance presents a dynamic, enriching experience of East and West: Chinese bamboo pole dancing; American Jazz, Charleston, Tango; acrobatics; stylized fights; heightened hyper-realist acting style from Chinese performance tradition, and so on. Chinese actors, according to Tina Kronis, have very good training and ability to adapt to and rise to new challenges thanks to their training in *jingju* (Peking opera) performing art. Although the original play was written in the 1940s America, its topical and thematic elements, such as love, family, power, resonate with Chinese culture and society today, especially when we extrapolate the most essential elements from the play (without unduly emphasizing its Americanness).

If measured against the Blanche as embodied by Vivian Leigh and others, Chen Haihua's Blanche may look a bit too innocent and inexperienced when she first arrives on stage the opening night December 19, 2014, at 77 Theatre (77剧场[21]), more like a young college graduate than a faded southern belle who has suffered more than her share of the slings of life. That innocence or naivete, however, turns out to be only a deceptively thin veneer. This Blanche has no speech for several minutes and can only express herself via physical performance, but she proves to be quite capable in expressing herself being torn between powerful forces of body and soul, kindheartedness and pretentiousness, and dream and despair The narrative is played out through a fast paced, flowing series of dramatized scenes, with occasional breakdown of the fourth wall, for example, Fang Yiheng/Mitch singing the 1943 no. 1 hit, "Paper Doll" ("I'm gonna buy a paper doll that I can call my own /A doll that other fellows cannot steal."[22]), a surprise turn for the audiences, which seems both thematically appropriate and entertaining.

The production travelled to the Edinburgh Festival in 2015, continuing its transcultural journey. One reviewer, at least, feels enriched by seeing this production:[23]

> I leave the theatre feeling that I know Tennessee Williams' play a little better—particularly enjoying the investigation of gender stereotypes (Eastern and Western) in this production. But I also feel that I've been in the hands of a creative team who are in control of their material, and not afraid to use the mores of popular culture in the telling of their tale.

Earlier, in October of that same year in Beijing, Theatre Movement Bazaar had staged their adaptation of Chekhov's *Three Sisters*, a play that Beijing theatergoers should be familiar with, at least via Lin Zhaohua's 1998 experimental adaptation *Three Sisters Waiting for Godot*.[24] Under the new title *Track 3*,[25] this new physical theatre adaptation mixes movement, dance, song, and humor and relocates the nineteenth-century Russian story to the twenty-first century wherein the characters are stranded, waiting and wanting something outside of themselves to give them happiness.

Although it did not garner as much international attention, the 2015 Beijing TinHouse and Theatre Movement Bazaar joint production *Poker Night Blues* reminds one of the 2011 production of *Streetcar* in Paris (*Un Tramway Nommé Désir*) directed by Lee Breuer (1937–2021), founding co-artistic director of Mabou Mines Theatre Company,[26] the first American play to be staged in the storied and proud Comédie Française. Noteworthy, as far as the subject of this book is concerned, is that fact that this Lee Breuer production incorporates considerable Japanese elements in creating "a fantasy world of sliding Japanese screens painted with menacing waterfalls and warriors, masked kurogo figures in black, and a longhaired Stanley in baggy pants and a satin tiger."[27] It seems that any audacious endeavor trying to blend different cultural and art forms into the same production would inevitably invite mixed responses. Nonetheless, "the intended marriage of all the creativity of Mabou Mines with all the traditions of the Comédie Française," one reviewer says, "could have ended like the collision of a sportscar and a freight train but this *Streetcar* never belches smoke or even loses steam."[28]

Shanghai Dramatic Arts Centre, 2016–

Two years after *Poker Night Blues*, Shanghai Dramatic Arts Centre, a professional theatrical company based in Shanghai and founded in 1995 after the merger of the Shanghai People's Art Theatre (上海人民艺术剧院, second probably only to the famed Beijing People's Art Theatre) and the Shanghai Youth Drama Troupe (上海青年话剧团), put out a noteworthy production of *Streetcar*.[29]

According to Wang Huan, translator and director of this production, who has a master's degree from the Royal Academy of Dramatic Art (London), a classic like Williams' play transcends time and space, but it is particularly resonant with China today. As alluded to at the opening of this chapter, Wang Huan believes that given the profound, transformative changes China has been undergoing, Chinese theatergoers should be able to resonate with and even see amongst themselves the kind of socioeconomic and psychological migrants and misfits as portrayed in Williams' plays.[30] Indeed, by 2016, China had already passed Japan to become the second largest economy in the world and the newest economic superpower.[31] However, although living standards for the Chinese people have seen significant improvement compared to the recent past, China's per capital income ($3600 vs. $46,000 in the US) is not much better than many less developed nations in the world. One of the important forces that contributed to this robust economic growth was internal migration, one of the most extensive in the world history. Hundreds of millions since 1979 have migrated from poor and rural regions to the metropolises such as Beijing, Shanghai, Guangzhou, Tianjin, Shenzhen, and many other cities, doing much of the heavy lifting for the economic boom although they are often excluded from local educational, housing, and welfare resources.[32] They are socioeconomic and psychological "migrants and misfits" in the modern cities they have helped build and are still building.

"Intrigued by the fate of ordinary people," Wang chose to downplay the American socioeconomic and cultural specifics of the play and focus on the human story.[33] Wang's *Streetcar* is lyrical, dreamy (or rather, nightmarish), and haunting, thanks to the noticeable touches of expressionism in its stagecraft, for example, big translucent white curtain fluttering in the backdrop; real rain drizzling or pouring down on both stage left and stage right (not a cleansing rain that washes away sins and the checkered past, but a repressive, ominous rain reminiscent of Hemingway's *A Farewell to Arms*); massive steam puffed onto stage; lighting that can shield or mercilessly expose; and rather moody theme music. It is also realistic, for example, bedding, table and chairs, even brutally naturalistic, especially in the final confrontation between Blanche (Xu Manman) and Stanley (Liu Xuanrui). It is a fairy tale that has gone awry; an urban legend loaded with tragic ethos and pathos.

The curtain rises, revealing a small apartment messily furnished and featuring a black TV set and a small refrigerator (modern gadgets indicating that the Kowalskis, though blue-collar working class, is doing fine socioeconomically before Blanche enters their world), and a few lights. Blanche enters stage right, as real as ethereal, like a ghost from another realm. She puts on a cape and a hat from the clothes stand, assumes the full vibe of a Southern belle, and is ready to face herself, to face the Kowalskis, and indeed to face the brave new world of New Orleans:[34]

> They told me to take a streetcar named Desire, and then transfer to one called Cemeteries and ride six blocks and get off at—Elysian Fields!

Wang Huan's adaptation, faithful to the original in both spirit and story development, takes considerable creative license in compressing the scenes (e.g., the opening scene in which Stanley tosses Stellar a piece of meat for her to catch) and streamlining characters (dispensing minor characters such as Eunice, the young collector, the negro woman, and the Mexican woman) so that the Chinese audiences, mostly young and college educated as they are, could follow and appreciate. Gone are also the Doctor and the Matron who in the original play appear near the end to take Blanche to the mental institution: "The gravity of their profession is exaggerated—the unmistakable aura of the state institution with its cynical detachment."[35] The "peculiarly sinister figure" of the matronly nurse does not step into the apartment to pinion Blanche's arms and handle her roughly. There is no sudden personalizing and indeed humanizing metamorphosis of the authoritative doctor either who speaks to the terrified Blanche softly, helps her up, "supports her with his arm and leads her through the portieres."[36] In Wang Huan's production, Blanche leaves by herself, much as she entered, her hands reaching out to the imaginary figures of the doctor and nurse in the semi-darkness offstage on the right, as massive steam being puffed onto stage, accompanied by the theme music—tender, moody, and ominous at the same time.

What has happened before this denouement scene is the final confrontation between Blanche and Stanley, merciless, brutal, dealing one last lethal blow on the fragilized psyche of a desperate Blanche. It is expressionistically framed and acted out as naturalistically as one could imagine or take.

Having been abandoned by Mitch, the onetime hope of escape, security, and perhaps love, Blanche knows that her game is over and she has to leave. As she hurriedly packs, stuffing the old relics—her real and fabricated history and her fragmented self—back into the suitcase, talking to herself, she suddenly jumps on a table, her figure silhouetted against the white translucent backdrop, spreading out her long limbs and indeed her wings, fluttering like a big, dark butterfly, indomitable, hauntingly beautiful, yet doomed.

It is at this moment that Stanley returns from the hospital. What ensues is the last battle between them, between the sexes, between a fading Southern belle (cultured, delicate, tenuously clinging to the falsehood of a romanticized past and a bygone world that has collapsed on her head) and a new urban male, raw, animalistic in physique and appetite, who moves shrewdly, leopard-like, on the perceived threat to the life, the love nest he has worked hard to build, on his prey. The beer bottle Blanche smashes on the table, clutching its broken top to defend herself as Stanley, having decided to "interfere with" her, moves on her, is as real as described in the original play, and as in the 1951 film adaptation starring Vivien Leigh and Marlon Brando. What happens next is not a "date," as Stanley sees it ("We've had this date with each other from the beginning!")[37] but a violent sexual assault: he carries the inert body of a crushed Blanche to the table (not the "bed" as in the original), lifts her skirt, spreads her still struggling yet "loosening" legs (one thinks of W. B. Yeats' "Leda and the Swan"), destroying the last remnants of her dignity. The stage darkens in time to shield the audiences from any more of the heartrending, horrific sight.

By now the audiences should have seen enough of the brutality to question whether anyone has the right to destroy another person's cocoon of falsehoods (to protect his or her fragilized psyche and sanity) and impose one's own ugly truths, half-truths—even when it seems to be justified—on him or her. The full three-hour performance (7:30 to 10:30), with no intermission, ends with the ghostly figure of Blanche, having recovered some resemblance of her former self, walking toward the imaginary doctor and nurse, leaving behind Stanley with his poker buddies (including Mitch), and her sister Stella. What will happen to Blanche? Will the love nest—or madhouse—of the Kowalskis go on as if nothing has happened? What, if any, "Chinese philosophy" Stella has cultivated will sustain her and enable her to continue to live under the same roof, and indeed in the same bed, with Stanley?

In a way this 2016 production of *Streetcar* is the "kindest" reinterpretation of all the productions discussed in this chapter thanks to its de-emphasis on the Americanness of the story and its highlighting instead universal humanness of the tragedy. It is a production that is based on a recognition that there are millions of migrants and misfits amongst us, in both social and psychological senses of the terms, and that such conflicts, which sometimes end in tragedies, happen every day because our desires and volitions sometimes run collusion courses. It is rooted in the human condition. As one reviewer put it, although we cannot bring ourselves to like any of the characters in the play and although we try to remind ourselves that what we see on the stage is make-believe, the power of the story, as retold by the theatre artists in this production, does get to us and arouse deep, indescribable, and heartfelt sympathy for each of them for his or her wretched existence,[38] including Stanley who may not have been as fully portrayed, with nuances, as in the original play.[39] It inspires us to transcend barriers, socioeconomic, cultural, linguistic, ideological, and otherwise and see others not as "strangers," but as ourselves, and be just a bit kinder to each other, or at least, as a "pessimistically optimistic" Wang Huan put it, to have a bit more "tolerance and acceptance" in our society.[40]

Wang Huan's *Streetcar* traveled to Beijing, Hangzhou, and other cities in 2017, 2018, and 2019 to spread the "gospel" of tolerance, acceptance, and kindness, and after a hiatus in 2020 due to the COVID-19 pandemic, resumed its journey in the summer of 2021 with another production.[41] What has changed over the last several years? For Wang Huan, the biggest change is that he now is in a position to be honest and true to himself and refuse to do what he doesn't want to do, to achieve a certain degree of "freedom": he doesn't mind working his heart out for what he wants to do, but would hate to do what he doesn't want to do. It is with this new, zen-like frame of mind that Wang took on *Streetcar* again, with the same passion, sorrow, and expectance. Five years ago, *Streetcar* felt like a storm and Wang was shaken by its cruelty and destructive power; five years later today, he would still be shaken emotively, but feels more empowered to have some distance and perspective to view it, like Chernobyl disaster that happened in 1986 (although Wang, as well as his crew and cast, and indeed the world are still in the midst of a pandemic that feels like a nightmare that has lasted for more than a year and half and still refuses to wake up):[42]

When mankind is disabled by our ignorance, nature has to take over everything. From this macro-worldview, it is meaningless and even naïve to pursue "perfection." The only thing we have the "sanctity" to do is to try and restore "wholeness."

To restore the "wholeness," Wang, during the rehearsal, sometimes found himself using a hammer to knock off some paint from the fridge and bathtub and make them look more used and rustier: beer bottles, rotary dial phones, wrinkled dollar bills, old fridges. He wanted the characters as portrayed by his actors, worn out by life, show their essential human essence. He even put an electronic remote-controlled moth inside the paper lantern to symbolically augment the sense of being doomed yet still struggling for another shot at happiness and indeed life for the scene between Blanche and Mitch on the Poker Night, when they open up to each other and seem to be connecting at some deep emotive and existential level. As ever before, Wang sees himself as a pessimistic idealist, disheartened by how intolerant people can be yet still hoping for more kindness toward each other:

> Characters portrayed by Tennessee Williams are complex and contradictory: There is affectation in sincerity, baseness in nobility, tenderness in malice, and vulgarity in chasteness. The hardest thing to do is to face ourselves honestly. Tennessee Williams tries to tear down "darkness" in dramatic works but do not indulge in presenting and protesting "darkness," hoping to lead us out of it.

That is the kind of "pessimistic idealism" Wang has tried to hold on to during the last five years.

This summer 2021 production has a brand-new cast of actors, each having his/her own take on Williams and the role he/she is to represent on the stage.[43] Zhao Sihan, cast in the role of Blanche, sees her character as someone who is naïve in believing that she can find the past, the lost glory of the old south because of who she is and what she loves (e.g., poetry); she does not understand that for each progress mankind makes there is a corresponding fall; she has been through cycles of life and death; she doesn't even know the difference between sex and love and is dumbfounded by how her sister could go back to her husband and sleep together (like a pair of lovebirds) after such a fight; her tragedy, therefore, is both accidental and inevitable. Echoing what Wang Huan, director of the production, has said, Zhao feels that we may not find people exactly like Blanche in the world we live today, yet what she embodies persists. He Yi, cast in the role of Stanley, insists that he is anything but Stanley in real life ("Thou dost protest too much," one may say to him. Who is anyway? Marlon Brando? Or rather, who isn't, albeit to varying degrees?). He Yi thinks that Stanley lives too much like an animal, aggressive, crude, lording it over everything and everyone whereas he, tender-hearted, soft-mannered, polite, is content with whatever little he has. Yet, his friends think he is a Stanley look-alike and he wants to present a "living" Stanley on the stage. Wei Lai, cast in the role of Stella, thinks of her character as a rebel of sorts who leaves home to pursue her own life and thinks she is saved by the man who takes her into a completely different world; Stella is content with a life of domesticity and physical intimacy, hangs on to that life despite being a battered woman, eventually betrays her sister, and therefore, like her sister, is doomed to tragedy. Xu Zihao, cast in the role of Mitch, thinks of his character as a deer that lingers by the edge of the "white woods" (Blanche Dubois) briefly and then goes on his way; the woods, deep, comes to life again, full of vitality, thanks to the deer who is thoughtful, tender, yet dull, boring, and even crude at the same time, full of contradictions, like everyone else in and outside the play; Mitch loves the idea of loving someone like Blanche, out of his league, but in the end, when the image both he and Blanche have conspired to conjure up collapses, Mitch retreats to the baser self and could love no one but himself.

The same play written by Tennessee Williams in 1947, the same Chinese director (albeit with a different cast), the same stage design and props— old TV set, old fridge, rain pouring down on both sides of the stage, the same ambience of desperate dream, desire, and doom—yet so much has happened and changed in China and indeed in the world since 2016; yet much remains the same.[44]

Guangzhou Spoken Drama Centre, 2020

In October 2020, as the COVID-19 pandemic raged on, Guangzhou Spoken Drama Centre put out an excerpt of *Streetcar*, as part of its classics series, a virtual theatre production with live audience interactions/comments.[45] Interesting enough, of the 11 scenes of *Streetcar*, the drama center chose Scene 9, when Blanche and Stanley have gone to the hospital and Mitch comes to confront Blanche about her past.

As the curtain rises for this short production (19 minutes, including one and half minutes of introduction to set up the scene for the audiences), we see Blanche, or rather her Chinese reincarnation, Bai Lanqi (白兰琪 White Orchid Jade), center stage, drinking and smoking at a small table loaded with full or empty bottles of Chinese liquor. Soon, Mitch, or Xiao Hai (小海 Little Sea), bespectacled, knocks on the door. Stanley becomes Zhao Xueqiang (赵学强 Zhao Studying Power) when he "appears" in the dialogues between Bai Lanqi and Xiao Hai; Allan becomes Ai Lun (艾伦); the merchant Kiefaber, a source of information of Bai Lanqi's past, is now Wang Hongwei (王宏伟 Wang Magnificent); Shaw, another informant, is now Li Baoliang (李宝亮 Li Treasure Glittering). All of these are possible, legitimate Chinese names. Even Flamingo, the hotel in Laurel where Bai Lanqi supposedly had stayed and scandalized the whole town, becomes Bai Yulan (白玉兰 White Magnolia) or Du Zhizhu (毒蜘蛛 Poisonous Spider) as Blanche calls it ("Flamingo? No! Tarantula was the name of it! I stayed at a hotel called the Tarantula Arms! … a big spider! That's where I brought my victims"[46]).

Apparently, this is a Sinicized adaptation that relocates the story to present-day China, which makes it, short as it is, more interesting and more relevant in the sense that the tragic story of Blanche could happen just about anywhere, including today's China. The two actors cast for the roles of Blanche/Bai Lanqi and Mitch/Xiao Hai are completely absorbed in the story they are telling on the stage, as if this was a full production in a physical theatre packed with audiences. Near the very end of the show, when Mitch/Xiao Hai, in a moment of pent-up frustration and desire, pushes Blanche/Bai Lanqi onto the small makeshift bed not far from the table, trying to get on top her, much more violently than being described in the Williams' play ("fumbling to embrace her"[47]), it reminds one of the scene toward the end of the play when Stanley attacks and rapes Blanche. Indeed, one wonders what a full production of the play by the Guangzhou Spoken Drama Centre would be like. It would certainly be different from the production staged by the Shanghai Dramatic Arts Centre, as directed by Wang Huan, as it should be. Members of the audience, while streaming the show, condemn Mitch/Xiao Hai as crude, rude, hypocritical, and ungentlemanly; they are sympathetic to Blanche/Bai Lanqi because, despite her weaknesses and flaws, "she has been living in a meat grinder and everyone else is a knife").

WHEN LESS IS NOT MORE? *THE GLASS MENAGERIE*

Another major play by Williams, *The Glass Menagerie*, has seen a few Chinese productions too. One notable production was also mounted by the Shanghai Dramatic Arts Centre in 2015 and 2016. It was directed by David Esbjornson, an American director and producer.[48] This is a classic *huaju* (spoken drama) adaptation in the sense that other than the language and actors being Chinese, it felt the same as any respectable productions seen in America and elsewhere. Believing in the "global" and "timeless" significance of the play, Esbjornson did not try to update or remake the play for the China of the twenty-first century. There was no attempt to indigenize, hybridize, or experiment with anything bold. Esbjornson said he would have taken much more creative license if it had been a Shakespearean play.

Esbjornson understands though that there are real cultural differences between him and the cast and tried to learn Chinese views and values in family, love and social taboos, but he insists that the significance of *The Glass Menagerie* is not limited to times or countries. Zhu Jie, cast in the role of Laura, however, thinks that the Chinese way of thinking wouldn't fit *Glass* and she would have to try to switch to the American way of thinking (although a person's way of thinking and behavior are deeply ingrained in the culture one is born and raised through long exposure, immersion, ritualized practice, and so on; it is not something that can be switched on and off easily). Song Ruihui, an award-winning actor cast for the role of Amanda, says that when she first got the script and read it, she could not even imagine what an American mother is like, let alone portraying her on the stage.[49]

To achieve some effect of the kind of timelessness he envisioned for the production, Esbjornson simplified the stage design, for example, dispensing with the two walls and curtains between the rooms for the Wingfield apartment as described in the original, whose loss (walls and curtains symbolizing emotional isolation of the family members) is compensated by the use of lighting.

There is now more fluidity in the dramatic space on the stage. Moreover, Esbjornson removed the "blown-up photograph of the father" supposed to be hanging on the wall of the living room, a move, unexplained, that considerably weakens the thematic as well as emotive tapestry of the play and dilutes its socio-historical and psychological significance, especially in the portrayal of the character of Tom Wingfield.

The actors performed to the best of their abilities. However, something seems lacking in this production. For one Chinese reviewer at least, it is the production's lack of "imagination" or "fantasy" (幻想).[50] According to this reviewer, illusion occupies a central place in the play, from the moment Tom enters stage, in the dual role of character and narrator, in this "memory" play:[51]

> Yes, I have tricks in my pocket, I have things up my sleeve. But I am the opposite of a stage magician. He gives you illusion that has the appearance of truth. I give you truth in the pleasant disguise of illusion.

All the characters in the play—Tom, Laura, Amanda, and even Jim, the gentleman caller, and the absent father figure, "a telephone man who fell in love with long distances," the shadow of his legacy hanging over the entire play—each live in his/her imaginary, fantasy world. By removing Mr. Wingfield's portrait, the door and window, and so on, this production may gain in "abstractness" but loses in the thematic and emotive depth and complexity. The actors, trying as hard as they did, seem to remain outside the American story they were trying to tell.

COLLEGE CAMPUS PRODUCTIONS

Chinese exposure to/experience with Western classics began on college campuses in the late 1800s and early 1900s. So, in so many ways, college campuses have always been on the forefront of transcultural experiences and encounters on the dramatic/theatrical scene.[52]

One of the earliest Chinese encounters with Western drama occurred on the campuses of mission schools set up by Western missionaries in the post-Opium War decades when their proselytizing activities were protected by treaties and law. In Shanghai alone, thousands of young Chinese were attending mission colleges. For example, St. John's University (*Shengyuehan*), a well-known Anglican university founded by American missionaries in 1879, provided a vibrant setting for the Chinese to experience Western drama both on and off stage, especially during its annual commencement exercises in July as the closing events and during the Christmas and holiday season near the end of the year. The annual commencement exercises at St. John's University saw students performing acts or scenes from *Julius Caesar* (1899), *Hamlet* (1901), *Merchant of Venice*

(1902), *Henry VIII* (1904), *As You Like It* (1906), and *The Taming of the Shrew* (1907).

College campus performances are very important in the history of modern Chinese drama. Some scholars have argued that student performances at Nankai University in Tianjin in the early decades of the twentieth century contributed significantly to the development of *huaju* and modern Chinese *xiju*. The new drama endeavors at this university included translations, adaptations, and performances of Westerns classics by Shakespeare, Wilde, Ibsen, and O'Neill. What young Nankai *Xin jushe* (new drama society) members saw in classic Western drama were powerful presentations of the inner realities—confusions and conflicts people experience when caught in the machines of modern times. Among Western classics adapted by Nankai University drama enthusiasts are Wilde's *Salomé*, Hauptmann's *The Weavers*, Ibsen's *An Enemy of the People*, Molière's *Tartuffe* and *The Miser*, and Galsworthy's *Strife*. In addition to Nankai University, campus drama activities at quite a few other universities, such as Fudan and Jiaotong in Shanghai, Qinghua (Tsinghua), Yanjing (Yenching), and Women's Normal University in Beijing, Southeastern (*Dongnan daxue*) in Nanjing, and Soochow (*Dongwu daxue*) in Suzhou, all contributed to the growth of modern Chinese drama. One of the most notable adaptations of Ibsen during those early decades is the May 5, 1923, performance of *A Doll's House*, under the Chinese title *Nala* (娜拉 Nora), by students of Peking Normal College for Women to commemorate the fourth anniversary of the May Fourth Movement. This early performance of the Ibsen play, based on a "faithful" Chinese translation still well-acclaimed today, is particularly significant because it was staged by young female students of one of the earliest women's colleges in a country where "Ignorance is a woman's virtue" (*nǚzi wu cai bian shi de* 女子无才便是德) and other such repressive "teachings" had held sway for millennia, and where lawful access to basic, elementary education for girls, let alone higher education, had not been won until only a decade or so before. About ten years later, in 1935, government officials in Nanjing, capital city of the Nationalist Government, tried to shut down another performance of *A Doll's House* staged by a normal school because they found the play morally corrupting; they fired the young teacher who performed the leading role Nora and banned all schools in the city from hiring her.[53]

Fast forward to the 1980s, the decade immediately after the Cultural Revolution (1966–1976) was over. In 1987, the graduating class at

Shanghai Theatre Academy staged a production of *Waiting for Godot*, a first in China which caught considerable attention from news media, theatre artists and critics, as well as the French Consul General in Shanghai. It was standing room only at the 1000-seat Changjiang Theatre on the Yellow River Road, formally the Carlton Theatre founded by the British in 1923, with an impressive run of 20 public performances. Another notable college campus production of *Waiting for Godot* was originally scheduled for December 31, 1989, as part of Meng Jinghui's master's degree program requirements at the Central Drama Academy in Beijing. But 1989 turned out to be an eventful year for the country[54] and the performance was shut down at the last minute. But the young theatre artist did not give up and staged his production in 1991 by way of reconfirming his belief 'in our existence' and his determination that "we shall never try to find any excuse for falling prey to the temptations of servitude, that we shall never become an ornament in the scenery of falsehood and affectations, that we shall never let our body and soul suffer the plight of weakening as we run for life."[55]

Several of Tennessee Williams plays, including *Summer and Smoke*, *Cat on a Hot Tin Roof*, *The Glass Menagerie*, and *A Streetcar Named Desire* have seen college campus productions, with *Streetcar* being the most popular of them all.

Summer and Smoke

Interesting enough, the first known (albeit not well publicized) college campus production of Tennessee Williams plays, or rather, the first known production of Williams plays in China by amateurs and professional theatre artists alike, was *Summer and Smoke* (*Xiari yanyun* 夏日烟云) staged by Class 85 acting students at Beijing Film Academy in 1986.[56]

Not much else is available today about this campus production other than what its director, Professor Li Ranran (李苒苒),[57] herself a well-known actor, says by way of introducing *Summer and Smoke* to the prospective theatergoers:[58]

> In this small circle of silver light, a group of people live in a country far away from ours, from our own time. They struggle in the limited time they have, trying desperately to light up their lives, pitiably short as they are under the infinitely vast sky, so they will sparkle. They entreat, they long, they hope … they walk to and fro in their long skirts, looking so strange, so faraway yet so familiar as if we have met him or her before, somewhere….

The most precious word in the entire world is—*ren* (human); *ren* is different from any other species; *ren* is the life endowed with noble spirits and therefore should not suffer from inhuman constraints and oppression. *Ren* should live, love, and be loved like *ren* although *ren* should also be ready to bear endless misery.

I love this monumental work by the great playwright Tennessee Williams. His passion, subtle, deep from his heart, hot like fire, attracts me, moves me, and inspires us in this collective creative project of ours.

If, when this small circle of silver light is out and the crowds are gone, there still lingers some quiet thinking and reflection, it would be our greatest satisfaction.

This is the earliest (known) full-throated celebration of Tennessee Williams without the usual cautionary note, as was the case of Ying Ruocheng, Guo Jide, and Wang Yiqun discussed in Chap. 3. One could still feel the palpable excitement and heartfelt celebration of essential humanness, humanist spirit liberated from the "puritanical" repression of the Cultural Revolution which ended ten years before.

Another interesting thing about this production is that there was no published Chinese translation of the play (as there is still none even today). Li and her team would have to resort to an in-house translation somehow. This would also be the case when students at the Communications University of China (based in Beijing) staged a production of *Summer and Smoke* in 2009.[59] Like its precursor back in 1986, there was not much publicity promoting this three-hour production directed by Chen Zidu (陈子度), who had by then directed the productions of quite a few Chinese and Western plays.[60] One of the audience members felt that *Summer and Smoke*, as staged via this campus production, is a "still waters runs deep" kind of play which dramatizes deep and fiery moral and emotive struggle, especially in Alma, despite the not so particularly intense plot; he felt that this play could serve as a lesson to young people about the tensions between flesh and soul, material and spirit in romantic relationships. The lesson he learned, or rather, he wanted the female audience members to learn (from his biased male perspective), goes like this:[61]

Women, if you love, just say so honestly. Please do not hide or camouflage it; do not wait till it is too late, like Alma, and regret for the rest of your lives. Women always like to be mysteries for men to puzzle out; however, if such puzzling goes on for too long and becomes too much, men will not play anymore. Also, please do not be obsessed with spirit at the expense of flesh.

> None of us are Plato and Plato himself, I believe, did not have a happy love life … Indeed, if I had to choose, I'd choose Nellie Ewell too [as John Buchanan, Jr. did].

The response of another male audience member seemed more cathartic than moralistic, and less gender biased (despite seeing the same production through the same male gaze):[62]

> The three-hour performance was tender, impassioned, and sometimes over-powering … I saw several female audiences moved to tears, which shows how touching it was in the theatre. I want this post to be the record of this illuminating thought that came to my mind then and there: Art is such a beautiful thing. When we are all so engrossed in our work and life's struggle, cracking our brains for ideas, we should take a break and come and enjoy a play like this: it is so refreshing, so relaxing, and so transcending [the worldly worries].

Cat on a Hot Tin Roof

Another early college campus production of Williams's plays was *Cat on a Hot Tin Roof* in 1987 by the graduating class at Shanghai Theatre Academy (the same graduating class that staged a production of *Waiting for Godot*, as alluded to earlier). This production of *Cat* was directed by Professor Zhang Yingxiang (张应湘) because, according to him, it has "pedagogical value" and more importantly because it is a complex play that deserves pondering over.[63] Although there is no detailed information available about this production, it is noteworthy because of the dismissive response (about Tennessee Williams) from Huang Zuolin it prompted, as alluded to elsewhere in this book.

In 2016, almost 30 years later, the graduating class of acting students at the recently founded Shanghai Institute of Visual Arts mounted a production of *Cat on a Hot Tin Roof*. It had a full week run from November 27 to December 3, to packed audiences.[64] Then, during the fall semester of 2018, *Woyuan jushe* (沃原剧社Fertile plain drama society) of East China University of Political Science and Law (*Huadong zhengfa daxue* 华东政法大学) staged a production of *Cat* as the society's 20th anniversary celebration and membership recruitment event. Although not much is known about the production, the promotional pitch the society put out characterizes the play as one that exposes and reflects on hypocrisy, deception, and lies caused by a familial struggle for inheritance. It mentions Brick's feeling of guilt due to the death of a very close friend (挚友), his drinking problem, and so on, but there is not a hint of the homosexual themes the play is known for. That silence in 2018, 20 years after the decriminalization of homosexuality in China, is so loud that anyone who has any knowledge or understanding of Tennessee Williams and *Cat* would have heard it.[65]

Indeed, Chinese theatre artists and amateur drama enthusiasts alike seem to stay away from this play despite the star power associated with the 1958 film adaptation (starring Elizabeth Taylor as Maggie and Paul Newman as Brick), which is very popular in China, and despite the fact that this play, including its homosexual themes, has been studied by Chinese scholars through various critical lenses.[66] It is interesting to note that *Cat on a Hot Tin Roof* was one of the three Williams plays staged during Shanghai Pride 2012,[67] the other two being *The Chalky White Substance* and *Something Unspoken*. It is probably the first and only time that *The Chalky White Substance* and *Something Unspoken* have ever been staged in China—by English-speaking amateur actors and for mostly English-speaking Western expatriates, much like during the late 1800s when Western expatriates built the first Western-style theatre in China, Lyceum Theatre (*lanxin dajuyuan* 兰心大剧院), that opened its doors in Shanghai in 1867 for Western troupes to come and stage Western plays.[68] Such performances may have the same effect of pushing the boundaries and opening up possibilities, albeit slowly, reminiscent, once again, of what happened in the late 1800s and early 1900s.

A Streetcar Named Desire

One of the most noteworthy college campus productions of Williams' plays happened in in 2002—a bold production of *A Streetcar Named Desire* staged at the Shanghai Theatre Academy.[69] As noted earlier, by this time, especially since Deng Xiaoping's 1992 southern tour (to reconfirm the "reform and opening up" policy for the post-1989 China), Chinese economy had been booming at an unprecedented double-digit growth rate and become the second biggest economy in the world. The decriminalization of homosexual sex had also happened in 1997, which signaled a green light for scholars to study homosexual themes in Williams plays too, including *A Streetcar Named Desire*.[70]

What is most noteworthy about this 2002 production of *Streetcar* is not how it treats the play's latent homosexual theme (which would be unimaginable at this time or anytime in the near future), but how it softens the portrayal of Blanche Dubois to make her a more sympathetic character. Directed by Acting Professor He Yan (何雁), this production takes considerable creative license to compress and streamline the dramatic action, dispense nonessential characters such as the negro woman, the Mexican woman, and the young collector Blanche could not help flirting with as she waits nervously for Mitch ("My Rosenkavalier!") to show up (with a bunch of roses). More noticeably, this production invents a narrator, very much in the manner of Tom Wingfield of *The Glass Menagerie* and inserts a fantastical party scene for Blanche's birthday, as if to give both Blanche and the audiences some much-needed festivity, a comic relief of sorts, before things go from bad to worse. What is gained and what is lost in this "kinder" reinterpretation of Williams play on the Chinese stage remains in the eye of the beholder.[71]

As the curtain rises in a small dimly lit theatre (450 square meters, 200 seats) at the Shanghai Dramatic Arts Centre, a young man, casually dressed, donning a fedora hat, comes on stage buoyantly:

> Ladies and gentlemen, good evening! Welcome to tonight's production of *A Streetcar Named Desire*, a representative play by the American playwright Tennessee Williams. The story takes place in the New Orleans of the 1940s. [walking down the stairway while talking] Here is the corner of a street near the Heavenly Square where the very air buzzes with wretched poverty under the grey sky and the smell of rotten bananas and automobile tires from warm breaths of the river that would kill your appetite for days. Here lives the young couple Stella and Stanley in a tiny two-room apartment. Despite the cramped space they live a comfortable life until one day Stella receives a telegraph from her elder sister.

The narrator, being a complete outsider, unlike Tom of *The Glass Menagerie*, who is "the narrator of the play, and also a character in it," and unequipped with his "magic" (tricks in his pocket to give the audience "truth in the pleasant disguise of illusion"),[72] can be seen as a Brechtian (epic theatre) narrator of sorts graphed onto an otherwise realistic theatre production. As the two-minute introduction by the narrator ends, we see a small apartment that reminds one of *tingzijian* (亭子间), a cramped studio underneath the stairway of buildings in old Shanghai, and Blanche and Stella talking excitedly while unpacking in the bedroom on stage left:

Stella: Big sister, why are you bringing so many dresses?
Blanche: I brought some nice clothes to meet all your lovely friends in.

Apparently, by beginning the play at this moment in the story, this pro-
duction cut the almost 7-page worth of exposition in the original play—
Stanley tossing Stella the red-stained meat package from the butcher's
("Catch!") and going off to play bowling with the guys, with Stella tailing
("Can I come watch"?); Blanche finding her way to her sister's home,
Eunice letting her in and chitchatting so we pick up bits of her backstory,
for example, the sisters' home-place in Mississippi ("A great big place with
white columns"), and Blanche being a school teacher; Blanche, half-dead
from the journey, helping herself to Stanley's whisky in a half-open closet
(pouring herself a half tumbler and tossing it down); the ecstatic joy of the
two sisters at the reunion, Blanche asking Stella for liquor ("you must have
some liquor on the place ...") as if she has not helped herself to it already;
Blanche explaining how she has left school ("on the verge of lunacy"); her
vain concern about her looks and fear of daylight ("never exposed so a
total ruin"); Blanche being shocked that Stella's home is small ("What?
Two rooms, did you say?"); and so on.[73]

Dispensing the 7-page worth of exposition in the original play may gain
in the pace of dramatic action but those dispensed details are indispensable
elements and motifs in the tapestry of the story as it builds up, one mini-
crisis after another, toward the climactic scene when Stanley corners
Blanche who desperately tries to get out ("Let me—let me get by you!"
"Stay back! Don't you come toward me another step or I'll—" "I warn
you, don't, I'm in danger!" "So I could twist the broken end in your
face!"), her defense proving futile, her personal space, and indeed her personhood, being violently violated[74] (this sexual assault scene is realistically
acted out on stage in this production as Blanche, horrified, screams for her
very life).

Although this production is essentially realist theatre, it does allow itself
a moment of levity or festivity now and then, even fantasy. One such
moment happens on the "Poker Night" (Scene Three) when Mitch walks
through the portieres and strikes up a conversation with Blanche. He
shows her his silver cigarette case that has a romantic inscription, lines
from Elizabeth Browning's Sonnet 43 ("if God choose, I shall but love
thee better after death"[75]) and she talks about her beloved Hawthorne,
Whitman, and Poe. They hit it off right away and begin to dance joyfully,
accompanied by lively jazz music, which turns out to be so infectious that

Stanley's card mates, Steve and Pablo, leave the table and join the dance, twisting and swirling their bodies suggestively. This moment of levity is cut short by a madhouse scene when Stanley dashes to where Mitch and Blanche are, smashes the music box, and hits Stella who is very close to the expecting day ("My sister is going to have a baby!").[76]

What is most notable in this 2002 production is the fantasy scene inserted into Blanche's birthday celebration (Scene 7 of the original play). In the lead up to the fantastical insertion, as Blanche bathes ("Soaking in a hot tub") to ready herself for the evening, Stanley lets Stella in on "th' dope" he has got on her "big sister" from "the most reliable sources and more:" "Sister Blanche is no lily! Ha-ha! Some lily she is!"; the "truth" about the loss of Laurels; and Mitch, now wised-up, not coming for cake and ice cream tonight. Then, magic happens, as if on cue (after one of Stanley's angry outbursts to Stella: "And you run out an' get her cokes, I suppose? And serve' em to Her Majesty in the tub?"),[77] a bunch of entertainers ("We are professionals!"), dressed like courtiers, led by Eunice, marches in from upstage, singing and dancing, creating palpable fanfare in the otherwise quite repressive scene.

During the fanfare that lasts for two and half minutes, in the midst of "Angel of Music" sung by Christine from *The Phantom of the Opera*, the revelers shower a perplexed Blanche, a small glittering crown on her head, with the most glowing clichés praising her elegant beauty; the two handsome young male revelers—princes charming—take turns to dance with her, one of them getting down on one knee in front of her as if ready to ask for her hand. As if waking up to the dream of her life that has finally come true, Blanche, being carried by the two princes charming, joins the celebration ("Father once spoke of an angel / I used to dream he'd appear / Now as I sing I can sense him / And I know he's here):[78]

> Blanche (ecstatic, looking at the candlelit birthday cake): Oh my God, I feel back home on our big plantation and I am in my sweet sixteen again!

However, there is no guardian angel of music, poetry, or otherwise, to protect Blanche from the harsh reality ("Christine, Christine you must have been dreaming / Stories like this can't come true"). With another angry outburst from Stanley who cannot take such festivity any longer, hits the table really hard, and sends the birthday cake crashing to the floor, we are all tossed back to "reality"—the repressive scene conjured up by Tennessee Williams as Stanley continues to prosecute his case against Blanche.

The play ends with Blanche running deep upstage, laughing "hysterically" and then the narrator returns, hat in hand, pensively:

Thus, Blanche leaves with the Doctor. Afterwards, some say Stella took the newborn baby with her and left Stanley. Others say she didn't leave. Either way, life goes on. Winter this year is particularly cold. As the holiday season gets nearer, grownups are decorating the Christmas tree. Children are dreaming of visits from Santa Claus. And Blanche? She gazes outside the window of the madhouse and keeps hoping—hoping, with all the dreams of her life, hoping.

There is no missing or mistaking the sympathy for Blanche in this ending, apparently out of a "kindness" as heartfelt as Tom at the end of *The Glass Menagerie* when he morphs into the narrator of the "memory play" again, chasing the long distance ("time is the longest distance between two places") and attempting ("to find in motion what was lost in space"), but he cannot just simply leave ("Oh, Laura, Laura, I tried to leave you behind me, but I am more faithful than I intended to be!").[79] This "kindness" for Blanche, which is evident throughout the 2002 Shanghai Theatre Academy production, offers an interesting counterpoint to how the original play ends with another sexually charged reconciliation between Stella and Stanley (consistent with the pathos and ethos established and developed throughout the original play) as their life returns to "normal:" Stella sobs "with inhuman abandon" and Stanley "kneels beside her and his fingers find the opening of her blouse:"[80]

Now, now, love. Now, love....
[The luxurious sobbing, the sensual murmur fade away under the swelling music of the "blue pianoz" and the muted trumpet.]

In 2011, Wuhan University's Zone-in Drama Society (*Zongdian jushe* 踪点戏剧社, founded in 1999) staged a full production of *Streetcar* (reproduced in 2015).[81] Among Western classics this young college campus drama society has staged are *A Midsummer Night's Dream* (2000), *Macbeth* (2002, in English), *Death of a Salesman* and *Waiting for Godot* (2003), *The Accidental Death of an Anarchist* (2006), *The Crucible* (*Salem Witches* as the play is known in China; 2010), *An Incident of the Enemy of the People* and *Salome* (2014), *No Exit* and *A Doll's House* (2015), *Seagull* and *Tartuffe* (2017), *How I Learned to Drive* (2018),[82] and *Three Sisters* (2019), quite an impressive list for a college drama society.

This is a bold, "extreme" adaptation, a sequel to Williams' play, much like *A Doll's House, Part 2*, a 2017 play written by Lucas Hnath which "picks up after Henrik Ibsen's 1879 play concludes."[83] It picks up where Williams' play ends: Blanche, now in a mental institution, reminisces of her life and fantasizes about the future. She dies near the end of the play. The dramatic action switches between memory and fantasy, mixing of traditional realistic theatre with expressionistic (fluidity of time and space) techniques. Here is the production's description, or rather, interpretation of the tragedy of Blanche:

> Blanche is an idealist caught in the crosscurrents of base desires; she has noble intellectual and artistic aspirations but, limited by her abilities, has to attach herself to the superficial social environments and therefore cannot help but end up being destroyed by desire.

The society continued to perform during the fall semester of 2020 once the city, the first epicenter of the COVID-19 pandemic, reopened and in 2021.

A particularly notable college campus full production of *Streetcar* during the COVID-19 pandemic was staged by The Seagull Drama Society (*Haiou jushe* 海鸥剧社) of the Ocean University of China (based in Qingdao) in December 2020.[84] The first thing that seemed so visibly "wrong" with this production was that this was December 2020, months before any COVID-19 vaccines, Sinovac, Sinopharm, Pfizer, or Moderna became widely available if they had been approved for emergency use at all, yet all the young student actors and the audience members in the packed theatre were maskless; they were all so engrossed in the theatrical event, performers and spectators alike, as if they were gleefully oblivious to what was going on in the world outside the theatre walls, as if they were living in a faraway COVID-19 free universe.

An interesting "trivia" associated with this production is that the Seagull Drama Society has quite a long history, going back to the early 1930s and that one of its founding members was Li Yunhe (李云鹤), who would soon afterwards metamorphose into Jiang Qing (江青), Madame Mao (1914–1991).[85]

During the last scene of this December 2020 production, as the student actor cast in the role of Stanley stripped to his waist and was readying himself to sexually assault Blanche, the audiences burst into uncomfortable laughs; they laughed again, uncomfortably, as Stanley hit Blanche, knocked her down, and got on top of her—laughing was possibly their way of coping with a rather disturbing scene they were witnessing (albeit in a make-belief theatre).

As Ralf Remshardt posits in Staging the Savage God: "if the horrible aspect is so dominant or manifest, laughter will almost always be a mechanism for counteracting the horror. When the comical element is dominant, horror becomes a response to the callousness of one's own laughter."[86] Indeed, it is said that Williams himself, sitting in the back of the theatre during Broadway performances of Streetcar, would "laugh hysterically" at the final scene when Blanche is taken away by the Doctor and the Matron.[87] However one copes with the grotesque in life and/or theatre, laughing, being horrified, or both, Chinese theatre artists and audiences seem to have come a long way in seeing Williams' characters such as Blanche DuBois not as strangers, American "other," but as amongst "us," which signifies considerable progress toward a kinder society although there is still a long way to go.

NOTES

1. Zhang Kun, "Streetcar at Home on China Stage," China Daily, April 6, 2017, http://www.chinadaily.com.cn/culture/2017-04/06/content_28811083.htm.
2. See Chap. 1, p. 12.
3. This brief overview of Chinese exposure to and adaptation of Western drama draws from Shouhua Qi, Adapting Western Classics for the Chinese Stage (London and New York: Routledge, 2018), viii–xviii, 1–10.
4. See Chap. 2, pp. 30, 40, 45–53.
5. See Shouhua Qi, "Pushing the Boundaries: Staging Western Modern(ist) Drama in Contemporary China," in The Edinburgh Companion to Modernism in Contemporary Theatre, edited by Adrian Curtin, et al (Edinburgh University Press, 2022).
6. See Qi, Adapting Western Classics, 86–102.
7. This portion of the discussion draws from Wei Zhang and Shouhua Qi, "The Kindness of Strangers: Tennessee Williams's A Streetcar Named Desire on the Chinese Stage," Comparative Drama 54.1 (2021): 99–102.
8. George C. White, "Directing O'Neill In China," The Eugene O'Neill Newsletter, IX–1 (Spring 1985), http://www.eoneill.com/library/newsletter/ix_1/ix-1g.htm.
9. The Chinese translation used for this production was rendered by Liang Bolong although, printed on low grade paper (of rather poor quality typi-

cal of the time) and distributed internally, he was not accredited as the translator on the title page. See Chap. 2 for more detailed discussion of this and other Chinese renditions of *Streetcar*.

10. This portion of the discussion draws from Phillip Kolin and Sherry Shao, "The First Production of *A Streetcar Named Desire* in Mainland China," *The Tennessee Williams Literary Journal* 2 (1990–1991): 19–32; and Wu Wenquan吾文泉, "*Kua wenhua wudu yu jieshou: Yuwangbao jieche zai zhongguo*" (跨文化误读与接受: 欲望号街车在中国Transcultural misreading and reception: *A Streetcar Named Desire* in China), *Journal of Sichuan International Studies University* 21–22 (2005): 11–14.
11. Qi, *Adapting Western Classics*, 27–59.
12. Kolin and Shao, 27.
13. Qi, *Adapting Western Classics*, 94–98.
14. Han Dexin 韩德新, "*Zhongguo dalu wutai shang de Tiannaxi weiliansi yanchu yanjiu*" (中国大陆舞台上的田纳西·威廉斯戏剧演出研究 Staging Tennessee Williams in Mainland China"), *Future Communication* (未来传播) 27.4 (August 2020): 111–138.
15. See Zhang Min, "*Tiannaxi weiliansi yanjiu zai zhongguo: huigu yu zhanwang*" (Tennessee Williams studies in China: review and future), *Dangdai waiguo wenxue* (Contemporary Foreign Literature) 3 (2011): 157–166.
16. See Beijing TinHouse Productions (北京铁皮屋剧社), http://www.tinhouseprod.com.
17. See Theatre Movement Bazaar, https://theatremovementbazaar.org/.
18. This discussion draws from Zhao Zhenjiang 赵振江, "*Xingti ju henduo linggan laizi zhongguo xiqu*" (形体剧很多灵感来自中国戏曲 Physical theatre production considerably inspired by Chinese *xiqu*), *East Morning Gazette* (东方早报), December 25, 2014, https://www.163.com/news/article/AEA60GKJ00014AED.html; and "Poker Night Blues," https://theatremovementbazaar.org/archives/poker-night-blues/.
19. Zhao Zhenjiang 赵振江.
20. Emily Feng, 'First Chinese-Language Production of *A Raisin In The Sun* is Staged in Beijing," *NPR*, September 3, 2020, https://www.npr.org/2020/09/03/908274058/first-chinese-language-production-of-a-raisin-in-the-sun-is-staged-in-beijing.
21. See "77 Theatre" (77剧场), https://baike.baidu.com/item/77%E5%89%A7%E5%9C%BA/19730020.
22. See "Paper Doll," https://en.wikipedia.org/wiki/Paper_Doll_(Mills_Brothers_song).
23. Dorothy Max Prior, "Theatre Movement Bazaar/Beijing TinHouse Productions: Poker Night Blues," August 17, 2015, https://totaltheatre.org.uk/theatre-movement-bazaarbeijing-tinhouse-productions-poker-night-blues/.
24. Qi, *Adapting Western Classics*, 143.

25. See "Track 3," https://theatremovementbazaar.org/archives/track-3/.
26. See "'*Un Tramway Nommé Désir*'—*A Streetcar Named Desire*," https://www.maboumines.org/production/a-streetcar-named-desire/. See also "Lee Breuer," https://en.wikipedia.org/wiki/Lee_Breuer.
27. Doreen Carvajal, "*Streetcar* in Paris, Hold the T-Shirt," *New York Times*, February 14, 2011, https://www.nytimes.com/2011/02/15/arts/15comedie.html?searchResultPosition=1. See also Judy Fayard, "French *Streetcar* Takes a Detour Via Japan," *Wallstreet Journal*, February 18, 2011, https://www.wsj.com/articles/SB10001424052748703584804576143853331643020.
28. Molly Grogan, "A Streetcar to Paris via New York," *Paris Voice*, n.d., accessed via https://www.maboumines.org/production/a-streetcar-named-desire/.
29. This portion of the discussion draws from Zhang and Qi, 106–110.
30. Zhang Kun.
31. David Barbozaaug, "China Passes Japan as Second-Largest Economy," *The New York Times*, August 15, 2010, https://www.nytimes.com/2010/08/16/business/global/16yuan.html.
32. See Andrew Scheineson, "China's Internal Migrants," Council on Foreign Relations, May 14, 2009, https://www.cfr.org/backgrounder/chinas-internal-migrants; and Sergio Gautreaux, "Understanding China's Internal Migration," *International Policy Digest*, March 3, 2013, https://intpolicydigest.org/2013/03/03/understanding-china-s-internal-migration/.
33. See Zhang Kun. This portion of the discussion is in part based on the production I saw at the Hangzhou Grand Theatre on May 20, 2017.
34. Tennessee Williams, *Tennessee Williams Plays 1937–1955* (New York: The Library of America, 2000), 471.
35. Ibid., 559.
36. Ibid., 562–564.
37. Ibid., 554–555.
38. "*Shuimu zhong ganshou shanghua ban Yuwanghao jieche*" (水幕之中感受上话版《欲望号街车》 Experiencing Shanghai Dramatic Arts Centre edition of *A Streetcar Named Desire* through water curtain), *Beijing Evening News*, May 3, 2017, http://bjwb.bjd.com.cn/html/2017-05/03/content_130703.htm.
39. Wu Gang 吴刚," *Geju jueding jieju: huaju Yuwanghao jieche guanhou*" (格局决定结局: 话剧《欲望号街车》观后 Interpretation determines representation: On spoken drama *A Streetcar Named Desire*), *Shanghai Theatre* (上海戏剧) 9 (2016): 25–27.
40. Fan, Jianghong 樊江洪, "*Shanghai huaju Yuwanghao jieche zai guojia dajuyuan xia le yi chang 'yu'*" (上海话剧《欲望号街车》在国家大剧院剧场下了一场"雨" Shanghai Dramatic Arts Centre edition of *A Streetcar*

Named Desire "rains" on the National Centre for the Performing Arts), *Shangguan* (上观), April 27, 2017, https://www.jfdaily.com/news/detail?id=51537.

41. This portion of the discussion draws from Shanghai Dramatic Arts Centre, "*Yong sanbu oumei jingdian juzuo silie heian de daoyan: Wang Huan* (用三部欧美经典剧作撕裂黑暗的导演：王欢 Director tearing open darkness with adaptations of three European and American classic plays: Wang Huan), April 5, 2021, https://www.sohu.com/a/459083776_740643.

42. Ibid.

43. See "*Jian zu ji luodi de juzu, gaosu de Yuwanghao jieche*" (建组即落地的剧组，高速的《欲望号街车》 Hit the ground running cast for a high-speed *Streetcar*), June 5, 2021, http://m.thepaper.cn/baijiahao_13012325; and Shanghai Dramatic Arts Centre, "*Yuwanghao jieche bu jiandan*" (《欲望号街车》不简单 *Streetcar* not a simple ride), June 2021, https://mp.weixin.qq.com/s?__biz=MjM5MTM3ODU4MA==&mid=2657638173&idx=1&sn=df3fae9eb3ac37fbcfbb70c4837b25ec&chksm=bd2a8ae68a5d03f0f49d705fe86658656b6d08eb6420cb647f098344a718c7912cd5be8f0657&mpshare=1&scene=1&srcid=06220sVUiGzZU5PVOdTrwwcr&sharer_sharetime=1624552885886&sharer_shareid=a357b1c856ac987d241e6c738b55262e#rd.

44. See Shanghai Dramatic Arts Centre, "*Lian yan wu nian de koubei huaju: Yi lie mingjiao yuwanghao de jieche*" (连演五年的口碑话剧，一列名叫欲望号的街车 A well-received spoken drama performed five-year on a roll: A *Streetcar Named Desire*), July 4, 2021, https://www.thepaper.cn/newsDetail_forward_13443452.

45. This brief discussion is based on the performance video released by Guangzhou Spoken Drama Centre, October 23, 2020, available at https://www.bilibili.com/video/BV15r4y1w7bE?spm_id_from=333.999.0.0.

46. Williams, *1937–1955*, 545.

47. Ibid.

48. This discussion is based on the performance I saw at the Shanghai Dramatic Arts Centre on May 15, 2016. It also draws from Mu Ye, "*Qudiao suoyou de xuanhua, congjian: Fang boli dongwuyuan daoyan Dawei aisibiyueengson*" (去掉所有的喧哗，从简:访《玻璃动物园》导演大卫·埃斯比约恩松 Clean out all the noise to make it really simple: An interview *The Glass Menagerie* director David Esbjornson. *Shanghai Theatre* 2 (2016): 18–19. See also "David Esbjornson," https://en.wikipedia.org/wiki/David_Esbjornson.

49. See Huang Qianqian 黄阡阡, "*Bailaohui Boli dongwuyuan zhongmei tong yanyi*" (百老汇《玻璃动物园》中美同演绎 Chinese-American joint production of Broadway play *The Glass Menagerie*", December 19, 2015, https://tw.mobi.yahoo.com/tech/%E7%99%BE%E8%80%81%E5%

8C%AF-%E7%8E%BB%E7%92%83%E5%8B%95%E7%89%A9%
E5%9C%92-%E4%B8%AD%E7%BE%8E%E5%90%8C%E6%BC%94%E7%B
9%B9-215005329%2D%2Dfinance.html.

50. Tan Yingzhou 谈瀛洲, "*Que de jiushi na yidian huanxiang: kan huaju Boli dongwuyuan*" (缺的就是那一点幻想:看话剧《玻璃动物园》What's missing is a bit of imagination: On spoken drama *The Glass Menagerie*," *Shanghai Theatre* (上海戏剧) 2 (2016): 20–21.

51. Williams, *1937–1955*, 400.

52. This portion of the discussion draws from Qi, *Adapting Western Classics*, 11–18.

53. This portion of the discussion draws from Shouhua Qi, "Misreading Ibsen: Chinese Noras on and off the Stage, and Nora in Her Chinese Husband's Ancestral Land of the 1930s—as Reimagined for the Present-Day Stage," *Comparative Drama* 50.4 (Winter 2016): 341–364.

54. See Jeff Hay, ed., *Perspectives on Modern World History: The Tiananmen Square Protests of 1989* (Farmington Hills, MI, Gale Cengage Learning, 2010).

55. Meng Jinghui 孟京辉, ed., "*Wa shiyan jutuan zhi guanzhong*" (蛙实验剧团致观众 To theatergoers from Frog Experimental Theatre), *Xianfeng xiju dangan* (先锋戏剧档案 Avant-Garde Theatre Archives) (Beijing: *Zuojia chubanshe* Writers Press 2011), 46–47.

56. This brief discussion is based on *Xiari yanyun* (夏日烟云 *Summer and Smoke*), the program for the production released by Beijing Film Academy in 2016.

57. See "Li Ranran" (李苒苒), https://baike.baidu.com/item/%E6%9D%8E%E8%8B%92%E8%8B%92/7940408.

58. *Summer and Smoke* (*Xiari yanyun* 夏日烟云).

59. This brief discussion is based on Zhang Aifeng 张爱峰, "*Xiari yanyun: aiqing ling yu rou de zhengzha* (《夏日烟云》: 爱情, 灵与肉的挣扎 Summer and Smoke: love and the struggle between flesh and soul), June 18, 2009, https://www.bfa.edu.cn/biaoyan/info/1005/1060.htm; and Fugui Caige 106 (富贵财哥_106), "*Guan zhongguo chuanmei daxue biaoyan ban biye daxi huaju Xiari yanyun* (观中国传媒大学表演班毕业大戏话剧《夏日烟云》Communications University of China acting students grand graduation spoken drama performance of *Summer and Smoke*) June 19, 2009, http://blog.sina.com.cn/s/blog_60a3e3190100du13.html.

60. Chen Zidu (陈子度), https://baike.baidu.com/item/%E9%99%88%E5%AD%90%E5%BA%A6/18749438.

61. Zhang Aifeng.

62. Fugui Caige.

63. Hang Dexin, 121.

64. See *"Biye daxi Re tiepi wuding shang de mao"* (Graduation performance *Cat on a Hot Tin Roof*, December 1, 2016, http://www.siva.edu.cn/site/site1/newsText.aspx?si=16&id=3787.

65. See *"Woyuan jushe zhaoxin daxi Re tie pi wuding shang de mao"* (沃原剧社招新大戏热铁皮屋顶上的猫 Fertile plain drama society recruitment play *Cat on a Hot Tin Roof*, October 2018, wwwJinciwei.cn/f39S674.html.

66. See Chap. 3, pp. 98–110, 114–122.

67. See "Shanghai Pride," https://en.wikipedia.org/wiki/Shanghai_Pride; and "Shanghai Pride," http://www.shpride.com/.

68. See Qi, *Adapting Western Classics*, 6–9.

69. This portion of the discussion draws from Zhang and Qi, 102–106.

70. See Chap. 1, p. 18.

71. This portion of the discussion is based on performance video provided by He Yan 何雁, director of the 2002 production and professor of acting at Shanghai Theatre Academy, https://www.sta.edu.cn/7f/39/c1559a32569/page.htm.

72. Williams, *Eight Plays* (Garden City, New York: Nelson Doubleday, 1979), 20.

73. Ibid., 95–102.

74. Ibid., 186–187.

75. Elizabeth Browning, "How Do I Love Thee?" (Sonnet 43), https://poets.org/poem/how-do-i-love-thee-sonnet-43.

76. Williams, *Eight Plays*, 129.

77. Ibid., 161–167.

78. "Angel of Music," https://genius.com/Andrew-lloyd-webber-angel-of-music-lyrics.

79. Williams, *Eight Plays*, 89–90.

80. Ibid., 196–197.

81. This brief discussion is based on *"Wuhan daxue zongdian jushe Yuwang hao jieche"* (武汉大学踪点戏剧社《欲望号街车》 Wuhan University's Zone-in Drama Society staging *A Streetcar Named Desire*), 2011, http://www.jsunion.net/Article/ShowArticle.asp?ArticleID=2599. See also *"Zongdian jueshe"* (踪点戏剧社 Zone-in Drama Society), https://baike.baidu.com/item/%E8%B8%AA%E7%82%B9%E6%88%8F%E5%89%A7%E7%A4%BE/3454514.

82. Given the sexually charged topic of this American play, and the fact that a US-China joint production of the play happened barely three years before, in 2015, it seemed quite gutsy for the young college theatre enthusiasts to take it on and for that matter, for the university to allow such performances to happen on its campus. See Qi, "Pushing the Boundaries."

83. See "A Doll's House, Part 2," https://en.wikipedia.org/wiki/A_Doll's_House,_Part_2.

84. This brief discussion is based on *"2020 Haiou jushe Yuwanghao jieche"* (2020 海鸥剧社《欲望号街车》 2020 Seagull Drama Society's *A Streetcar Named Desire*), the performance video available at https://www.bilibili. com/video/BV1RN411X71K?spm_id_from=333.905.b_7265 6c61746564.4. See also Zhou Jiechen and Zhang Zhenglai 周洁辰 张钲来, *"Huangdan huangyan yuwang jiaozhi: Haiou jushe Yuwanghao jieche shangyan* (荒诞谎言 欲望交织: 海鸥剧社《欲望号街车》 上演 Absurd lies and interwoven desires: Seagull Drama Society stages *A Streetcar Named Desire*), Watch and Listen to the Sea Waves 观海听涛, December 13, 2020, http://news.ouc.edu.cn/2020/1213/c78a103670/page.htm.
85. See *"Haiou jushe"* (海鸥剧社), https://baike.baidu.com/item/%E6%B5 %B7%E9%B8%A5%E5%89%A7%E7%A4%BE/4936943.
86. Quoted in Saddik, 7. Ralf Remshardt, *Staging the Savage God: The Grotesque in Performance* (Carbondale, IL: Southern Illinois University Press, 2004), 85. For a "behind the scene" view of how Hollywood handles the rape scene, see Nancy M. Tishler, "'Tiger—Tiger!' Blanche's Rape on Screen," in *Magical Muse: Millennial Essays on Tennessee Williams*, edited by Ralph E. Voss (Tuscaloosa, Al: University of Alabama Press, 2002), 50–69.
87. Saddik, 7.

CHAPTER 5

Conclusion

Although Tennessee Williams never had a chance to set foot in China and see with his own eyes the country, people, and culture he invoked in *A Streetcar Named Desire*, *The Night of Iguana*, and a few other works, most likely as an "exotic other" (rather than as a spiritual home and final resting place he was so longing for, as some Chinese scholars would like to believe), and although for decades he was rejected and/or viewed with misgivings thanks to perceived decadence in his dramatic works and therefore remained a "stranger" to the Chinese, Williams has come a long way in his reception in China since the early 1980s.

As discussed in the chapters of this book, much of the early Chinese rejection and/or misgivings of Tennessee Williams were shaped and conditioned by the dominant ideology and discourse in arts and literature and by Chinese sexual mores which had decried homosexuality as a degenerate, decadent lifestyle until more recently. Indeed, the reception of Tennessee Williams in China, from rejection and/or misgivings to cautious curiosity and to full-throated acceptance, has developed through literary translation, critical interpretation, and theatric adaptation in the context of profound changes in China's socioeconomic and cultural life and sexual mores during the decades since the end of the Cultural Revolution (1966–1976) and the beginning of "reform and opening up." During those decades, China has developed from an economy teetering

© The Author(s), under exclusive license to Springer Nature
Switzerland AG 2022
S. Qi, *Culture, History, and the Reception of Tennessee Williams in China*, Chinese Literature and Culture in the World,
https://doi.org/10.1007/978-3-031-16934-2_5

on the edge of collapse to that of the second largest in the world. Its socio-cultural life has also become exponentially richer despite censorship, "The Great Firewall," and other seemingly capricious limits and constraints. The decriminalization of homosexual sex in 1997 and its removal from the list of mental disorders in 2001 by the Chinese Society of Psychiatry signi-fied a big step forward toward a kinder, more accepting society although even today homosexuals could still face prejudice and harassment of vari-ous kinds.

A larger context for understanding the reception of Williams in China is the country's encounter and reception of Western ideas, including arts and literature, since the post-Opium War (1839–1841) decades as genera-tions of Chinese searched for ways to save and strengthen the ancient civi-lization in the brave new world and reclaim its glory, real and imagined, on the world stage. Indeed, cultural and people renewal for national sur-vival has been the motivating force behind much of the Chinese transla-tion, interpretation, and adaptation endeavors since the turn of the twentieth century. Viewed from this national and civilizational perspective and given what is at stake, it is no wonder that translation, interpretation, adaptation, and such literary, artistic, and intellectual practices have, inevi-tably, been molded and conditioned by the complex dynamics of texts (literary and/or artistic and socio-historical), contexts (Chinese and Western), and intertexts (source texts/culture and target texts/culture in the forms of translations, adaptations, and/or performances) of domi-nance (language, culture, ideology) and resistance, and of tension and convergence.

Translation, carrying ideas from the source language/culture to the target language/culture, especially in the context of China, is so much more than the "technical" question of being faithful or freewheeling, and/or rendered for the stage/performability or for the reader/readability (in the case of dramatic works) although they are all pertinent, important questions. It is fraught with politics, morality, and social and cultural norms. This is even truer in the case of Tennessee Williams, given how his literary reputation was maligned for quite some time even in the US and the West due to his open homosexuality. Translating Tennessee Williams, from Ying Ruocheng's 1963 rendition of *Something Unspoken* to the vari-ous renditions, since the 1980s, of *The Glass Menagerie, A Streetcar Named Desire, Cat on a Hot Tin Roof, The Night of Iguana*, and Williams' *Memoirs*, has been filtered and complicated by sociopolitical, cultural, and moral forces at work during those decades.

From the cautioning note Ying Ruocheng wrote to accompany his 1963 rendition of *Something Unspoken* to the serious yet cautious interest shown by scholars such as Guo Jide and Wang Yiqun in the early 1990s and then to the enthusiastic deep dive undertaken by aspiring scholars in the first two decades of the twenty-first century, equipped with various critical lenses, for example, psychology, psychoanalysis, gender and politics, and so on, Chinese critical reception of Tennessee Williams has made significant headway during the decades. The achievement is remarkable despite the occasional overzealous and/or unsubstantiated claims and false notes.

Similarly, when theatre artists such as Wang Huan in 2016 (and thereafter) encourage his actors to see Blanche Dubois as amongst the many migrants and misfits in China's big metropolises such as Shanghai and Beijing, both in the socioeconomic and psychological senses, it seems such a far cry from Huang Zuolin's dismissal of Williams as an American "other" in response to the 1987 staging of *Cat on a Hot Tin Roof* by Shanghai Theatre Academy students, and such a far cry from the 1988 staging of *A Streetcar Named Desire* by Tianjin People's Art Theatre, when the actors were, at first, perplexed by characters as flawed and complex as Blanche Dubois, and tried hard to understand in order to channel them on the stage. This decades-long journey should also have to be viewed in the context of dramatic developments in the politics, culture, and sexual mores in China to see its full significance.

Where will this journey go from here, not just in terms of the reception of Williams, but more importantly, in terms of the reception of all things Western, including arts and literature, seems somewhat uncertain at this time, given recent developments in China. As has been reported by Western media, there has been a gradual tightening of cultural and ideological control in China for the last decade or so. A favorite metaphor journalists and pundits like to use to characterize what is going on in China is "culture war."[1] It is true that the pendulum seems to be swinging back for some cooling off of all things Western, as China is on track to overtake the United States in the not distant future, in terms of the overall GDP (not the per capita income), as the biggest economy and a major powerhouse of scientific and technological development. Inside China, there has been call and argument for "cultural self-confidence" by scholars and policymakers alike.[2] For many, it is high time that China gave (or rather, exported its cultural practices and products) rather than took (imported) from the outside world, especially the West. This call for

Chinese culture to "go out" and the policies to push and make it happen, to build, spread, and wield its "soft power" in the world,[3] is an important part of China's strategic initiatives, including the "Belt and Road" initiative.[4]

The reality, though, may be more complicated than the war metaphor hypes. For one, the tug of war—if, for the sake of discussion, we may continue to use the rather jarring metaphor that puts cultures on a war footing with each other—between preservation of native cultural traditions and practices and adaptation and appropriation of foreign (Western) ideas and practices has never stopped since China was forced to open its doors in the post-Opium War decades, or more recently, since China began "reform and opening up" when the Cultural Revolution ended in the late 1970s.[5] In important ways, what happened in the spring/summer of 1989 in China, which culminated rather tragically on the Tiananmen Square, was a disastrous flare-up of such continued tug of cultural forces long at work. It seems that this time around, the swinging back, cooling off, or correction, if you will, is orchestrated from top down (with support from large portions of the populace although many scholars, alarmed and gravely concerned, struggle to make their voices heard at the risk of being censored, censured, or paying even dearer prices); it is being carefully managed to avoid a repeat of 1989 or, even worse, the ten-year nightmare of 1966–1976, a Cultural Revolution 2.0. Moreover, "culture wars" are not unique to China. They have been going on in the United States, Europe, and almost everywhere else in the world. Just look at these news headlines and titles of books: *Culture Wars: The Struggle to Define America*; "America's Culture Wars Will Intensify. The Defeat of Donald Trump will not Help;" "The World Is Trapped in America's Culture War;" "How Culture Wars Start—Is the UK Going Down the Same Road as the US?"; "Culture Wars in the EU;" "The Culture War Dividing Europe: Historically Catholic Poland and Ireland Offer Divergent Visions of the Continent's Future;" *Populism and the European Culture Wars: The Conflict of Values between Hungary and the EU*;[6] the list can go on.

It is unlikely, albeit not entirely impossible, for China to regress to the scorched earth sociocultural policies and practices of the Cultural Revolution days when all things Western (as well as traditional Chinese culture and literary classics) were denounced as being poisonous. Xi Jinping, who assumed the helmsmanship of the Communist Party and China in 2012 and is poised to serve an unprecedented third term, has frequently touted his avid reading of Western classics during his formative years. "It can be said that, literally," Xi said in a 2013 interview, "I read nearly all the literary classics I could find during that time."[7] Among these: Russian classics such as *Eugene Onegin* (Alexander Pushkin), *A Hero of Our Time* (Mikhail Lermontov), *Quiet Flows the Don* (Mikhail Sholokhov), and *War and Peace* and *Resurrection* (Leo Tolstoy); German classics by Johann Wolfgang von Goethe and Friedrich Schiller (he read *The Sorrows of Young Werther* at age 14; while receiving reeducation in rural China, young Xi walked 30 kilometers to borrow a copy of *Faust* from a friend of his although it proved to be too dense for him to understand); American classics such as *Leaves of Grass* (Walt Whitman) and *The Adventures of Huckleberry Finn* (Mark Twain), *The Old Man and the Sea* (Ernest Hemingway; Xi looked for the spots where Hemingway wrote the novel when he visited Cuba); French classics such as *The Red and The Black* (Stendhal), *The Human Comedy* (Honoré de Balzac); *Les Misérables* (Victor Hugo; one of the moments that touched Xi the most was when Bishop Myriel helps Jean Valjean and encourages him to be a better man); and English classics by Shakespeare, Wordsworth, Jane Austen, and Charles Dickens.[8] A total regression with a Cultural Revolution 2.0 of sorts would amount to a total rejection of the well-cultured, cosmopolitan image or persona Xi has taken pains to portray and project on the world stage.

A quick look at the theatre scene in the metropolises such as Beijing and Shanghai in winter/spring 2022,[9] at the time of this writing, shows that what is being staged, in terms of Western drama, is a mix of "old" classics and a few more modern/contemporary titles, for example, *Electra* (Sophocles); *The Red and the Black* (Stendhal) and *The Good Person of Szechwan* (Brecht), both adapted by Meng Jinghui; *Turandot* (Puccini); hi-definition screenings of *Romeo and Juliet*, *Hamlet*, *The Merchant of Venice*, *Measure for Measure*, and *A Midsummer Night's Dream*; *The Zoo Story* (Albee); popular musicals such as *Man of La Mancha* (Dale Wasserman); *A Rock-and-Roll Faust* (이지나 Gina Lee); *Tick, Tick … Boom!* (Jonathan Larson); and *I Love You* (Joe DiPietro). One gets a clear sense that there is tightening of control (as is true in education and almost every other facet of the sociocultural and economic life[10]) and that theatre artists are mostly playing it (relatively) safe. Yet, there is still palpable life and theatre artists can still find ways to channel their creativity by way of speaking to the sociocultural reality of the present day. In April 2020, when China was gingerly reopening for life again, after months of being locked down due to the coronavirus pandemic, Wang Chong mounted a bold production of Beckett's *Waiting for Godot* (1953), with the cast and crew, all sheltering in their homes in Beijing, Guangzhou, Wuhan (the first epicenter of the pandemic), performing online, for the hundreds of thousands of "theatergoers" to see through live streaming. The fact that Wang Huan's production of *A Streetcar Named Desire* had a run from 2016 to 2021 suggests that once the door of the country is opened, it cannot be (completely) shut again.

Indeed, China seems to be committed to "reform and opening up,"[11] although that commitment may take different forms and there will be pendulum swings and even setbacks, as the country continues to evolve, define, and redefine itself (as every other country in the world does), and learns to live with its newly minted superpower status and with the rest of the world, its neighbors, allies (all such alliances, by nature, are temporary, conditional, and precarious) as well as adversaries (real and/or perceived, especially the United States).[12] China's reception of Western arts and literature will continue to be an uneasy tug of confluence and divergence, native and foreign (Western), traditional and modern, and different literary/artistic, moral, and sociopolitical proclivities. In that continued, albeit uneasy and oftentimes contentious, intermingling of cultures will be Tennessee Williams dramatic oeuvre (including some of his "grotesque" later plays)—to enrich and deepen our understanding of our shared humanity (despite all the differences, real and hyped) and to make the world a more accepting and kinder place for everyone to live in.

Notes

1. See "Xi Jinping's Culture Wars," *China File,* November 12, 2014, https://www.chinafile.com/conversation/xi-jinpings-culture-wars; "Xi Jinping on What's Wrong with Contemporary Chinese Culture," *China File,* October 26, 2015, https://www.chinafile.com/reporting-opinion/culture/xi-jinping-whats-wrong-contemporary-chinese-culture; Chang Che, "China's Cultural Crackdown: A Guide," MCLC Resource Center, December 7, 2021, https://u.osu.edu/mclc/2021/12/07/chinas-cultural-crackdown-a-guide/; Howard W. French, "China's Culture Wars Are Just Getting Started," September 15, 2021, https://www.worldpoliticsreview.com/articles/29958/a-rising-china-s-culture-wars-are-just-getting-started; **Hongwei Bao,** "What Does China's 'Cultural War' Say About Culture? Film Quarterly, September 17, 2021, https://filmquarterly.org/2021/09/17/what-does-chinas-cultural-war-say-about-culture/; James Griffiths, "Xi Jinping's Culture War Comes to China's

Campuses as Communist Party Prepares to Mark 100 Years," CNN, April 20, 2021, https://www.cnn.com/2021/04/20/china/xi-jinping-universities-intl-hnk/index.html; Vincent Ni, and Helen Davidson, "China's Cultural Crackdown: Few Areas Untouched as Xi Reshapes Society," *The Guardian*, September 10, 2021, https://www.theguardian.com/world/2021/sep/10/chinas-cultural-crackdown-few-areas-untouched-as-xi-reshapes-society; and Damien Ma, "Beijing's 'Culture War' Isn't About the U.S.—It's About China's Future," January 5, 2012, https://www.theatlantic.com/international/archive/2012/01/beijings-culture-war-isnt-about-the-us-its-about-chinas-future/250900/.

2. See *"Jiandin 'wenhua zixin xu dudong Xi Jinping zhe liu pian zhongyao jianghua* (坚定"文化自信," 须读懂习近平这6篇重要讲话 To firm up 'cultural self-confidence these are six must-read Xi Jinping speeches), *Xinhuanet*, June 16, 2019, http://www.xinhuanet.com/politics/xxjxs/2019-06/19/c_1124642114.htm; *"Women weishemo yao wenhua zixin"* (我们为什么要文化自信 Why do we need to have cultural self-confidence?), *China.com.cn*, June 1, 2020, http://xitheory.china.com.cn/2020-06/01/content_76112707.htm; and *"Xi Jinping: Zengqiang wenhua zijue jiandin wenhua zixin zhanshi zhongguo wenyi xin qixiang zhujiu zhonghua wenhua xin huihuan"* (习近平:增强文化自觉坚定文化自信 展示中国文艺新气象铸就中华文化新辉煌 Xi Jinping: Strengthen cultural self-consciousness, firm up cultural self-confidence, showcase China's new vibrance in arts and literature, and mold and promote Chinese cultural glory), *Xinhuanet*, December 14, 2021, http://www.court.gov.cn/zixun-xiangqing-337181.html.

3. See Yang Liying 杨利英, *"Jin nian lai zhongguo wenhua "zou chu qu" zhanlue yanjiu zongshu"* (近年来中国文化"走出去"战略研究综述 Overview of China culture "going out" strategy research in recent years), *China Culture*, February12, 2009, http://cn.cccweb.org/pubinfo/2020/04/28/200001004001/ebfe00815baa4b48900309964718b2a3.html; Wang Yuling 王玉玲, *"Zhongguo wenhua 'zou chu qu' de lishi jiyu* (中国文化"走出去"的历史机遇 Historical opportunities for Chinese culture "going out"), *China Today*, January 24, 2017, http://www.chinatoday.com.cn/chinese/sz/zggc/201701/t20170124_800086207.html; and Li Xiaoqun 李潇君, "推动中华文化走出去 增强国家文化软实力" (*Tuidong zhonghua wenhua zou chu qu zengqiang guojia wenhua ruan shili* (Pushing for Chinese culture going out, strengthening national cultural soft power), *People*, June 16, 2021, http://theory.people.com.cn/n1/2021/0616/c40531-32131322.html.

4. See "Belt and Road Initiative," World Bank, https://www.worldbank.org/en/topic/regional-integration/brief/belt-and-road-initiative; and "China's Massive Belt and Road Initiative," Council on Foreign Relations,

https://www.cfr.org/backgrounder/chinas-massive-belt-and-road-initiative.

5. See Shouhua Qi, *Western Literature in China and the Translation of a Nation* (New York: Palgrave Macmillan, 2012).

6. James Davison Hunter, *Culture Wars: The Struggle to Define America* (Basic Books, 1991); "America's Culture Wars Will Intensify. The Defeat of Donald Trump will not Help," *The Economist*, November 17, 2020, https://www.economist.com/the-world-ahead/2020/11/17/americas-culture-wars-will-intensify?gclid=Cj0KCQiAoY-PBhCNARIsABcz773jir3ke_iZabkNizE4jnw8wvnXAZdwuoVKPhhVgogJCcOD-muyKR8AaAu3UEALw_wcB&gclsrc=aw.ds; Helen Lewis, "The World Is Trapped in America's Culture War," *The Atlantic*, October 27, 2020, https://www.theatlantic.com/international/archive/2020/10/internet-world-trapped-americas-culture-war/616799/; Bobby Duffy and Kirstie Hewlett, "How Culture Wars Start—Is the UK Going Down the Same Road as the US?" Kings College London News Centre, May 24, 2021, https://www.kcl.ac.uk/news/how-culture-wars-start; Marek Jan Chodakiewicz, "Culture Wars in the EU," *Active Measures Journal*, July 23, 2021, https://www.iwp.edu/articles/2021/07/23/culture-wars-in-the-eu/; Yaroslav Trofimov, "The Culture War Dividing Europe: Historically Catholic Poland and Ireland Offer Divergent Visions of the Continent's Future," *The Wall Street Journal*, March 29, 2019, https://www.wsj.com/articles/the-culture-war-dividing-europe-11553872752; and Frank Furedi, *Populism and the European Culture Wars: The Conflict of Values between Hungary and the EU* (Routledge, 2018).

7. "A Look at What's on Chinese President Xi Jinping's Shelves," *People's Daily*, October 18, 2016, http://en.people.cn/n3/2016/1018/c90000-9128892.html.

8. See also *"Zhexie zuopin yingxiang Xi Jinping shu shi nian"* (这些作品，影响习近平数十年 These works have influenced Xi Jinping for many years), October 20, 2016, https://news.12371.cn/2016/10/20/ARTI1476942635132147.shtml; and "Xi Jinping 'dianzan' guo de gu jin zhong wai wenxue zuopin (习近平"点赞"过的古今中外文学作品 Chinese and foreign ancient and modern classics Xi Jinping has 'thumbed up'), *People's Daily*, May 27, 2015, http://culture.people.com.cn/n/2015/0522/c87423-27039953-3.html.

9. Based on information gleaned from Damai Wang (大麦网 Damai Net), https://detail.damai.cn, a Chinese equivalent of Box Office that sells tickets of all kinds of leisure and entertainment, e.g., concerts, sports events, theatre performances, and so on.

10. See for example Karin Fischer, "China's Higher-Ed Ambitions Are at Odds with Its Tightening Grip on Academic Freedom," *Chronicle of Higher*

Education, September 24, 2019, https://www.chronicle.com/article/chinas-higher-ed-ambitions-are-at-odds-with-its-tightening-grip-on-academic-freedom/.

11. Cao Desheng, "Nation Remains Committed to Reform, Opening-Up," *China Daily*, August 26, https://www.chinadaily.com.cn/a/202008/26/WS5f4596a3a310675eafc55753.html; Tom Fowdy, "China Continues Reform and Opening Up to Further Integrate with the Global Economy," December 28, 2021, http://www.china.org.cn/opinion/2021-12/28/content_77956308.htm; and Jacques Delisle and Av Ery Goldstein, "China's Economic Reform and Opening at Forty: Past Accomplishments and Emerging Challenges," https://www.brookings.edu/wp-content/uploads/2019/04/9780815737254_ch1.pdf.

12. Thomas Barker, "The Real Culture War: China vs U.S.: Soft Power in the Age of Covid," The Institute of Art and Ideas, July 22, 2021, https://iai.tv/articles/the-real-culture-war-china-vs-u-s-auid-1844.

SELECT BIBLIOGRAPHY

CHINESE LANGUAGE SOURCES

An, Man 安曼, trans. *The Night of Iguana* (*Xiyi de yewan* 蜥蜴的夜晚) by Tennessee Williams, in *Foreign Contemporary Plays* (*Waiguo dangdai juzuo xuan* 外国当代剧作选). Beijing: China Drama Press (中国戏剧出版社), 1992: 363–552.

Chen, Liangting 陈良廷, trans. *Cat on a Hot Tin Roof* (*Re tiepi wuding shang de mao* 热铁皮屋顶上的猫) by Tennessee Williams, in *Cat on a Hot Tin Roof* (*Re tiepi wuding shang de mao* 热铁皮屋顶上的猫). Beijing: Chinese Social Sciences Press (中国社会科学出版社), 1982, 224–382.

Dong, Xiu 东秀, trans. *The Glass Menagerie* (*Boli dongwuyuan* 玻璃动物园) by Tennessee Williams. *Contemporary Foreign Literature* (当代外国文学) 4 (Oct. 1981): 111–147.

Fan, Jianghong 樊江洪. "*Shanghai huaju Yuwanghao jieche zai guojia dajuyuan xia le yi chang 'yu'*" (上海话剧《欲望号街车》在国家大剧院剧场下了一场"雨" Shanghai Dramatic Arts Centre edition of *A Streetcar Named Desire* "rains" on the National Centre for the Performing Arts). *Shangguan* (上观), April 27, 2017. https://www.jfdaily.com/news/detail?id=51537.

Feng, Qianzhu 冯倩珠, trans. *Memoirs* (*Tiannaxi weiliansi huiyilu* 田纳西·威廉斯回忆录) by Tennessee Williams. Zhengzhou: Henan University Press (河南人民出版社), 2018.

Feng, Tao 冯涛, trans. *A Streetcar Named Desire* (*Yuwanghao jieche* 欲望号街车) by Tennessee Williams. Shanghai: Shanghai Translation Press (上海译文出版社), 2015.

© The Author(s), under exclusive license to Springer Nature Switzerland AG 2022
S. Qi, *Culture, History, and the Reception of Tennessee Williams in China*, Chinese Literature and Culture in the World,
https://doi.org/10.1007/978-3-031-16934-2

Gao, Ruisen 高芮森, ed. *Foreign Classical Tragedies* (*Waiguo zhuming beiju xuan* 外国著名悲剧选), vol. 3. Zhengzhou: Henan People's Press, 1991.

Gao, Xianhua 高鲜花. *The Legend of Encouragement and Decadence: The Study of Tennessee Williams and His Drama* (*Lizhi yu tuifei de chuanqi: Tiannaxi weiliansi jiqi xiju yanjiu* 励志与颓废的传奇: 田纳西·威廉斯及其戏剧研究). Beijing: China Drama Press (中国戏剧出版社), 2019.

Guangzhou Spoken Drama Centre 广州话剧艺术中心. *Mingzhu xilie huaju Yuwanghao jieche* (名著系列话剧《欲望号街车》 Drama classics series *A Streetcar Named Desire* excerpt) performance video. October 23, 2020. https://www.bilibili.com/video/BV15r4y1w7bE?spm_id_from= 333.999.0.0.

Guo, Jide 郭继业. *History of American Drama* (*Meiguo xiju shi* 美国戏剧史). Zhengzhou: Henan People's Press (河南人民出版社), 1993.

Han, Dexing 韩德星. "*Zhongguo dalu wutai shang de Tiannaxi weiliansi yanchu yanjiu*" (中国大陆舞台上的田纳西·威廉斯戏剧演出研究 Staging Tennessee Williams in Mainland China) *Future Communication* (未来传播) 27.4 (August 2020): 111–138.

Han, Xi 韩曦. *Broadway Troubadour: Tennessee Williams* (*Bailaohui de xingyin shiren* 百老汇的行吟诗人). Beijing: Qunyan Press (群言出版社), 2013.

Huo, Xinchun 霍新村. "*Tiannaxi weiliansi zuopin zhong de zhongguo yuansu* (田纳西·威廉斯作品中的的中国元素 Chinese Elements in Tennessee Williams Dramatic Works). *Northeast Asia Forum* (东北亚外语论坛) 6 (2018): 27–31.

Jiang, Xianping 蒋贤萍. *Reimagining the Past: Southern Belles in Tennessee Williams' Plays* (*Chong xin xiangxiang guoqu: Tiannaxi weiliansi juzhuo zhong de nanfang shunü* 重新想象过去: 田纳西·威廉斯剧作中的南方淑女). Beijing: Guangming Daily Publishing House (光明日报出版社), 2013.

Li, Li 李莉. *Woman's Growth: Feminist Approach to Tennessee Williams' Works* (*Nüren de chengzhang licheng: Tiannaxi weiliansi zuopin de nüxing zhuyi jiedu* 女人成长历程:田纳西·威廉斯作品的女性主义解读). Tianjin: Tianjin People's Press (天津人民出版社), 2004.

Li, Shanghong 李尚宏. *The Homosexual Subtext in Tennessee Williams* (*Tiannaxi weiliansi xinlun* 田纳西·威廉斯新论). Shanghai: Shanghai Foreign Language Education Press (上海外语教育出版社), 2010.

Li, Ying 李英. *A Psychoanalytic Critique of Desire in Tennessee Williams Plays* (*Tiannaxi weiliansi xiju zhong yuwang de xinli toushi* 田纳西·威廉斯剧中欲望的心理透视) Beijing: Modern Education Press (现代教育出版社), 2008.

Li, Yinhe and Wang Xiaobo 李银河 王小波. *Tamen de shijie: Zhongguo nan tongxinglian qunluo toushi* (他们的世界--中国男同性恋群落透视 *Their World: A Study of Male Homosexuality in China*). Hong Kong: Cosmos Press, 1992; Xi'an: Shanxi People's Press (陕西人民出版社), 1993.

Liang, Bolong 梁伯龙, trans. *A Streetcar Named Desire* (*Yuwanghao jieche* 欲望号街车) by Tennessee Williams. Tianjin: Tianjin People's Art Theatre (天津人民艺术院), 1987.

Liang, Chaoqun 梁超群. *Presence and Absence of the Father in Tennessee Williams' Theatre* (*Tiannaxi weiliansi xiju zhong fuqin de zaichang yu quexi* 田纳西·威廉斯戏剧中父亲的在场与缺席). Shanghai: Shanghai Sanlian Books (上海三联出版社), 2010.

Liang, Zhen 梁真. *The Study on Tennessee Williams from the Perspective of "Heterology"* (*Linglei rensheng: yizhi shiyu xia d Tiannaxi weiliansi yanjiu*另类人生:异质视域下的田纳西·威廉斯研究). Ningbo, Zhejiang: Ningbo Publishing House (宁波出版社), 2020.

Lu, Jin 鹿金, trans. *The Glass Menagerie* (*Boli dongwuyuan* 玻璃动物园) by Tennessee Williams. In *Foreign Classical Tragedies* (*Waiguo zhuming beiju xuan* 外国著名悲剧选), vol. 3, edited by Gao Ruisen 高芮森. Zhengzhou: Henan People's Press (河南人民出版社), 1991.

Lu, Xun 鲁迅. "*Guanyu fanyi*" (关于翻译About translation, 1933), *Contemporary Foreign Literature* (*Dangdai waiguo wenxue*当代外国文学) 4 (Oct. 1981): 33.

———. "*Xianjin de xin wenxue de gaiguan*" (现今的新文学的概观 An overview of today's new literature, 1929), ibid., 37.

———. "*Nalai zhuyi*" (拿来主义 On take-ism, 1934a), ibid., 110.

———. "*Muke jicheng xiaoji*" (木刻纪程小记Preface of "Woodcut", 1934b), ibid.

Meng, Jinghui 孟京辉, ed. "*Wa shiyan jutuan zhi guanzhong*"(蛙实验剧团致观众 To theatergoers from Frog Experimental Theatre). *Xianfeng xiju dangan* (先锋戏剧档案Avant-Garde Theatre Archives). Beijing: Writers Press (作家出版社), 2011, 46–47.

Mu, Ye 木叶. "*Qudiao suoyou de xuanhua, congjian: Fang boli dongwuyuan daoyan Dawei aisibiyueengson*" (去掉所有的喧哗，从简:访《玻璃动物园》导演大卫·埃斯比约恩松Clean out all the noise to make it really simple: An interview *The Glass Menagerie* director David Esbjornson. *Shanghai Theatre* (上海戏剧) 2 (2016): 18–19.

Qi, Qing 奇青, trans. *A Streetcar Named Desire* (*Yuwanghao jieche* 欲望号街车) by Tennessee Williams, in *Foreign Contemporary Plays* (*Waiguo dangdai juzuo xuan*外国当代剧作选). Beijing: China Drama Press (中国戏剧出版社), 1992, 101–225.

Seagull Drama Society 海鸥剧社. *2020 Haiou jushe Yuwanghao jieche* (海鸥剧社《欲望号街车》 2020 Seagull Drama Society's *A Streetcar Named Desire*), performance video available at https://www.bilibili.com/video/BV1RN411X7 1K?spm_id_from=333.905.b_72656c61746564.4.

Sun, Baimei 孙白梅, trans. *A Streetcar Named Desire* (*Yuwanghao jieche* 欲望号街车) by Tennessee Williams. Shanghai: Shanghai Translation Press (上海译文出版社), 1991.

Tan, Yingzhou 谈瀛洲. "*Que de jiushi na yidian huanxiang: kan huaju Boli dong-wuyuan*" (缺的就是那一点想象:看话剧《玻璃动物园》 What's missing is a bit of imagination: On spoken drama *The Glass Menagerie*." *Shanghai Theatre* (上海戏剧) 2 (2016): 20–21.

Wu, Gang 吴刚. "*Geju jueding jieju: huaju Yuwanghao jieche guanhou*" (格局决定结局:话剧《欲望号街车》观后 Interpretation determines representation: On spoken drama *A Streetcar Named Desire*). *Shanghai Theatre* (上海戏剧) 9 (2016): 25–27.

Wu, Wenquan 吾文泉. "*Kua wenhua shixue yanjiu yu wutai biaoshu: Tiannaxi weiliansi zai zhongguo*" (跨文化诗学研究与舞台表述: 田纳西·威廉斯在中国 Transcultural poetics studies and theatric expressions: Tennessee Williams in China." *Xiju* (Drama) 4 (2004): 67–74.

———. "*Kua wenhua wudu yu jieshou: Yuwanghao jieche zai zhongguo*" (跨文化误读与接受:欲望号街车在中国 Transcultural misreading and reception: *A Streetcar Named Desire* in China). *Journal of Sichuan International Studies University* 21–22 (2005): 11–14.

Xu, Huaijing 徐怀静. *Masculinity Crises: Troubled Men in Tennessee Williams' Major Plays* (*Tie beixin: Tiannaxi weiliansi juzuo zhong kunhuo de nanren men* 铁背心: 田纳西·威廉斯剧作中困惑的男人们). Beijing: Tongxin Press (同心出版社), 2007.

Ying, Ruocheng 英若诚, trans. *Something Unspoken* (*Meiyou jiang chulai de hua* 没有讲出来的话) by Tennessee Williams. *World Literature* (世界文学) 3 (1963), 44–61.

———. "Postface" (*houji* 后记), ibid., 61–62.

Yuan, Kejia 袁可嘉. "Preface" (*Yinyan*引言). *Selections from Foreign Modernist Literature* (*Waiguo xiandai pai zuopin xuan* 外国现代派作品选), vol. 4-1 (Shanghai: Shanghai Literature and Arts Press 上海文艺出版社, 1985a), 1–4.

———. "Western Modernist Literature as I Understand it" (*Wo suo renshi de xifang xiandai pai wenxue* 我所认识的西方现代派文学), *Selections from Foreign Modernist Literature* (*Waiguo xiandai pai zuopin xuan* 外国现代派作品选), vol.4-2 (Shanghai: Shanghai Literature and Arts Press 上海文艺出版社, 1985b), 1136–1142.

Zhang, Min 张敏. "*Tiannaxi weiliansi yanjiu zai zhongguo: huigu yu zhanwang*" (Tennessee Williams studies in China: review and future). *Dangdai waiguo wenxue* (Contemporary Foreign Literature) 3 (2011a): 157–166.

Zhang, Xinying 张新颖. *The Thematic Study of Margin in Tennessee Williams' Plays* (*Tiannaxi weiliansi juzhuo de bianyuan zhuti yanjiu* 田纳西·威廉斯剧作的边缘主题研究). Beijing: Science Press (科学出版社), 2011b.

Zhao, Quanzhang 赵全章, trans. *The Glass Menagerie* (*Boli dongwuyuan* 玻璃动物园) by Tennessee Williams, in *Modernist Foreign Literary Works* (*Waiguo xiandaipai zuoping xuan* 外国现代派作品选), vol. 4. Shanghai: Shanghai Literature and Art Press (上海文艺出版社), 1985.

Zhao, Zhenjiang 赵振江. "*Xingti ju henduo linggan laizi zhongguo xiqu*" (形体剧很多灵感来自中国戏曲Physical theatre production considerably inspired by Chinese *xiju*). *East Morning Gazette* (东方早报), December 25, 2014. https://www.163.com/news/article/AEA60GKJ00014AED.html.

Zhou, Jiechen and Zhang Zhenglai 周洁辰 张铤来. "*Huangdan huangyan yuwang jiaozhi: Haiou jushe Yuwanghao jieche shangyan*" (荒诞谎言 欲望交织: 海鸥剧社《欲望号街车》上演 Absurd lies interwoven desires: Seagull Drama Society stages *A Streetcar Named Desire*). *Watch and Listen to Sea Waves* (观海听涛), December 13, 2020. http://news.ouc.edu.cn/2020/1213/c78a103670/page.htm.

Zhou, Peitong 周培桐. "*Duju yige de meiguo juzuojia: Jieshao Tiannaxi weiliansi*" (独具一格的美国剧作家--介绍田纳西·威廉斯 An idiosyncratic American playwright: an introduction of Tennessee Williams). *Theatre Gazette* (戏剧报) 8 (1987): 33–34.

Zuo, Yi 左宜. "Tennessee Williams' Early Works" (*Tiannaxi weiliansi de zaoqi zuopin* 田纳西·威廉姆斯的早期作品). *Contemporary Foreign Literature* (当代外国文学) 4 (Oct. 1981), 143–147.

ENGLISH LANGUAGE SOURCES

Allen, Graham. *Intertextuality*. New York: Routledge, 2000.

American Ethical Union. The. *The Standard*, vol. iii. New York: the American Ethical Union, 1916–1917.

"Anti-Rightist Campaign." https://en.wikipedia.org/wiki/Anti-Rightist_Campaign.

Bak, John S. ed. *Tennessee Williams and Europe: Intercultural Encounters, Transatlantic Exchanges*. Amsterdam and New York: Rodopi, 2014.

Barbozaaug, David. "China Passes Japan as Second-Largest Economy." *The New York Times*, 15 August, 2010. https://www.nytimes.com/2010/08/16/business/global/16yuan.html.

Barnes, Clive. "Theater: *In the Bar of a Tokyo Hotel*." *New York Times*, May 12, 1969. https://archive.nytimes.com/www.nytimes.com/books/00/12/31/specials/williams-tokyo.html.

Bassnett, Susan. "The Translator in the Theatre." *Theatre Quarterly* 10.40 (1981): 37–48.

———. "Translating for the Theatre: The Case Against Performability." *TTR* (Traduction, Terminologie, Redaction) 4.1 (1991): 99–111.

Biberman, Matthew. "Tennessee Williams: The American Shakespeare." *Huffington Post*, 26 March, 2011. https://www.huffpost.com/entry/tennessee-williams-the-am_b_838552.

Bigsby, C. W. E. "Tennessee Williams: the Theatricalising Self." In *Modern American Drama, 1945–2000.* Cambridge, UK: Cambridge University Press, 2000, 31–68.

Blankenship, Mark. "In the Bar of a Tokyo Hotel." *Variety,* February 6, 2007. https://variety.com/2007/legit/reviews/in-the-bar-of-a-tokyo-hotel-1200510564/.

Boxill, Roger. *Tennessee Williams.* London: Macmillan, 1987.

Butler, Judith. *Gender Trouble: Feminism and the Subversion of Identity.* New York: Routledge, 2006.

———. *Bodies That Matter: On the Discursive Limits of "Sex."* New York: Routledge: 1993.

Cardullo, Bert, ed. *Conversations with Stanley Kauffmann.* Jackson, MI: University Press of Mississippi, 2003.

Carvajal, Doreen. "Streetcar in Paris, Hold the T-Shirt," *New York Times,* February 14, 2011. https://www.nytimes.com/2011/02/15/arts/15comedie.html?searchResultPosition=1.

Casanova, Pascale. "Consecration and Accumulation of Literary Capital: Translation as Unequal Exchange." Translated by Siobhan Brownlie, in *Critical Readings in Translation Studies,* edited by Mona Baker. London and New York: Routledge, 2010, 286–303.

Chaussende, Damien. "Chen Shu 陈书." In *Early Medieval Chinese Texts: A Bibliographical Guide,* edited by Cynthia Louise Chennault, et al. Berkeley, CA: Institute of East Asian Studies University of California, 2018.

"Cold War." https://www.britannica.com/event/Cold-War.

"Commune." https://www.britannica.com/topic/commune-Chinese-agriculture.

Criscitiello, Alexa. "Photo Flash: *In The Bar of A Tokyo Hotel* Opens Tomorrow at 292 Theatre," *Broadway World,* March 14, 2017. https://www.broadwayworld.com/article/Photo-Flash-IN-THE-BAR-OF-A-TOKYO-HOTEL-Opens-Tomorrow-at-202-Theatre-20170314.

"Cuban Missile Crisis." https://www.britannica.com/event/Cuban-missile-crisis.

de Man, Paul. *Allegories of Reading: Figural Language in Rousseau, Nietzsche, Rilke, and Proust.* New Haven: Yale University Press, 1979.

Debusscher, Gilbert. "Creative Rewriting: European and American Influences on the Dramas of Tennessee Williams." In *The Cambridge Companion to Tennessee Williams,* edited by Matthew C. Roudane. Cambridge, UK: Cambridge University Press, 1997, 167–188.

Devlin, Albert J. ed. *Conversations with Tennessee Williams.* Jackson, MI: University Press of Mississippi, 1986.

Dowling, Robert M. *Eugene O'Neill: A Life in Four Acts.* New Haven, CT: Yale University Press, 2016.

Eliot, T.S. "Tradition and Individual Talent," in *The Sacred Wood: Essays on Poetry and Criticism*. New York: Alfred A. Knopf, 1921, 42–53.

Embassy of Japan, The. *Japan Report* (日本), 6–8, April 15, 1960, 5. https://books.google.com/books?id=7VeHgPX7m1MC&printsec=frontcover&source=gbs_ge_summary_r&cad=0#v=onepage&q&f=false.

Emerson, Caryl. *The Cambridge Introduction to Russian Literature*. Cambridge, UK: Cambridge University Press, 2008.

Fayard, Judy. "French Streetcar Takes a Detour Via Japan." *Wallstreet Journal*, February 18, 2011. https://www.wsj.com/articles/SB10001424052748703584804576143853331643020.

Fedder, Norman J. *The Influence of D. H. Lawrence on Tennessee Williams*. Berkely, CA: University of California Press, 1966.

Feng, Emily. 'First Chinese-Language Production of *A Raisin In The Sun* is Staged in Beijing." *NPR*, September 3, 2020. https://www.npr.org/2020/09/03/908274058/first-chinese-language-production-of-a-raisin-in-the-sun-is-staged-in-beijing.

Freud, Sigmund. "Mourning and Melancholia" (1917). In *General Psychological Theory*, edited by Philip Rieff. New York: Macmillan Publishing Co., Inc., 1978.

Fu, Youde and Wang Qiangwei. "A Comparison of Filial Piety in Ancient Judaism and Early Confucianism." Translated by Noah Lipkowitz. *Journal of Chinese Humanities* 1 (2015), 280–231. https://brill.com/view/journals/joch/1/2/article-p280_6.xml?language=en.

Gantz, Arthur. "A Desperate Morality." In *TW: A Collection of Critical Essays*, edited by Stephen S. Stanton. Englewood Cliffs, NJ: Prentice-Hall, 1977.

Gautreaux, Sergio. "Understanding China's Internal Migration." *International Policy Digest*, March 3, 2013. https://intpolicydigest.org/2013/03/03/understanding-china-s-internal-migration/.

Gelder, Lawrence Van. "*East Palace, West Palace*: Powerful Drama and Courageous Politics." *The New York Times*, July 24, 1998. https://archive.nytimes.com/www.nytimes.com/library/film/072498palace-film-review.html.

Gindt, Dirk. "Tennessee Williams and the Swedish Academy: Why He Never Won the Nobel Prize." In *Tenn at One Hundred: The Reputation of Tennessee Williams*, edited by David Kaplan. East Brunswick, NJ: Hansen Publishing Group, 2011. 152–167.

Gittings, John. "China Drops Homosexuality from List of Psychiatric Disorders." *The Guardian*, March 7, 2001. https://www.theguardian.com/world/2001/mar/07/china.johngittings1.

"Great Leap Forward." https://www.britannica.com/event/Great-Leap-Forward.

Grode, Eric. "A Touch of Eugene O'Neill." *The Sun*, April 25, 2007. http://www.nysun.com/arts/touch-of-eugene-oneill/53172/.

Grogan, Molly. "A Streetcar to Paris via New York." *Paris Voice*, n.d., accessed via https://www.maboumines.org/production/a-streetcar-named-desire/.

Heintzelman, Greta and Alycia Smith-Howard. *Critical Companion to Tennessee Williams: A Literary Reference to His Life and Work*. New York: Infobase Publishing, 2014.

Henley, Christopher. "Review: *The Lady from the Village of Falling Flowers*," December 11, 2019, *DC Theatre Scene*, https://dctheatrescene.com/2019/12/11/review-the-lady-from-the-village-of-falling-flowers/.

Hinsch, Bret. *Passions of the Cut Sleeve: The Male Homosexual Tradition in China*. Oakland, CA: University of California Press, 1990.

"Hundred Flowers Campaign." https://www.britannica.com/event/Hundred-Flowers-Campaign.

Ip, Hung-yok. *Intellectuals in Revolutionary China, 1921–1949*. London and New York: Routledge, 2005.

Johnson, Sarah Elizabeth. *The Influence of Japanese Traditional Performing Arts Tennessee Williams Late Plays*. MFA (Master of Fine Arts) thesis, University of Iowa, 2014. https://doi.org/10.17077/etd.92wlztti.

Kang, Wenqing. *Obsession: Male Same-Sex Relations in China, 1900–1950*. Hong Kong: Hong Kong University Press, 2009.

Kaplan, David. "*The Day on Which a Man Dies:* Chicago 2007, Chicago, East Hampton, Provincetown 2009." http://davidkaplandirector.com/the-day-on-which-a-man-dies/.

Kaplan, David, ed. *Tenn at One Hundred: The Reputation of Tennessee Williams*. East Brunswick, NJ: Hansen Publishing Group, 2011.

Keith, Thomas. "Pulp Williams: Tennessee in the Popular Imagination." In *Tenn At One Hundred: The Reputation of Tennessee Williams*, edited by David Kaplan. East Brunswick, NJ: Hansen Publishing Group, 2011, 169–181.

Kolin, Phillip and Sherry Shao. "The First Production of *A Streetcar Named Desire* in Mainland China." *The Tennessee Williams Literary Journal* 2 (1990–1991): 19–32.

Kristof, Nicholas D. "China Bans One of Its Own Films; Cannes Festival Gave It Top Prize." *The New York Times*. August 4, 1993. https://www.nytimes.com/search?query=Nicholas+D.++Kristof%2C+%22China+Bans+One+of+Its+Own+Films%3B+Cannes+Festival+Gave+It+Top+Prize%22.

Lahr, John. *Tennessee Williams: Mad Pilgrimage of the Flesh*. New York: Norton, 2014.

Lane, Beverly. "History of Tao House." http://www.eugeneoneill.org/about-tao-house/.

Lefevere, André. "Chinese and Western Thinking on Translation," in Susan Bassnett and André Lefevere, *Constructing Cultures: Essays on Literary Translation*. Bristol, UK: Multicultural Matters, 1998), 12–24.

Lester, Neal A. "27 Wagons Full of Cotton and Other One-Act Plays." In *Tennessee Williams: A Guide to Research and Performance*, edited by Phillip C. Kolin. Westport, CT: Greenwood Press, 1998), 1–12.

Li, Kwok-sing. *A Glossary of Political Terms of the People's Republic of China.* Translated by Mary Lok. Hong Kong: The Chinese University of Hong Kong Press, 1995.

Lian, Xi. *Blood Letters.* New York: Hachette Book, 2018.

Liu, Haiping and Lowell Swortzell, eds. *Eugene O'Neill in China: An International Centenary Celebration.* Westport, CT: Praeger, 1992.

Lupton, Julia Reinhard, et al. *After Oedipus: Shakespeare in Psychoanalysis.* Ithaca, NY: Cornell University Press, 1993.

"Lu-shan Conference." https://www.britannica.com/topic/Lu-shan-Conference.

Miller, Arthur. "In China." *The Atlantic Monthly,* March 1979, 90–117.

———. *Salesman in Beijing.* New York: Viking, 1983.

Miller, Arthur and Inge Morath. *Chinese Encounters.* New York: Farrar Straus Giroux, 1979.

Miller, Arthur and Phillip Gelb. "Morality and Modern Drama." *Educational Theatre Journal* 10–13 (Oct., 1958), 190–202.

Miller, J. Hillis. "Walter Pater: A Partial Portrait." *Daedalus* 105.1 (Winter 1976): 97–113.

———. "The Critic as Host." *Critical Inquiry* 3.3 (Spring 1977): 439–447.

Mountford, Tom. *China: The Legal Position and Status of Lesbian, Gay, Bisexual and Transgender People in The People's Republic of China,* 2009. https://outrightinternational.org/content/china-legal-position-and-status-lesbian-gay-bisexual-and-transgender-people-people%E2%80%99s.

Moussa, Maher. *The Re-Invention of the Self: Performativity and Liberation in Selected Plays by Tennessee Williams.* PhD dissertation. Ann Arbor: Michigan State University, 2001.

Nikolarea, Ekaterini. "Performability versus Readability: A Historical Overview of a Theoretical Polarization in Theater Translation." *Translation Journal* 6.4 (October 2002). https://translationjournal.net/journal/22theater.htm.

Paller, Michael. *Gentlemen Callers: Tennessee Williams, Homosexuality, and Mid-Twentieth-Century Drama.* New York: Palgrave Macmillan, 2005.

"Peng Dehuai." https://en.wikipedia.org/wiki/Peng_Dehuai.

Prior, Dorothy Max. "Theatre Movement Bazaar/Beijing TinHouse Productions: Poker Night Blues," August 17, 2015, https://totaltheatre.org.uk/theatre-movement-bazaarbeijing-tinhouse-productions-poker-night-blues/.

"Provincetown Tennessee Williams Theater Festival-2013 Shows." https://www.twptown.org/archives.

Qi, Shouhua. *Adapting Western Classics for the Chinese Stage.* London and New York: Routledge, 2018.

———. "Misreading Ibsen: Chinese Noras on and off the Stage, and Nora in Her Chinese Husband's Ancestral Land of the 1930s—as Reimagined for the Present-Day Stage." *Comparative Drama* 50.4 (Winter 2016): 341–364.

———. "Pushing the Boundaries: Staging Western Modern(ist) Drama in Contemporary China." In *The Edinburgh Companion to Modernism in Contemporary Theatre*, edited by Adrian Curtin, et al. Edinburgh University Press, 2022.

———. *Western Literature in China and the Translation of a Nation.* New York: Palgrave Macmillan, 2012.

Qi, Shouhua and Wei Zhang. "Total Heroism: Reinterpreting Sartre's *Morts sans sépulture* (The Victors) for the Chinese Stage." *Theatre Research International* 44.2 (2019): 171–188.

Richardson, Jack. "Unaffected Recollections." *New York Times Book Review*, November. 2, 1975. https://www.nytimes.com/1975/11/02/archives/unaffected-recollections-memoirs.html?searchResultPosition=1.

Saddik, Annette. "From Broadway Darling to Outrageous Outlaw: Tennessee Williams and the American Theatre." Invited Faculty Lecture (via WebEx), October 8, 2020, Western Connecticut State University, Danbury, CT.

———. "The Grotesque and Too Funny for Laughter: Publishing the Late Tennessee Williams," in David Kaplan, 260–278, n.d.

———. *The Politics of Reputation: The Critical Reception of Tennessee Williams' Later Plays.* Plainsboro, NJ: Associated University Presses, 1999.

———. *Tennessee Williams and The Theatre of Excess: The Strange, The Crazed, The Queer.* Cambridge, UK: Cambridge University Press, 2015.

Sartre, Jean-Paul. *Existentialism Is a Humanism.* Translated by Carol Macomber. New Haven: Yale University Press, 2007.

Scheineson, Andrew. "China's Internal Migrants." Council on Foreign Relations, 14 May 2009. https://www.cfr.org/backgrounder/chinas-internal-migrants.

Shaland, Irene. *Tennessee Williams on the Soviet Stage.* Lanham, NY and London University Press of America, 1987.

"Shanghai PRIDE 2012 Theater." http://www.shpride.com/pride2012theater/?lang=en.

"Socialist Education Movement." https://en.wikipedia.org/wiki/Socialist_Education_Movement.

Stoltenberg, John. "Tennessee Williams's *Lady from the Village of Falling Flowers* Returns." *DC Metro*, December 19, 2020. https://dcmetrotheaterarts.com/2020/12/19/natsu-onoda-power-crafts-a-tennessee-williams-puppet-show/.

Tyler, Patrick E. "China's Censors Issue a Warning." *The New York Times*, September 4, 1993. https://www.nytimes.com/search?query=Patrick+E.+Tyler%2C+%22China%27s+Censors+Issue+a+Warning%22.

United Christian Society, The. *They Went To China: Biographies of Missionaries of the Disciples of Christ.* Indianapolis, Indiana: The United Christian Missionary Society, 1948. https://digitalcommons.acu.edu/crs_books/477.

Venuti, Lawrence. *The Translator's Invisibility: A History of Translation*. London and New York: Routledge, 1995.

Wakeman, Frederic, Jr. *Policing Shanghai, 1927–1937*. Oakland, CA: University of California Press, 1995.

White, George C. "Directing O'Neill In China." *The Eugene O'Neill Newsletter* 9-1 (Spring 1985). http://www.eoneill.com/library/newsletter/ix_1/ix-1g.htm.

Williams, Tennessee. *A Streetcar Named Desire*, with an Introduction by Arthur Miller. New York: New Directions, 2004.

———. *Eight Plays*. Garden City, New York: Nelson Doubleday, 1979.

———. *In the Bar of a Tokyo Hotel*. New York: Dramatist Plays Service, 1969.

———. *Memoirs*. New York: New Directions Publishing, 2006.

———. *Tennessee Williams Plays 1937–1955*. New York: The Library of America, 2000.

———. *Tennessee Williams Plays 1957–1980*. New York: The Library of America.

———. *The Traveling Companion and Other Plays*, edited by Annette J. Saddik. New York: New Directions, 2008.

Williams, Tom. "*The Day On Which A Man Dies*: Unique Lost Tennessee Williams One Act is Riveting," *Chicago Critic*, https://chicagocritic.com/the-day-on-which-a-man-dies/.

Woods, Eddie. *Tennessee Williams in Bangkok*. Dixon, CA: Inkblot Books, 2013.

Worell, Judith, ed. *Encyclopedia of Women and Gender: Sex Similarities and Differences and Impact of Society on Gender*. San Diego, CA: Academic Press, 2001.

Wright, Andy. "The Hole Truth about Why We 'Dig to China.'" October 19, 2015. https://www.atlasobscura.com/articles/the-hole-truth-about-why-we-dig-to-china.

Ying, Ruochen and Claire Conceison. *Voices Carry: Behind Bars and Backstage during China's Revolution and Reform*. New York: Roman and Littlefield, 2009.

Zhang, Wei. *Chinese Adaptations of Brecht: Appropriation and Intertextuality*. New York: Palgrave Macmillan, 2019.

Zhang, Wei and Shouhua Qi. "The Kindness of Strangers: Tennessee Williams's *A Streetcar Named Desire* on the Chinese Stage." *Comparative Drama* 54.1 (2021a): 97–115, https://scholarworks.wmich.edu/compdr/vol54/iss1/5.

Zhang, Kun, "'Streetcar' at Home on China Stage." *China Daily*, April 6, 2017. http://www.chinadaily.com.cn/culture/2017-04/06/content_2881 1083.htm.

Zhang, Wei and Shouhua Qi. "The Kindness of Strangers: Tennessee Williams's A Streetcar Named Desire on the Chinese Stage." *Comparative Drama* 54.1 (2021b): 99–102.

Zhou, Xun. *The Great Famine in China, 1958–1962: A Documentary History*. New Haven, CT: Yale University Press, 2012.

INDEX[1]

A

Adaptation, 9, 17–19, 31, 38, 56, 63, 77, 122, 135–138, 140, 141, 143, 145, 146, 150, 151, 153, 157, 162, 163n3, 166n41, 171, 172, 174

Afreds, Mike, 138–140

See also Adaptation; *Streetcar Named Desire, A*

Allan, *see* Homosexuality; *Streetcar Named Desire, A*

Alma, *see* *Summer and Smoke*

Alvaro, *see* *Rose Tattoo, The*

Amanda (Amanda Wingfield), 42, 57, 84, 93, 96, 98, 116–118, 151, 152

See also *Glass Menagerie, The*

An, Man (安曼), 41, 53, 71n46

Anti-Rightest Campaign, 35, 81

Artaud, Antonin, 13, 103

Auto-da-Fé, 106

B

Bakhtin, Mikhail, 13, 103

Bangkok, 8, 9, 11

Bassnett, Susan, 29

See also Performativity; Readability

Beijing TinHouse Productions (北京铁皮屋剧社), 122, 141

Belle Reve, 3, 64

See also *Streetcar Named Desire, A*

Belt and Road, 174

Big Daddy, 45–47, 49, 51–53, 56, 90, 99, 107–109, 111

See also *Cat on a Hot Tin Roof*

Big Mama, 49, 50

See also *Cat on a Hot Tin Roof*

Blanche DuBois, 1, 84, 93, 108, 112, 116, 135–163, 173

See also Homosexuality; *Streetcar Named Desire, A*

[1] Note: Page numbers followed by 'n' refer to notes.

M

Mao, Zedong (毛泽东), 11, 14,
22n29, 35, 38, 70n27, 80
Margaret (Maggie), 45–51, 53, 56,
89, 95, 107–109, 113, 157
See also Cat on a Hot Tin Roof
Maxine (Maxine Faulk), *see Night of
Iguana, The*
Memoirs, 19, 23n45, 41, 54–56, 68,
125n5, 172
Memory play, 59, 84, 93, 138, 152, 161
See also Glass Menagerie, The
*Milk Train Doesn't Stop Here Anymore,
The*, 10, 78, 94, 103, 124
Miller, Arthur, 1, 8, 11, 12, 20n3, 28,
30, 41, 69n10, 71n41, 74n103,
88, 89, 91–94, 127n41, 137,
139, 140
See also Death of a Salesman
Mishima, Yukio, 9, 10, 23n45,
122, 124
See also Japanese theatre
Mitch, 2, 3, 45, 64, 99, 141, 142,
146, 148–150, 158–160
See also Streetcar Named Desire, A

N

Naturalizing (naturalization), 61
See also Translation
New Culture and New Literature
Movement, 29
Night of Iguana, The, 1, 2, 5–8, 13,
54, 61, 62, 84, 94, 96, 99, 110,
113, 115, 123
Noh, 9, 10, 124
See also Japanese theatre
Nonno, *see Night of the Iguana, The*

O

O'Neill, Eugene, 1, 8, 12, 19, 20n3,
28, 89–92, 94, 126n29,
126–127n31, 137, 139, 153

Opium War, the, 136
Orpheus Descending, 13, 15, 84, 93,
99, 102, 115

P

Paper lantern, 2–4, 121, 148
See also Streetcar Named Desire, A
Peng, Dehuai (彭德怀), *see* Lushan
Conference
People's Commune, 80
Performability, 28–30, 64, 67, 172
See also Translation
Performativity, 116, 117
Period of Adjustment, 93, 99
Plastic theatre, 84
See also Glass Menagerie, The
Poker Night Blues, 122, 141–144
See also Streetcar Named Desire, A

Q

Qi, Qing (奇青), 41, 44, 45, 63, 65

R

Readability, 28, 30, 64, 172
See also Translation
Reform and opening up, 8, 18, 30, 77,
90, 139, 157, 174, 176
Rose Tattoo, The, 93, 95, 101, 102

S

Seagull Drama Society, the (海鸥
剧社), 162
Sebastian (Sebastian Venable), *see*
Homosexuality; *Suddenly
Last Summer*
Serafina (Serafina Delle Rose), *see Rose
Tattoo, The*
Sexual mores, 11–20, 30, 38–56, 124,
171, 173
See also Homosexuality

Printed in the USA
CPSIA information can be obtained
at www.ICGtesting.com
LVHW011637161123
764105LV00006B/295